STUDIES IN CHRISTIAN HISTORY AND THOUGHT

The Ground of Election

Jacobus Arminius' Doctrine of the Work and Person of Christ

STUDIES IN CHRISTIAN HISTORY AND THOUGHT

A full listing of all titles in this series
appears at the close of this book

STUDIES IN CHRISTIAN HISTORY AND THOUGHT

The Ground of Election

Jacobus Arminius' Doctrine of the Work and Person of Christ

F. Stuart Clarke

Foreword by Herbert Boyd McGonigle

Wipf & Stock
PUBLISHERS
Eugene, Oregon

Wipf and Stock Publishers
199 W 8th Ave, Suite 3
Eugene, OR 97401

The Ground of Election
Jacob Arminius' Doctrine of the Work and Person of Christ
By Clarke, F. Stuart
Copyright©2006 Paternoster
ISBN 13: 978-1-59752-919-8
ISBN 10: 1-59752-919-2
Publication date 9/19/2006
Previously published by Paternoster, 2006

This Edition Published by Wipf and Stock Publishers
by arrangement with Paternoster

Paternoster
9 Holdom Avenue
Bletchley
Milton Keyes, MK1 1QR
Great Britain

STUDIES IN CHRISTIAN HISTORY AND THOUGHT

Series Preface

This series complements the specialist series of *Studies in Evangelical History and Thought* and *Studies in Baptist History and Thought* for which Paternoster is becoming increasingly well known by offering works that cover the wider field of Christian history and thought. It encompasses accounts of Christian witness at various periods, studies of individual Christians and movements, and works which concern the relations of church and society through history, and the history of Christian thought.

The series includes monographs, revised dissertations and theses, and collections of papers by individuals and groups. As well as 'free standing' volumes, works on particular running themes are being commissioned; authors will be engaged for these from around the world and from a variety of Christian traditions.

A high academic standard combined with lively writing will commend the volumes in this series both to scholars and to a wider readership.

Series Editors

Alan P.F. Sell, Visiting Professor at Acadia University Divinity College, Nova Scotia, Canada

David Bebbington, Professor of History, University of Stirling, Stirling, Scotland, UK

Clyde Binfield, Professor Associate in History, University of Sheffield, UK

Gerald Bray, Anglican Professor of Divinity, Beeson Divinity School, Samford University, Birmingham, Alabama, USA

Grayson Carter, Associate Professor of Church History, Fuller Theological Seminary SW, Phoenix, Arizona, USA

To
my daughters
Susanna and Katherine
and
in memory of my son
Paul

Contents

Foreword by Herbert Boyd McGonigle xi

Acknowledgements xv

Introduction xvii

Chapter 1
Arminius Studies from 1609–2000 1

Chapter 2
The Reluctant Theologian: Pastorate and Predestination
from 1591–1603 10

Chapter 3
The Christology of a General Practitioner, 1599–1603 40

Chapter 4
Synopsis: The Roots of Arminius' Christology 61
Prolegomena: Do Christ and his Work Matter Most to Arminius? 61
Very God?: The Doctrines of the Trinity and the Person of Christ 63
The Good God and the Good Universe he Made 67
God's Dominion, Providence and the Covenants 69
   Sin 73
   Grace 75
   The Mediator 78
The Threefold Office: Priest, Prophet, King 79
Humiliation and Exaltation 85
Atonement 88
Predestination in its Proper Setting 90
The Call to Repentance 91
   Faith 95
   Union with Christ 97
   Communion and Redemption 98
   Regeneration 101
   Assurance 102
   Justification 103
   Holiness 105
Christ and the Church 108
   The Yoke of Bondage and the Freedom of the Christian 111
   The Head and the Body 115

One, Holy and Catholic 117
Sacraments 119
Summary...121

Chapter 5
The Return of Controversy, 1604–1608 ....**125**

Chapter 6
Epilogue: How Great the Harvest **165**

Bibliography..**175**

General Index..**181**

Foreword

The eighteenth-century Evangelical Revival in England was marked by a number of theological wrangles among the 'Methodists' of the day. The most serious of these divisions concerned the doctrines of election and predestination. The literary war between the two groups spread over some fifty years and the names of John Calvin and James Arminius were bandied about by both sides. In a moment of exasperation in 1770, John Wesley wrote: 'To say, "This man is an Arminian" has the same effect on many hearers, as to say, "This is a mad dog." It puts them into a fright at once: they run away from him with all speed and diligence; and will hardly stop, unless it be to throw a stone at the dreadful and mischievous animal.' Interestingly Wesley wrote this in a pamphlet entitled, *'The Question, "What is an Arminian?" answered. By a lover of Free Grace'*.

Two centuries on from Wesley's strictures there is still misapprehension and division among evangelicals about the theology of James Arminius (1558-1609). One reason for this is that Arminius' Latin text has suffered at the hands of his main English translators. James and William Nichols in the 1820s and 1870s, and William Bagnall in the 1850s, produced almost 1,800 ponderous pages and only the most dedicated reader is likely to study the full text with care and even-handedness. Arminius' theology has been waiting for a scholar to give it a systematic treatment and now Dr Stuart Clarke has done that. This book is the re-working of his PhD thesis and it gives us a very valuable and much-needed exposition of Arminius' theological system. As a result of careful and critical research, Dr Clarke highlights a number of very significant conclusions about what James Arminius believed and taught.

First, Arminius was not an anti-Calvinist if that phrase means being an opponent to all or most of what John Calvin (1509-64) taught. Arminius did not reject a doctrine of election and predestination, as is popularly thought. All his writings on this subject show clearly that he believed God deals with men and women according to His purposes in predestination and Arminius even set out these purposes in terms of four decrees. Arminius' protests were not against the teachings of John Calvin as such but against the strict supralapsarian 'Calvinism' being promulgated in his Dutch homeland. Arminius was drawn into the controversy simmering in the Netherlands when two prominent Dutch Calvinists found it difficult to defend the supralapsarian doctrine that emanated from the teaching and influence of Theodore Beza (1519-1605). Dr Clarke demonstrates very convincingly that Arminius was not anti-Calvinist; rather he should be described as a Calvinist revisionist.

Second, this book offers incontrovertible evidence that James Arminius was an evangelical and reformed theologian. In doing so he has also demonstrated that the description 'Reformed' is not restricted to classic 'Five Point' Calvinism. Arminius believed and taught and wrote on what are commonly called the doctrines of grace. He foundationed all his theology on the understanding that the Bible is the full and final revelation of the one, true God. He emphasised a doctrine of original sin that is very close to Augustine's position. He taught salvation by faith alone in Christ. Sinners are justified through saving faith in Jesus Christ and are enabled by the Holy Spirit to grow in the grace of sanctification. In his anthropology Arminius was not Pelagian, in his Christology he was not Arian, and in his soteriology he was not Roman Catholic.

Third, Dr Clarke distinguishes between what Arminius believed and what has often been dubbed 'Arminianism' in the subsequent centuries. Among his followers in Holland, the Remonstrants, a number of them moved away from Arminius' Christological convictions, as did some seventeenth-century English Latitudinarian 'Arminians'. But these deviant teachings did not represent what Arminius himself believed. It was against this misrepresentation of Arminius' theology that John Wesley protested so vigorously. And even today there are evangelical scholars who, whether from ignorance of the facts or by deliberate propaganda, still lump Arminianism with Pelagianism, Arianism, Socinianism and whatever other 'ism' they don't like. Is it too much to hope that such people will carefully read this book and be willing to be factually informed?

Fourth, Dr Clarke has made a most significant, and in many ways original, contribution towards a better understanding of Arminius' theology. This relates to his insight that Arminius' foundation, in his whole theological system, was essentially and deliberately Christological. So his title is carefully and accurately chosen, *The Ground of Election: Jacobus Arminius' Doctrine of the Work and Person of Christ.* Our election is in Christ, not in God's so-called 'hidden' purposes or in secret prelapsarian decrees. God loves the world of sinners in His Son and all His plans for our salvation, Arminius never tired of emphasising, are in the birth, life, death, resurrection, ascension and intercession of his beloved Son. While Dr Clarke rightly points out that Arminius' doctrine of the person and work of the Holy Spirit is left unfinished, part of the reason for this is that for most of his comparatively short life, he was rescuing soteriology from hard-line Calvinism. God is known to us in the revelation of His Son Jesus Christ, and all our salvation is grounded, guaranteed and offered to us, and to all mankind, in the finished, and still ongoing work, of our blessed Redeemer. Evangelical theology needs to give far more attention than it has previously done to James Arminius' theology of grace and this book is the primary text to point us in that direction.

Herbert Boyd McGonigle
Senior Lecturer in Historical Theology and Church History
Nazarene Theological College
Manchester
February 2006

Acknowledgements

This book has been so long (fifty years!) in preparation that, sadly, many of the people to whom I owe acknowledgements have already passed to their reward.

Perhaps the first name I should mention is that of my Church History tutor, the Revd Professor E. Gordon Rupp, who recognised the enthusiasm that inspired me to write an unusually long, if mediocre, essay on 'Arminianism', and recommended me to pursue this line of study. I should also thank for their encouragement my other tutors at college, the Revd Drs R. Newton Flew, William F. Flemington, and Philip S. Watson, all now deceased, as is the Revd Dr Carl O. Bangs, the one outstanding Arminius scholar I have had the privilege of knowing personally. Another scholar who helped me, the Revd Benjamin Drewery, then of Manchester University, is happily still with us.

I wish also to express thanks to the staff and students of St John's College, Bramcote, Nottingham, for much help in the Graduate Seminars and otherwise, to the Revd Adrian Chatfield, my tutor for the first year, and especially to Canon Dr Christina Baxter, the present Principal, who acted as my tutor for the rest of the course. Also I would like to mention with gratitude the Revd Dr Herbert B. McGonigle and Dr John Darch of St John's, my examiners.

Thanks are also due to friends who helped with suggesting or obtaining the relevant literature; Dr Carl Trueman, the Revd Professor Paul Ellingworth, the late Revd Graham Slater, and my daughter Susanna and Dr Colin Greenland of Cambridge.

With a subject as controversial as Arminius, I have inevitably met scholars who have disagreed with me. A few have thought I should not study such a man at all, but most have encouraged me to say what I can for Arminius and his views. So I would like to thank those Calvinists and Reformed who, by their criticisms, have helped to refine my thinking and to eliminate weak arguments; especially those I have met through the Tyndale Fellowship.

Finally, it is traditional for authors to acknowledge a debt to their partners. This is not always just conventional. The subject of this work went to his aunt's wedding reception on 10 December 1596, saw a theologian he had wanted to meet for years, and the two of them rudely ignored other wedding-guests, and even the bride and groom, to engage in lengthy theological discussion! Theologians can be very poor company. So I would like to thank my wife, Janet, for all the practical support she gave me during the long process of composing this study.

Introduction

I have been interested in Arminius himself, as distinct from 'Arminianism', since 1956, when I wrote an essay on him for Part 3 in Church History of the Cambridge Theological Tripos. I took him as my special subject for my examinations as a Methodist probationer minister from 1956-8. In 1957 I visited the Netherlands for the first time, and also purchased copies of the recently republished *Writings* of Arminius in the Nichols-Bagnall edition. I attended the Arminius Symposium in Amsterdam for the supposed 400th anniversary of his birth in 1960.

Between 1960 and 1996 other duties largely kept me from following up this interest, but in 1972 I included two chapters on Arminius, 'Clearing the Ground' and 'A Reconstruction of His Theology' in a thesis on 'The Doctrine of Predestination in Protestant Theology with particular reference to the period between 1560 and 1610'.

Some of what I had studied stayed in my memory, and on retirement in 1996 I took up my interest again. The situation had changed from 1956-70. There was more interest in Arminius, and varying degrees of sympathy and criticism. Bangs, Muller, Dekker and others had published significant works, and it soon became clear that my original idea to write about the general theology of Arminius was superfluous. Muller had studied Arminius' doctrines of God and theological prolegomena, and with his exhaustive knowledge of the background had produced the definitive work on these aspects, far more fully than I could hope to do—though I find his study of Arminius' doctrines of creation and providence in the same book, while very valuable, slightly less definitive. My second idea, to write on Arminius' doctrines of grace and predestination, had already been done by Dekker, but Dekker had placed them in the context of human freewill, which I considered was wrong, and still do. I had to place them where I believe they belong, in the context of the whole work of Christ, which meant doing what no one has yet done, studying Arminius' doctrine of the work and person of Christ as a whole.

My method involved a two-pronged approach. There was undoubtedly development in Arminius' doctrine of predestination between his earliest theological pronouncements of 1591, and the delivery of the *Declaration of Sentiments* in 1608. On this subject in particular, it was important to note to whom Arminius was responding, whether a friend like Uitenbogaert or an adversary like Gomarus, so that I could understand the context of his writing.

On other doctrines evidence for development is scanty. Muller finds his Public Disputation of 1607 *On the Righteousness and Efficacy of the Providence of God Concerning Evil* much clearer than the theses of the 1605 *Disputation* on the same subject with the same title, and 'quite incapable of being interpreted in the direction of the accusations being made'.[1] Dekker *perhaps* finds some development in Arminius' doctrines of grace and faith between the *Examination of Perkins* and later works like *Ep. 85* of 1606, *Public Disputation 16* of 1609 and the *Articuli Nonnulli*,[2] but he is more concerned to stress the *onhelderheid* (lack of clarity) which he considers links them all. But it remains true that traceable development in Arminius' theology is largely confined to predestination.

This is the reason for the two 'prongs'. The first prong is historical; the development of the doctrine of predestination which is followed through from beginning to end and which is represented in the book primarily in chapters 2 and 5, with chapter 3 mentioning other subjects as and when they surface up to 1603. There was originally to have been a chapter on Arminius' life and career which, in consultation with my supervisor, I decided to omit from the published edition of this research.

The second 'prong' might be described as thematic. I have taken various theological subjects which have to do with, or are linked to, the work and person of Christ, and noted all the places where Arminius discussed these themes and what he had to say on them. This approach ran concurrently with the more historical approach described above. These subjects included the following:

> The Divine Knowledge
> The Divine Will
> Creation
> Providence
> Covenant
> The Fall and Sin
> The Divine Nature and the Appointment of Christ
> The Love of God
> The Person of Christ and whether Arminius' doctrine is subordinationist.
> The Holy Spirit
> The Trinity
> Grace
> The Priesthood of Christ
> Atonement
> Christ's Prophetical and Regal Offices
> Christ's states of Humiliation and Exaltation
> Predestination in its position in Arminius' thought

---

1 R.A. Muller, *God, Creation and Providence in the Thought of Jacob Arminius* (Grand Rapids, MI: Baker Book House, 1991), pp.257-8.

2 E. Dekker, Rijker *dan Midas: Vrijheid, Genade en Predestinatie in de Theologie van Jacobus Arminius (1559-1609)* (Zoetermeer: Uitgeverij Boekencentrum BV, 1993), pp.161-77.

> Call and repentance
> Faith
> Justification
> The Union of believers with Christ
> The Communion of believers with Christ in His Death and Life
> Sanctification
> Christ and the Church
> The Church of the Old Testament under the Promise
> The Church of the New Testament under the Gospel
> Christian Liberty
> The Head and Marks of the Church
> The Catholic Church
> Sacraments

As I progressed with this thematic approach to Arminius' doctrines, it became increasingly clear that the right order in which they should be discussed, was the order adopted by Arminius himself in his *Private Disputations* (systematic theology). This meant that he would be studied, evaluated and judged in his own terms and not in those of others (e.g., later standard Reformed theologians). Much of the material, which is contained mainly in chapter 4 ('Synopsis') also comes from the *Private Disputations* and follows their pattern, but sometimes the *Public Disputations* are followed, or other material, e.g., for the priesthood of Christ most of the pattern and material are taken from Arminius' inaugural *Oration IV*, his fullest treatment of the subject.

This research also enabled me to see some of the emphases which I now advance as the core of my research, namely that Arminius firmly believed the following:

> 1. That God's creation is good in itself and is not merely subservient to the greater good of redemption and of God's glory in determining individual human destiny;
>
> 2. That 'the Lord is good to all, and his tender mercies are over all his works' (Psalm 145:9).
>
> 3. That God deals with his human creation in the form of covenant, which is not just an occasional arrangement which God makes with humanity from time to time, but a permanent principle which God has adopted in his dealings with humanity, right through from Adam and Eve before the Fall, to the current and final New Covenant. In other words, he deals with them as persons who can and must respond, not as inanimate things.
>
> 4. That the work and person of Christ is central to all God's dealings with his human creation since the Fall, and in particular that predestination is an integral part of the work of Christ, not just God's response to human faith.

This very important thematic approach, represented primarily in chapter 4, is inserted at the point of 1603 in the historical narrative, to mark the big change in Arminius' life from pastor at Amsterdam to professor at Leiden. Although, as we shall see, he began his *Synopsis* (later to be called *Private Disputations*) in 1599, he began with the doctrine of God and probably did not reach the work and person of Christ till about the time he moved from Amsterdam to Leiden. He then continued to produce his systematic theology, which remained largely unaffected by the storms that continued to gather around him. The historical story is resumed in the following chapter 5.

Finally, the last chapter continues the evidence of his private notes, the *Articuli Nonnulli*, and what they and other writings have to tell us about his approach to certain issues, particularly predestination, which have caused continued division since his time.

In places I have recognised that I was arguing against reputable scholars who give a different interpretation of the material, and I have sought to engage with this at appropriate points in my exposition of Arminius' ideas, making clear the reasons in his text, or its background, why I suggest an alternative interpretation.

For original texts I have used the English translation of James and William Nichols, the so-called London Edition. This is generally recommended by Muller, one of the best Latinists, if not the best, who has studied Arminius in the original, as 'a solid and serviceable translation that faithfully renders Arminius's thought', which 'deserves to be modernized and emended (as) the basis of any subsequent English-language edition' and on which 'readers will note my grateful reliance'.[3] Muller also has legitimate criticisms of Nichols. This has been supplemented by Hoenderdaal's edition of the original Dutch version of the *Declaration of Sentiments*, and by the Latin versions of Arminius' extant letters, many of which have never appeared in translation. I also have read the original Latin version of other works as appropriate, as included in the 1631 edition of Arminius' *Opera Theologica* and the 1645 edition of the *Examination of Gomarus's Theses*. I have not felt it necessary to read every word Arminius wrote in Latin, as there are passages in his works which, when read in English, clearly have no bearing on his doctrine of the work and person of Christ. Such are the long philosophical *Treatise on Permission*, inserted into the *Examination of Perkins*; much of *Private Disputations I—XXV*, which deal with the doctrine of God philosophically; and parts of the *Dissertation* on Romans 7 and *Analysis* of Romans 9, where the concern is with human psychology rather than the work of Christ, but I have read all parts of the works in the original languages that are relevant to the subject.

---

3 Muller, *God*, Preface , p.x.

CHAPTER 1

Arminius Studies from 1609–2000

While some valuable work has been done on certain aspects of Arminius' theology, especially since 1970, no-one has yet studied the heart of his theology, the work and person of Christ, as a whole. The present study is designed to fill this gap.

Jacobus (James) Arminius died on 19 October 1609 and was condemned as a heretic nearly a decade later by the Reformed churches at the Synod of Dort in 1618-19, at which his followers were expelled from the Dutch Reformed Church and eventually became the Remonstrant Brotherhood.

The Synod of Dort's conclusions about certain doctrines, in particular that of limited atonement, were of questionable orthodoxy judged even by previous Reformed standards, but they were effective as a statement of Reformed orthodoxy as it had developed by 1619, and as a foreshadowing of further developments of Reformed orthodoxy during the seventeeth century. The Synod of Dort was not the complete success it appeared to some of its participants; even at the Synod itself a certain reaction may have occurred, like that of John Hales, Provost of Eton and chaplain to the English ambassador to the Hague, who was present at the Synod and after listening to the Remonstrant Episcopius expounding John 3:16, is said to have commented afterwards, 'There I bid John Calvin good-night.'[1] Nevertheless, most seventeenth-century Reformed theologians followed Dort or even went beyond it; the *Second Helvetic Confession* of 1675 is considered to represent the high-water mark of Calvinism. But there were also exceptions, like John Goodwin the 'Arminian' Puritan in his *Banner of Justification* of 1659, and Arminius' *magnum opus*, the *Declaration of Sentiments*, which had been translated into English by Tobias Conyers in 1657.

The progress of Arminius studies during the eighteenth century has been well studied and need not be given in detail here.[2] Briefly, Gerard

---

1 Recent Reformed study of Hales has questioned whether this can be taken at face value as summarising his later relationship with Calvinism.

2 A useful introduction to the various publications involved can be found in the Introduction (dated 1986) by Carl Bangs to the reprint of James Nichols' and William Nichols' *The Works of Arminius* (3 vols; Grand Rapids, MI: Baker Book House, 1991 [1825, 1828 and 1875]), pp.xx-xxix (hereafter *Works*).

Brandt's *Historie der Reformatie en andre Kerkelijke Geschiedenissen in en ontrent de Nederlanden*, written from a Remonstrant standpoint, appeared in four volumes from 1671 to 1704, and was translated into English in 1720-3, and Brandt's son Caspar published his *Historia vitae Jacobi Arminii* in 1725, which eventually appeared in English translation in England in 1854 and in the USA in 1857. Meanwhile early leaders of the Evangelical Revival of 1711 onwards, like Jonathan Edwards, were Calvinist/Orthodox Reformed in their views, but the conversion of the Wesley brothers in 1738 and their discovery of their 'Arminian' principles in 1739-41, produced a new form of evangelical 'Arminianism' which the Reformed found difficult to fit into their preferred categories. By the early nineteenth century Evangelical Arminianism was expanding and appeared to be prospering more than its Calvinist counterpart. James Nichols, an Anglican layman, not a Methodist, published in 1824 his *Calvinism and Arminianism Compared* and followed it the following year with the first volume of his translation of the Latin *Opera* of Arminius, which presented his five University *Orations* in English for the first time and also the first English translation of the *Declaration of Sentiments* since 1657. The second volume in 1828 included other important material, notably the *Public Disputations* and the *Private Disputations*, the latter in effect Arminius' uncompleted systematic theology. But as Bangs says,

> The remaining contents of the *Opera* were to have been in a third volume, but the response to the first two was minimal. The Puritan-Arminian controversy in the Church of England was increasingly forgotten.... In both [England and the USA] Anglicans were turning their attention to other matters and would be completely distracted by the rise of the Oxford Movement. Nichols was discouraged and never completed his project.[3]

In the 1620s and 1630s the Calvinist Puritans had used 'Arminian' as a term of opprobrium for their high-church Caroline opponents, as in the so-called 'Arminian nunnery' of Little Gidding, and Bangs suggests that these opponents may have come to accept it for themselves.[4] If so, one might have expected the leaders of the Oxford Movement to have respected Arminius. The evidence suggests the reverse. The novelist and educator Charlotte Mary Yonge (1823-1901), friend and protegee of John Keble, who had made her name by publishing her novel *The Heir of Redclyffe* four years before, published in 1857 the final volume of her *Landmarks of History, Modern History: From the Reformation to the Fall of Napoleon*, which includes the following:

---

3 *Works*, I, p.xxvi.
4 *Works*, I, p.xxii.

A great heresy broke out in Holland, taught by a Leiden professor, Jacob Arminius, who denied the doctrine of the Holy Trinity, and exaggerated the Calvinist theory of predestination. Maurice of Nassau tried to silence him, but he was protected by two of the most respected of the Dutch, Barneveldt and Hugo Grotius, who were anxious to maintain toleration. Disputes ran high, and there was such a tumult in Utrecht, that Maurice marched in his troops and arrested both Barneveldt and Grotius.... The Arminian heresy was never quite weeded out of Holland.[5]

Maurice's arrest of Oldenbarneveldt and Grotius took place in 1618, nine years after Arminius' death; and Arminius hardly 'exaggerated' Calvinist doctrine! There is just one point in this travesty that is worth further investigation, Yonge's claim that Arminius denied the Trinity. But if this most theologically aware and personally saintly of greater novelists could produce this, it shows that Anglo-Catholics had no more time for Arminius than contemporary Calvinists had, and it places a question-mark against the so-called 'Arminianism' of Caroline high-churchmen.

There was a movement away from dogmatic theology in the later nineteenth century towards biblical exegesis, probably a result of the growth of theological liberalism and of critical theories concerning authorship, date and the textual history of the biblical books. Arminius was not a biblical commentator and his only works which bore any resemblance to commentaries were two early and in some ways immature works, the *Dissertation* on Romans 7 and the *Analysis* of Romans 9. The original versions were produced for his own use in defending himself before the Amsterdam Consistory from two charges brought against him. Arminius had said, in sermons on *Romans*, that Romans 7:14-25 refers to an unregenerate and not a regenerate man, and that Romans 9 teaches not a decree of God to save some and condemn others for reasons hidden to us but the salvation of those who seek righteousness by faith and the condemnation of those who seek it through the law. Both the *Dissertation* and *Analysis* attempt to justify these positions. The extremely influential commentary of 1895 by Sanday and Headlam in the International Critical Commentary series mentions these in the introduction to commentaries of the Reformation and Post-Reformation periods:

As a typical example of the opposite school of interpretation to that of Calvin may be taken Arminius.... Two tracts (sic) of his were devoted to explaining Romans vii and ix. He admirably illustrates the statement of Hallam that 'every one who had to defend a cause, found no course so ready as to explain the Scriptures consistently with his own tenets.'[6]

---

[5] *Landmarks of Modern History...by the Author of the "Heir of Redclyffe", "Kings of England"* etc. (London: J. and C. Mozley, and Masters, 1857), p.167.

[6] William Sanday and Arthur C. Headlam, *A Critical and Exegetical Commentary on the Epistle to the Romans* (Edinburgh: T&T Clark, 1895), p.civ.

In the section 'A History of the Interpretation of Romans ix.6-29' there is a longer summary of Arminius' views:

> Arminius represents absolute antagonism on every point to (Calvin's) views. The purpose of the chapter is, he says, the same as that of the Epistle...to prove 'Justification by Faith'.... The image of the potter and the clay is introduced to prove, not the absolute sovereignty of God, but his right to do what he will, that is to name his own conditions.... The condition is Justification by Faith.... At the beginning of the present [nineteenth] century the defects or inadequacies of both views became apparent.... Against Arminius Calvin's interpretation of c.ix was correct, that St. Paul's object in it was not to prove or defend justification by faith, but to discuss...why...some had obtained justification by faith and others had not. But equally clear was it that Calvin's interpretation...was inconsistent with c.x, and the language which St. Paul habitually uses elsewhere.[7]

By 1860 the Remonstrant Brotherhood had shrunk to a small rump, but it received a new lease of life when, around this date, many who had been influenced by critical views of the Bible left the Reformed Church to join it. In 1865, H.C. Rogge published a biography of Coolhaes, 'the forerunner of Arminius and the Remonstrants', and followed it with the letters and works of Uitenbogaert, Arminius' friend from early days and his life-long supporter and correspondent. He also produced a biography of Uitenbogaert, but there was no further biography of Arminius himself till Maronier's Dutch work of 1905. Maronier largely repeated Brandt and filled out his story with extracts from the letters of Arminius and others, and his work has largely been superseded by that of Bangs. While Maronier has little to say about Arminius' theology, his book has one continuing useful feature; he summarises the contents of Arminius' letters, including some not translated out of the Latin, nor mentioned by Nichols or Bangs. Meanwhile in Britain Methodists were largely concerned with their own internal divisions and reunification, and the first important historical work to appear on Arminius in English after William Nichols completed the translation of the *Works* begun by his father, in 1875, was Archibald W. Harrison's *The Beginnings of Arminianism to the Synod of Dort*,[8] which appeared in 1926. This again has largely been superseded by the works of Bangs, but remains a useful historical account. Harrison's later work, *Arminianism*, produced for the Duckworth series in 1937, is disappointing and contains little new material for the early period, the first few chapters being a summary of the previous book. Harrison missed the opportunity to give a precise definition of 'Arminianism', which makes his book compare unfavourably with Dakin's work of 1940 on *Calvinism* in the same series. We should also

---

7 Sanday and Headlam, *Romans*, p.274.
8 London: University of London Press, 1926.

mention the work by Howard Watkin-Jones, *The Holy Spirit from Arminius to Wesley*.[9] Neither Bangs, Muller or Dekker appears to have heard of Watkin-Jones, but his work has been useful in preparing the sections on the Holy Spirit and the Trinity in this book.

The supposed 400th anniversary of Arminius' birth, October 10 1960, was celebrated by an 'Arminius Symposium' in Amsterdam, organised by the Remonstrant Brotherhood in connection with the meeting that year of the International Congregational Council to which they belong. Various articles were produced, and also an edition in Dutch of the *Verklaring (Declaration of Sentiments)* with a new introduction by Dr G.J. Hoenderdaal.[10]

The most significant publication on Arminius has been Carl Bangs' biography *Arminius: A Study in the Dutch Reformation* of 1970,[11] which went into a second edition in 1985 with additions, mostly of a biographical nature. This will remain the standard biography for the foreseeable future, and was at the time of publication the best introduction to his theology. Dr Bangs is concerned not to overstress differences between Arminius and his Reformed contemporaries, and wishes to see him as essentially a Reformed theologian who was 'Reformed' in a rather different way from some contemporaries and most later Reformed. For example:

> In both...assurance and perseverance, Arminius develops Reformed theology in a manner somewhat apart from the later mainstream, but it is a development of Reformed theology, not an intrusion of Pelagianism or humanism from the outside. And there were many in the Reformed church of his day who agreed with him.[12]

There is no copyright on the word 'Reformed'. In a sense any church that arose out of the Reformation, including Lutherans and Anabaptists, could be called that; even the Roman Catholic Church would qualify for the title in the sense that its life, if not its doctrine, was reformed at the Council of Trent. It is, however, more helpful to confine the word to the 'later mainstream' and the theology of which that mainstream was a continuation. The other weakness of Bangs' work from a theological point of view is that it concentrates on the theological subjects which became controversial in Arminius' own time, and later writers, particularly Muller, have shown that this is to ignore important aspects of Arminius' theology.

---

9 London: Epworth Press, 1929.
10 De Tijdstroom: Lochem, 1960.
11 Nashville: Abingdon Press, 1970; 2nd edition edited Joseph D. Allison, Grand Rapids: Zondervan Publishing House, 1985.
12 Bangs, *Arminius*, p.349.

Since Arminius' orthodoxy was first questioned in 1592 by Plancius, strict Calvinists or Reformed scholars have tended to treat Arminius as a congenital deceiver whose statements can never be relied upon even as a description of his own beliefs. A comparatively recent example of this is the booklet *The Manifold Grace of God*, papers read at the Puritan and Reformed Studies Conference of 1968.[13] In such instances there is no point in quoting from what Arminius said, and there are no quotations.[14] During the 1970s this changed, perhaps as a result of Bangs' great biography which at last showed the Calvinists and Reformed that they could not continue to ignore the views of Arminius himself. The first work by a Reformed theologian to take Arminius' statements seriously was perhaps R.T. Kendall's *Calvin and English Calvinism to 1649*.[15] Dr Kendall is concerned with the doctrine of faith and with stressing the difference between Calvin's doctrine of faith and that of later Calvinists. He has a chapter on Arminius because he (Kendall) finds the same doctrine of faith in his works as in William Perkins, and argues that Perkins' doctrine of faith lays him open to the criticisms which Arminius made in his *Examination of Perkins's Pamphlet*. Kendall is hostile to Arminius; he calls his 'bringing the decrees [the Calvinist decrees of predestination] in line with his voluntaristic view of faith' 'his sin', and accuses Arminius of *stealing* from Reformed theology Calvin's conviction that Christ died for all men, as if this insight were Calvin's own personal property and not to be found in a number of New Testament texts like 2 Corinthians 5:14, as well as in later writers.[16] But Kendall may be the first Reformed theologian to allow Arminius to speak for himself and to assume that he really means what he says; and only when this is assumed can there be meaningful dialogue.

We may also briefly mention Paul K. Jewett's *Election and Predestination*,[17] a fairly brief overview which resuscitates the old infralapsarian Calvinism of Corneliszoon and Donteklok. However, Jewett also selects the doctrine of Karl Barth for criticism, and implies a comparison between Barth and Arminius that Barth himself was unwilling

---

13 See especially John R. de Witt's comments on pp.9-10. E.g., 'The man pledged himself to adhere in his teaching to the doctrine of the Church...and then set out in private ways to undermine and alter it, he was guilty of a very serious fault indeed.'

14 But the supposed followers of Arminius have also often avoided direct quotation of Arminius and have contented themselves with the vague entity of 'Arminianism'. This is true of the nine Methodist theologians who prepared the symposium *Freedom and Grace* as an 'exploration of the Arminian emphasis on divine grace' (London: Epworth Press, 1988).

15 Oxford: Oxford University Press, 1979; 2nd edition with new Preface, Carlisle: Paternoster Press, 1997.

16 Kendall, *Calvin*, pp.147, 150.

17 Grand Rapids: Eerdmans/Carlisle: Paternoster Press, 1985.

to make.[18] The same comparison is made by the Dutch writer Dr C. Graafland in his 'Van Calvijn tot Barth: Oorsprong en ontwikkeling van de leer der verkiezing in het Gereformeerd Protestantisme' ('From Calvin to Barth: Source and Development of the Doctrine of Election in the Protestant Reformation').[19] He also finds a link between election and righteousness in both Arminius and Barth. There is also useful material in B. Loonstra's *Verkiezing-Verzoening-Verbond; Beschrieving en Beoordeling van de leer van het PACTUM SALUTIS in de gereformeerde theologie* (*Election-Reconciliation-Union: Description and Evaluation of the Doctrine of the Covenant of Salvation in Reformed Theology*), concerned with Arminius' doctrine of covenant.[20]

However, Arminius' own followers were not idle. Two symposia edited by Clark H. Pinnock, *Grace Unlimited* (1975) and *The Grace of God and the Will of Man* (1989) both include useful material; in the former volume essays by Osborne, Strauss, Skevington Wood and particularly Donald M. Lake are helpful introductions to the subject; in the latter those by Pinnock himself and Rice. The most useful work from the 'Arminian' side of recent times is the article 'The Righteousness of Saving Faith: Arminian versus Remonstrant Grace', by J.M. Hicks.[21] Two other articles in the Evangelical Quarterly of the early 1990s are worth mentioning: Charles M. Cameron's 'Arminius—Hero or Heretic?',[22] and the apparently unconnected 'The Declaration of Sentiments: The Theological Testament of Arminius'[23] by A. Skevington Wood, his last published work. Both articles are sound while containing little new material. The recent work by Roger E. Olson on the history of doctrine recognises Arminius' importance by devoting a whole chapter to him, 'Arminius's Attempt to Reform Reformed Theology', but again there is little that is new.[24]

We turn finally to two Reformed theologians who have published important works concentrating on Arminius' own opinions. Richard A. Muller's interest in 'Arminianism' dates back at least to 1982 and his article on 'The Federal Motif in Seventeenth Century Arminian Theology'.[25] A main concern of Muller's is the link between medieval scholasticism and the theology of the sixteenth and seventeenth centuries, whether Roman Catholic, Reformed, Lutheran or 'Arminian', and in

---

18 Jewett, *Election*, p.92 and n.55 on the same page.
19 's-Gravenhage: Uitgeverij Boekencentrum BV, 1987.
20 's-Gravenhage: Uitgeverij Boekencentrum BV, 1990, pp.21-28.
21 *Evangelical Journal* 9 (1991), pp. 27-39.
22 Vol. LXIV/No. 3, July 1992, pp.213-28.
23 Vol. 65.2, April 1993, pp.111-29.
24 *The Story of Christian Theology* (Leicester: Apollos, 1999).
25 *Nederlands Archief voor de Kerkgeschiedenis* (hereafter *NAKG*), 62 (1982), pp.102-22.

1986 he published *Christ and the Decree: Christology and Predestination in Reformed Theology from Calvin to Perkins*,[26] which considers the Christological foundations of the doctrine of predestination of early Reformed theologians. In 1988 he published an article directly on Arminius, 'The Christological Problem in the Thought of Jacobus Arminius',[27] which in a sense does for Arminius what he had done for Reformed theologians in the earlier book; it is, however, highly critical of Arminius. The argument of the article will receive fuller consideration later. His most useful work on Arminius is a later book, *God, Creation and Providence in the Thought of Jacob Arminius: Sources and Directions of Scholastic Protestantism in the Era of Early Orthodoxy*,[28] in which he brings his great knowledge and understanding of scholasticism to bear on early orthodoxy in general and Arminius in particular. This is an exceptionally valuable study which has shown the importance of Arminius' work in many spheres, notably theological prolegomena and the subjects of the title, which, with the exception of providence, have not aroused controversy in Arminius' time or later. The present study will, however, re-examine some of Muller's conclusions, particularly on the subjects of the nature of God, creation and providence.

The other important recent study is that by Evert Dekker, *Rijker dan Midas: Vrijheid, Genade en Predestinatie in de Theologie van Jacobus Arminius*,[29] (*Richer than Midas: Freedom, Grace and Predestination in the Theology of Jacobus Arminius*), which, as the title says, considers issues like grace and predestination as well as God's will and human freewill.

Both Muller and Dekker stress the influence of sixteenth-century Catholic thinkers like Suarez and Bellarmine, and especially Luis de Molina (1535-1600), the Jesuit theologian, on Arminius. They would see the Calvinist-Arminian controversy over predestination and other doctrines as a Protestant parallel to the slightly earlier Dominican-Jesuit controversy in the Roman Catholic Church. This point deserves further consideration.

The important work of Dr H.B. McGonigle, *Sufficient Saving Grace: John Wesley's Evangelical Arminianism*,[30] appeared too late to be taken into full consideration when preparing this study, but its opening chapter considers Arminius' theology before moving to that of Wesley.

We see that although some theologians, notably Hicks, have considered important aspects of the work and person of Christ in Arminius'

---

26 Studies in Historical Theology 2 (Durham, NC: Labyrinth Press, 1986; 2nd edition Grand Rapids, MI: Baker Book House, 1988).
27 *NAKG* 68 (1988), pp.145-63.
28 Grand Rapids: Baker Book House, 1991.
29 Zoetermeer: Uitgeverij Boekencentrum BV, 1993.
30 Carlisle: Paternoster Press, 2001.

theology, there remains room and need for a full-scale study of the subject.

CHAPTER 2

The Reluctant Theologian: Pastorate and Predestination from 1591–1603

Most of Arminius' theological career was a process of discovery, and Christology was at the very centre of this. Hence it would necessarily somewhat distort the picture to begin with a crystal-clear thesis which is worked out inexorably in the remainder of this book. As we shall see, Bertius in his *Funeral Oration* came close to this approach by suggesting that everything resulted from a request to Arminius to answer Corneliszoon and Donteklok's pamphlet, while in our own time Dekker and Kendall have taken as their starting-point that Arminius discovered that predestination is of believers, and built up all his theology on that basis. But Arminius' theology was not the result of startling revelation of unfamiliar truth early in his ministry, which he then worked out step by step. If it had been, this study would have been easier to write. He was originally reluctant to get involved at all, and when he became convinced that he must, he had to find out what he needed to say over the years, while all the time his opponents were watching with deepening suspicion and hostility. There was no inevitable outcome to this process, except perhaps in the recesses of Arminius' own personality. Perhaps most theologians who had undertaken this work would have finished by accepting the supralapsarian doctrine of predestination which was to become more and more dominant for three-quarters of the seventeenth century, whether they accepted it through conviction, desire for a quiet life, or sheer laziness. Arminius could not do this.

His doctrine of Christ is at least as important as his (undoubtedly important) doctrines of theological prolegomena, and of God (which Muller has highlighted), and which certainly had a more positive influence on seventeenth-century Reformed theology. I would argue that the doctrine of Christ is even more important and fundamental, using chronological evidence at both ends of his career. There is much earlier evidence for his concern with the doctrine of Christ (1591, as against 1599 for theological prolegomena and the doctrine of God), and he returned to it in his final controversies of 1604-09.

Arminius did not start writing systematic theology till comparatively late in his career, around the age of forty, but it would be a mistake to think that his earlier experiences did not influence his later thought.

We should not begin with the actual outbreak of Christological controversy in 1606. As early as 1599 Arminius had privately expressed views similar to those which caused trouble at the later date. These views had been, and continued to be, developed in his controversies over predestination, which, as we shall see in chapter 4, is for Arminius a part of Christology. Predestination is not a matter of the eternal decrees of God determining the individual's fate irrespective of that individual's choices, nor is it an aspect of human psychology and free-will, as perhaps it became for later Remonstrants.

The life of Arminius has been described in detail elsewhere, and this study does not seek to provide a biography. For the fullest, most up-to-date account of Arminius' life and times readers are referred to the second (1985) edition of Carl Bangs' *Arminius: A Study in the Dutch Reformation*. A shorter account, which adds to and occasionally corrects Bangs' work, is given in Evert Dekker's *Rijker dan Midas*, especially in Hoofdstuk (Chapter) 2 and Bijlagen (Appendices) 2, 3 and 4. Chapter 2 of Richard A. Muller's *God, Creation and Providence* is concerned with the theological influences brought to bear on Arminius at various stages of his life, and his reactions to them.[1]

There are, however, a few biographical points which have not, in my opinion, been given full weight in earlier works, of which two should be mentioned at the outset. The first is the influence of Johannes Drusius, whom Arminius came to know when Drusius arrived in Leiden as Professor of Hebrew in 1577. Arminius himself left Leiden in 1581, and the two may not even have met personally afterwards, yet Arminius kept up occasional correspondence with Drusius at least between 1595 and 1608, and we have more of his letters to Drusius than to any other correspondent with the exception of Uitenbogaert. In view of this it seems surprising that Muller never mentions Drusius, and that Dekker, though he lists all Arminius' letters to him, only mentions Drusius briefly and occasionally. But one of Arminius' last letters is evidence for a particularly deep and lasting impression made by the older man on the younger:

> You have two qualities, above all others, which I cannot but extol; The FIRST is, that you openly declare that you are still in doubt and suspend your judgment, where, after the arguments have been produced, you are afraid of giving a full assent. The SECOND is, that you do not refuse at this period of your life to change your opinions, even after you have been for many years so well versed in these matters. I

---

1 C. Bangs, *Arminius: A Study in the Dutch Reformation* (Nashville, TN: Abingdon Press, 1971); E. Dekker, *Rijker dan Midas: Vrijheid, Genade en Predestinatie in de Theologie van Jacobus Arminius (1559-1609)* (Zoetermeer: Uitgeverij Boekencentrum B.V., 1993); Richard A. Muller, *God, Creation and Providence in the Thought of Jacobus Arminius* (Granda Rapids, MI: Baker Book House, 1991).

love these two properties so much the more, because they are very close to my own intentions.... All religious doctrines are not equally necessary. For this [belief]...I am calumniated by many persons, who carry *the knowledge of all things* enclosed within the casket of their own breast, from which, whenever they are interrogated on any subject, they suppose that they utter nothing less than oracles which must be received with open hearts and ears. Nor am I ashamed to have occasionally forsaken some sentiments instilled by my masters, since it appears to me that I can prove by the most forcible arguments that such a change has been made for the better.[2]

Drusius was at this time (6 April 1608) Professor at Franeker, and an opponent of Arminius' opponent Lubbertus, who was also teaching at Franeker. We see that even before Arminius went to Geneva, he had learned from Drusius not to accept blindly everything he was told, but to examine it, suspend judgment if necessary, and not to fear to change his opinions if he must. It is likely that he stuck to this approach during his university career and after.

The second point is that when he signed the agreement in 1581 to devote his life to the service of the Amsterdam church on completion of his studies, he had no expectation of doing anything else, and when he finally took up his duties in 1588 nothing had changed, in that respect at least. Unlike some theologians who then as now spent little or no time in pastoral work in churches, Arminius spent over two-thirds of his ministry in them. This cannot have failed to influence his views. He wanted to give all he could to preaching and pastoral work, and at the same time not to neglect philosophical and theological studies, but to keep abreast of contemporary developments and to let ministerial work and academic studies cross-fertilise. There is plenty of general evidence for this in his letters and writings, but it is harder to pinpoint the precise effect of his pastoral experience on his theology. The clearest, longest and most interesting evidence unfortunately comes from almost the end of his pastoral career, during the plague of 1602. The subject matter is the nature of justifying faith, and we know that he had been concerned about the nature of faith and its relation to salvation at least since his letter to Uitenbogaert of 8 September 1592. In 1602, a man and a woman from Arminius' church, unknown to each other, both ill of the plague, who were 'of good life and unspotted reputation, and in my opinion true Christians', were concerned that they did not have assurance of the remission of sins and the testimony of the Holy Spirit in their hearts. As they believed that this assurance and testimony were equivalent to justifying faith, they despaired. Arminius investigated and confirmed that

---

2 *Praestantium ac Eruditorum Virorum Epistolae Ecclesiasticae et Theologicae* (Amsterdam, 1704), no.115; hereafter referred to as *Ep.*, translation by Nichols, *Works*, I, p.168 (revised).

they believed fully in Jesus Christ as Saviour, then told them that this is justifying faith, of which remission of sins is the fruit, and the sense of remission (assurance) necessarily follows, though possibly later (cf. Romans 5:1). 'Two days after', says Arminius, 'the man died in the Lord.'[3] A fuller theological consideration is appropriately left to the next chapter, but this shows how he developed his views on the work of Christ as a pastor in Amsterdam.

His first extant writing is a letter to Burckhardt Leemann, professor of Hebrew at Zurich, written from Geneva in August 1585. It is reprinted in volume 1 of De Vries de Heekelingen's *Genève: Pepinière du Calvinisme Hollandais*.[4] Some writers mention this letter, but fail to note that it has no theological content and was written to an older scholar whom he had met on a recent visit, commending his young friends who were travelling to Zurich and asking for similar kindness to be extended to them. The next letter is to Uitenbogaert on 10 February 1591, answering a letter of the 7th from Uitenbogaert; the only matter to notice is the postscript, asking Uitenbogaert to think about the question of original sin in Romans 5, which Arminius himself was investigating, doubtless as part of his preaching through Romans.[5] Up to this point we have really no firm knowledge of Arminius' theology, and can only guess at what it might have been from the concerns of his teachers and his own later views.

According to Bertius' *Funeral Oration*, early in his time at Amsterdam Arminius received a request to engage in theological controversy.[6] In 1589 two ministers of Delft, Arent Corneliszoon and Reynier Donteklok, had published a manuscript which may not have appeared as a printed book and is now lost, entitled (in English) *Answer to Certain Arguments of Beza and Calvin: from a Treatise on Predestination on the Ninth Chapter of the Epistle to the Romans*. It was based on an argument they had had as long ago as 1578 with the veteran humanist critic of Reformed theology, Dirck Volckertszoon Coornhert. The two authors had decided that the supralapsarian standpoint of Beza, according to which God's predestinating decree antedated the fall, could not be maintained, and that critics like Coornhert could only be answered from an infralapsarian position (God's predestinating decree coming after the Fall). According to Bertius, Martin Lydius, formerly minister at Amsterdam and since 1583 professor at Franeker, sent a copy of the manuscript to Arminius requesting that he defend the doctrine of his master Beza. According to Brandt, the Consistory of Amsterdam had already made a similar request

---

3 *Ep.* 56, in *Works*, I, pp.176-9; cf. Bangs, *Arminius*, p.174.

4 Fribourg: Fragnière Frères, 1918, vol. 1, pp.240-42 (being the earliest known letter of Arminius)

5 *Letter* III, in H.C. Rogge, *Brieven en onuitgegeven stukken van Johannes Uitenbogaert*, dl. [volume] 1 (Utrecht, 1868), pp.7-8.

6 See *Works*, I, pp.29f.

to Arminius.⁷ Bertius claimed that Arminius was at first happy to make the attempt, but was then first convinced by the arguments of Corneliszoon and Donteklok, and afterwards became dissatisfied with both forms of predestinarian doctrine. In other words, reading this pamphlet marked his conversion from Calvinism.

This account has been reproduced by most writers without further examination, but it was challenged, rightly, by de Vries in the early twentieth century, and more importantly by Bangs. It has done harm because it implies, first that Arminius held a Calvinist view of predestination, and second that a particular event—the reading of a manuscript—marked the beginning of a change of opinion. It seems that up to about 1590, Arminius had given no particular attention to predestination or to any specific Christian doctrine. His personal interests had been in philosophy, not theology. If asked for his opinion, he would probably have answered in the words of his church's confessional standards, the *Belgic Confession* and the *Heidelberg Catechism*. In this sense he might loosely have been described as a 'Calvinist', but one with no personal commitment to any doctrine of predestination. Reading Corneliszoon and Donteklok, if he ever did, settled nothing.

As Bangs recognises, the next letter to Grynaeus, of 10 March 1591, disproves both parts of Bertius' thesis. While Bangs' analysis of this letter⁸ is helpful, except for his slight rearrangement of the material, it requires more detailed analysis. Bangs finds the mood of the letter 'one of surprise', but I would describe it as troubled:

> The confusion of opinions and heresies among us is incredible. Nothing was formerly so certain that it will not be called into question, nothing is so holy as to be immune from blasphemy. What shall I say? Everyone knows everything, no one is ignorant in any way, so they maintain whatever intolerable impudence they like, yet it is to be tolerated, because it seems that no agreement can remove it. When I think about these things they make me incurably sad, a sadness increased by the almost supine indifference of nearly all our people, and their neglecting to seek remedies, and there is similar confidence in many of us in asserting and saying what you like before whom you like.... I wish that we too would imitate the prudence of the apostle to the *Hebrews* and the ancient fathers in dispensing divine mysteries.

It is at this point that he mentions many and great controversies about predestination, original sin, free will etc., and his inability to extricate himself from them, which it appears he would dearly have loved to do. Such controversies may well have included requests to refute the Delft ministers and Coornhert, but there were obviously many more, and

---

7 Caspar Brandt, *The Life of James Arminius, D.D.* (trans. John Guthrie; London 1854, and Nashville 1857), p.61.

8 Bangs, *Arminius*, pp.139f.

Bertius is clearly wrong in supposing that Arminius reacted by calmly investigating the subject of predestination and equally calmly deciding that he disagreed with what was being taught. On the contrary, Arminius remained confused and worried. His unwelcome involvement, he says, has led him to read, enquire, search the scriptures and recognised theologians, and pray, and he has decided that many aspects of these subjects are obscure and the average Christian does not need to know all about them in order to be saved.[9]

This did not mean that he was dismissing the whole subject and washing his hands of it. Instead, he reacted positively, asking himself, What do I really believe? What are the foundations of my faith?

> I console myself with this thought alone, that while I hold on to the foundations [*fundamenta*], I cannot err so as to endanger my own salvation, nor can I be the author or cause of error in others. I believe that our salvation rests on Christ alone, and that we are made participants of this salvation by grace alone, through the working of the Holy Spirit by faith, for the forgiveness of sins and the renewing of life.[10]

These two sentences are in effect Arminius' manifesto at the beginning of his theological career, and his whole doctrine of the work of Christ can be seen as unpacking the implications of this statement. It would be going too far to suggest that Arminius had this statement consciously in mind every time he formulated his later views of the work of Christ. But the remainder of this study will show that he never went back on any part of this statement, and much of his later theology illustrates it. Bangs uses it as if it were the letter's conclusion, but, perhaps significantly, it is not. Arminius goes back to the subjects he has mentioned, and speaks of them in more detail.

Some, he says, make the subject of predestination man, not only before the fall but even before his creation (the 'creabilitarian' view, later called supralapsarianism); others make it man created but not yet fallen (a variant of the supralapsarian view); while others make it man fallen and liable to damnation (later called infralapsarianism). The definition of original sin and (possible) ways of its propagation are discussed, and whether the corruption of human nature comes before guilt or not; then the point about opponents who deny original sin altogether, which, as

---

9 *Letter* IX, in *Bibliotheca Historico-Philologico-Theologica* (= *Bibliotheca Bremensis*), *Classis Tertiae, Fasciculus Secundus* (Amsterdam, 1720), pp.384-7 (my translation); cf. Bangs, *Arminius*, pp.139f.

10 *Letter* IX, p.386: 'Hoc unico me consolor, quod dum fundamenta teneo, cum periculo salutis errare non possum, nec aliis author aut causa erroris esse. Credo in unico Christo salutem nostram positam, huius nos mera gratia per Spiritus Sancti efficaciam fide participes fieri ad remissionem peccatorum et vitae renovationem.'

Bangs says, must mean the humanist followers of Coornhert—who want proved everything about original sin, Adam's fall, God's supernatural gifts to Adam and his posterity, and what gifts Adam lost by sin and what took their place—for they deny them one by one. There are problems with (human) free will too; is it merely passive in an unregenerate man or active in his conversion; if active, is it prevenient or subsequent, or is it at the same time operating and contributory?[11]

Why did he go back to discuss these views? It is because he saw them as unhelpful. At best they obscured the foundations (*fundamenta*) of Christ and the Holy Spirit, of grace, salvation, faith, forgiveness of sins and renewing of life, that he had mentioned. At worst, they denied them and introduced error in their place. Henceforth, all he has to say about Christ's work will be devoted to two ends; either affirming the *fundamenta*, or examining and rejecting the 'confusion of opinions and heresies' which threaten them.

In this sense there was a negative, reactionary element in Arminius' theology from the start, but he was reacting, not against any particular Calvinist or Reformed doctrine, but against the hated 'confusion of opinions'. The only doctrines to which he states his own opposition are not any of the Calvinists, but those of the 'libertines' who deny original sin and Adam's fall. It was only much later, probably after Gomarus' theses of 1604, certainly before the *Declaration of Sentiments* in 1608, that he would single out the supralapsarian doctrine of predestination as uniquely dangerous, and devote his energies above all to attacking it. But this, too, had a positive purpose; to ensure that the foundation doctrines of the work of Christ and his Holy Spirit were neither denied nor obscured. In practice, he sometimes stressed the negative (opposing wrong opinions and heresies), at other times he stressed the positive (describing Christ's work). The former appears more in disputes with Junius, Perkins, Gomarus and in the *Declaration of Sentiments*; the latter is shown above all in the *Disputations*, both private and public.

Finally, in this letter Arminius was asking for Grynaeus' help. Whether he received a helpful reply, or any reply, we do not know. It would be some years before he worked out a doctrine of predestination which satisfied him, and till then he would not feel in a position to challenge anyone else's doctrine.

The next text is the *Dissertation* on Romans 7, a response to the challenge to Arminius' interpretation in his sermons late in 1591, a challenge emanating primarily from Plancius. Was the man described by Paul in Romans 7:14-25 regenerate or unregenerate? The difficulty of using the *Dissertation* to describe Arminius' views in 1591-92 is that it was only published after his death in 1612, and Arminius may have

---

11 *Letter* IX, pp.386f.

altered it as his views developed. This interpretation is suggested by the 'Dedication' from his 'nine orphan children', which states that 'if God had granted him longer life, he would have corrected his production with greater accuracy, as he had already begun to do'.[12] With this proviso, we may examine the *Dissertation* as we have it; presumably a work designed to answer the question whether the man of Romans 7 concerned is regenerate or unregenerate must contain some definition of regeneration.

Arminius is concerned to appeal to recognised Reformed authorities in support of his views; to Beza's *Refutation of the Calumnies of Til(e)man(n) Heshusius*, the Lutheran whose challenge to the Reformed doctrine of predestination in 1560 marked the break between the Lutherans and the Reformed on the subject, and to Calvin's work on *Initial Fear* to the same effect and also to the *Institutes*, Book 3 Chapter 3. In the cited work, Beza makes what Arminius calls a 'charming distinction' between 'the things which precede regeneration' and 'regeneration itself'.[13] To Arminius there is only one kind of regenerate man, one whom Christ frees from the rigour of the law through his Spirit; a sinner whom Christ came to call, in a call which precedes justification and sanctification, which, taken together, Arminius equates with regeneration; and justification is also through Christ (Galatians 2:16).[14] In the detailed exposition, Christ overcomes the armed strong man, binds him hand and foot and casts him out, then occupies his house (the human person), and dwells in it by faith through the Holy Spirit.[15] There is also a beautiful description of regeneration summing up the interpretation of Romans 7:18:

> The unregenerate are SINNERS, whom Christ came to call; LABOURING and HEAVY-LADEN, to whom He came with refreshment and rest; SICK and INFIRM, who need a physician; POOR and NEEDY, to whom He came with the Gospel; CAPTIVES and PRISONERS IN BONDS, whom He came to deliver; CONTRITE IN SPIRIT and BROKEN-HEARTED, whom He came to bind up, etc. But when Christ's Spirit acts on such, the same persons become BELIEVERS, JUSTIFIED, REDEEMED, SANCTIFIED, REGENERATED, and LIBERATED, GRAFTED INTO CHRIST, MADE ONE BODY WITH HIM, BONES OF HIS BONES AND FLESH OF HIS FLESH, etc.[16]

But,

---

12 *Works*, II, pp.484f.
13 *Works*, II, pp.495f.
14 *Works*, II, pp.492-5.
15 *Works*, II, p.529, on Romans 7:17; cf. Romans 6:2 and Galatians 2:20.
16 *Works*, II, p.543; Arminius' emphases, which in the original *Opera Theologica* (Frankfurt, 2nd edn, 1631), are marked not with capitals, but in heavier small type. Nichols' translation replaces this here, and elsewhere, with capitals.

an unregenerate man is—not only he who is entirely blind, ignorant of God's will, knowingly and willingly contaminating himself with sins without any remorse of conscience, affected with no sense of God's wrath, terrified with no compunctious visits of conscience, not oppressed with the burden of sin, and inflamed with no desire of deliverance....

Clearly the man of Romans 7:14-25 is not *that* sort of man. But an unregenerate man

is also he who knows God's will and does it not, who is acquainted with the way of righteousness but departs from it; who has God's law written in his heart...who receives God's word with gladness and for a season rejoices in its light; who comes to baptism but...does not receive the word itself with a good heart or...does not bring forth fruit; who is affected with a painful sense of sin, is oppressed with its burden, and who sorrows after a godly sort; who knows that righteousness cannot be acquired by the law

but who has not yet fled to Christ. *That* is the sort of unregenerate man pictured in Romans 7.[17]

Yet the whole passage from Romans 7:14 onwards is oddly Christ-less for Paul; there is no mention of Christ between 7:4 and 7:25. Consequently, in this earliest and longest treatise of Arminius, there is comparatively little about Christ either. It is concerned mainly with the psychology of the sinner and of the regenerate. This point can be overstated; Arminius wanted all men seriously to consider how God leads us to faith in his Son, and to the obedience of this faith; and how he converts a sinner through the Law and Gospel, through the Holy Spirit uniting us to Christ and so regenerating us.[18] Nor has he, as we have seen, entirely forgotten the points he had made in his letter of the previous year, that salvation rests on Christ alone and that our sins are forgiven and our life renewed through the grace of the Holy Spirit. But the *Dissertation* remains more psychological than theological. The argument is summed up in the fifth part, where 'it is shown that the opposite opinion is injurious to Grace'.[19] His opponents (including Plancius?) had argued that 'those who explain this passage in reference to a man living under the law, [hold] a doctrine which has some affinity to the...heresy of Pelagius...and...ascribe to man, without the grace of Christ, some true and saving good'.[20] At the end Arminius turns the tables and argues that

an injury is inflicted on grace, not only by him who attributes to nature or free will that which belongs to grace...but likewise by him who attributes to it less than its

---

17 *Works*, II, p.497f.
18 *Opera*, p.881; *Works*, II pp.587f.
19 *Works*, II, p.656.
20 *Works*, II, p.489.

due.... The Scriptures ascribe to Divine Grace that in the regenerate, it works not only to will but also to do (Philippians 2:13)...but this modern opinion [says] that its only effect in the regenerate is to will, not to do, that it is too weak to crucify the old man, to destroy the body of sin, or to conquer the world, the flesh, and Satan. For the regenerate man, according to this opinion, is said to obey sin in its lusts, and to walk after the desires of the flesh, though...compelled by the violence of sin, in opposition to conscience, and with a reluctant will.

This was why St Augustine interpreted the chapter as referring to concupiscence; he perceived that if he interpreted it concerning actual sins, he would be inflicting injury upon grace.[21]

Arminius confirms this by his own pastoral experience. He knew a man who was admonished not to commit a crime but who replied 'that it was indeed his will so to refrain, but that he must declare, with the apostle, "We are unable to perform the good that we would"', and a woman who was blamed for something 'which she knew she had perpetrated against God's law and her own conscience', who replied even more coolly, 'that as she had done that...with a reluctant will and not with a full consent, in this she experienced something similar to what the apostle Paul endured when he said, "The evil that I would not, that I do."' On the other hand, some, both men and women, young and old, to whom Arminius explained Romans 7 in the sense he gave it in the *Dissertation*, confessed,

> that they had always previously entertained the opinion that if they had...perpetrated any evil with a reluctant mind, or had omitted the performance of any good when their conscience exclaimed against [it)], it was not necessary...to care much...or deeply to lament it, since they considered themselves...to be similar to St. Paul.

Such people thanked Arminius for delivering them from a false opinion.[22] There is, therefore, much in the *Dissertation* to indicate that Arminius had Christ and his work, and the need for it, in his mind when writing; yet most of the time Arminius seems more interested in the psychological difference between the regenerate and the unregenerate, and if this is what concerned his critics of the Classis in Amsterdam, they may have had a point.

As Dekker hardly mentions the 1591 letter to Grynaeus, so Bangs does not mention the important letter of 6 September 1592 to Uitenbogaert. Dekker mentions it briefly,[23] mainly as an introduction to the *Collatio* with Junius. In this letter Arminius expresses his wish to meet Junius and discuss theology with him. Arminius was writing to his friend about a book he had recently received, *De Efficitate Christi servatoris in omnibus*

---

21 *Works*, II, pp.656f.
22 *Works*, II, pp.659f.
23 Dekker, *Rijker dan Midas*, p.33 n.75.

et singulis hominibus quatenus homines (*Of the efficacy of Christ as a saviour to all individual men as human beings*), by Franciscus Puccius Filidenus, an Italian Roman Catholic who tried to prove from scripture and the Fathers that all men are saved through Christ by the kindness and universal grace of the Father, so that no one will perish eternally, unless by his own perpetual ingratitude and wickedness he prepares eternal punishment for himself in this life. From what we know of his later views, we might have expected Arminius to agree with Puccius. Interestingly, he does not at this stage of his career. As Dekker says, this went much too far for him. But he understood that Junius had taken it upon himself to refute this book, and was now doing so. Possibly disappointed in the lack of helpful response from Grynaeus, Arminius rejoiced that such an opportunity had been given to 'the most learned of men' to benefit the churches so much, and to pacify the minds of many who were wavering round that heresy. This is surprising in more than one way. Months after Arminius had fallen foul of Plancius by his views on Romans 7, and after that particular dispute had subsided, he was still identifying himself with the Reformed, rather than with their critics, on the subject of predestination. Bangs' comment that 'the issue of predestination was just under the surface of Arminius' treatment of Romans 7, but he never let it come to light'[24] looks very dubious; it seems that in spite of Plancius' accusations Arminius had not made up his mind about predestination by September 1592 and was looking to Junius to solve the problem. However, Arminius himself has something to say. He considers that Puccius has raised two questions; first, whether Christ by God's decree died for all men individually, without discrimination being made between men by predestination; second, what the means is by which man comes into the communion of Christ, whether by a faith in Christ alone which rests upon knowledge of his person and office, or by 'something universal in God'. In other words, whom and what sort of men has God in Christ and through Christ decided to save? Arminius posits a double decree of God and a definite (*certam*) condition of salvation to be followed in and through Christ. He repeats the question about predestination put eighteen months before to Grynaeus, whether God decided to save some and damn others from men neither created nor fallen, or from men already fallen; or to put it another way, whether predestination is prior to the fall, and the fall is a subordinate means of executing the decree, or whether the fall was the occasion of making the decree. He also wants the question fully treated, what things it is absolutely necessary to know and believe in order to be saved. He has

---

24 Bangs, *Arminius*, p.193.

great hopes of Junius and wants to confer with him on this and similar matters, and asks for Uitenbogaert's help in arranging an introduction.[25]

Clearly, Arminius was at this time still uncertain about many aspects of predestination. So far from being converted to final views around 1589-90, he was still doubtful in 1592, and ignored requests to debate the subject because he had not made up his own mind. He also retained his Reformed aversion to any doctrine of God's universal salvific will, which appeared to ignore predestination. He was still looking to Junius to resolve the issues. But there is a hint in his 'second question', as also in the query whether election was made from men already reconciled with (God) himself through Christ, that there may be a condition in predestination. A few months later, preaching on Romans 9, he appears to have identified faith as that condition.

Whatever Arminius had to say in his sermons about the passage which actually mentions predestination in Romans 8:29-30, it appears to have escaped the eagle eyes of Plancius and his friends. Presumably there can be no better proof that it was non-committal and innocuous from their standpoint. But on 25 March 1593, Arminius was challenged on his interpretation of Romans 9:18, 'God has mercy on anyone he wishes and makes stubborn anyone he wishes'. It is not clear whether the doctrine in the *Analysis* of Romans 9, sent to Snecanus in 1596, represents exactly what Arminius had preached three years earlier and defended in the Consistory, the meeting of the elders of the church. At this March meeting he agreed that he interpreted Romans 9:18 differently from the *margin* of the *Confession* but argued that his brethren often used similar liberty in interpretation. At a later meeting of the Consistory on 27 May he argued that his interpretation of Article 16 of the *Belgic Confession*, that God saves and preserves all whom he in his goodness has elected in Jesus Christ our Lord, as referring to believers, was acceptable; and the Consistory agreed. So we may assume that the *Analysis* is a fair representation of his preaching of 1593.

In the *Analysis* Christ is mentioned quite frequently, but usually as the object of faith in a way that could suggest he had no more to do with the actual procuring and distribution of salvation than the bronze serpent which Moses lifted up in the wilderness; as if God exhibited both serpent and Christ as passive objects of faith to be seen and believed on. Christ is called the 'Mediator' by whom God enters into the covenant of grace with us, and this is further explained: 'on whom that cause of mankind might be laid, to be conducted and carried through before the tribunal of justice, whereby man might be a vessel for illustrating goodness and justice in the highest and most excellent manner'.[26] His later explanations

---

25 Rogge, *Brieven, Letter* VI, pp.15ff.
26 *Works*, III. pp.591, 497, 513.

of how Christ is Mediator will, as we shall see, give a much more active role to Christ himself. He recognises that there was another covenant before this covenant of grace, the 'word of the covenant entered into with the Jews' whose condition was 'the perfect obedience of the law'.[27] Otherwise the point he makes in this still immature work is that election and predestination are of believers.

This is the point taken up by Dekker, who sees it as the most important clue to Arminius' whole doctrine of predestination. He notes that Arminius had interpreted 'all whom God has elected' in the sixteenth article of the *Belgic Confession* as referring to believers, and that this interpretation, which he terms 'eigenschappen-predestinatie', is found again in the *Analysis*. Indeed, he argues that 'in all later works he will presuppose that (when he talks of predestination) it is a matter only and solely of "eigenschappen-predestinatie"'.[28]

Since this concept is clearly so important for Dekker's understanding of Arminius' doctrine of predestination, we need to examine it carefully. First, the word eigenschap (literally 'own-thing') means a quality, property, characteristic, distinguishing feature. 'Eigenschappen-predestinatie', therefore, means predestination on the basis of someone's innate qualities. Secondly, although the term is apparently Dekker's own coinage, the idea is not new; in fact it goes back to Arminius' own lifetime when Gomarus, in a letter to Lubbertus dated 23 October 1607,[29] says that predestination in Arminius' understanding is not of individual persons, but of qualities. This letter, however, is from one opponent of Arminius to another, and can hardly be taken as a dispassionate interpretation of Arminius' view. Thirdly, it is true that in his appearance before the Consistory and in the *Analysis* Arminius stated that predestination is of believers (virtually the only point he makes about predestination), and that it reappears in his later writings on the subject up to and including the *Declaration of Sentiments*; though it is hardly so prominent later as one would gather from Dekker.

But is faith in Christ an innate quality of those predestined to salvation, in Arminius' view, or something which they make for themselves? For Arminius faith is a gracious and gratuitous gift of God to men, and in no sense either an innate quality or a personal achievement. It is a gift which men may reject or neglect to accept, but that makes it no less a gift. Dekker appears to assume that this eigenschappen-predestinatie is the foundation of Arminius' doctrine of predestination and that other elements were added later in the manner of a child using building-blocks. Arminius certainly developed his doctrine, and never rejected the

---

27 *Opera*, pp.780, 784: 'verbum foederis cum Iudaeis initi....conditionem....in perfecta legis obedientia', cf. *Works*, III pp.488, 495.

28 Dekker, *Rijker dan Midas*, pp.32, 184.

29 Quoted in Dekker, *Rijker dan Midas*, p.184 n.26

predestination of believers, but, as we shall see in what he learned from Junius, some new elements he introduced changed subtly what was already there. Arminius ends the *Analysis* with the 'neither sublime nor pathetic'[30] verse, in which he asks for correction if he is mistaken, and may well be implying that he is not entirely satisfied with the *Analysis*, and is at least aware that there is more to be said about predestination than that it is of believers. Bangs' view that Arminius' doctrine is one of predestination of classes, criticised by Dekker in the same footnote wherein he quotes Gomarus, at least has the advantage of going back to Arminius himself, as Dekker recognises, and does not predetermine the issue whether God predestines on the basis of something innate in man, or on the basis of his own gift. The *Analysis* is an unsatisfactory and provisional statement of Arminius' doctrine, but it is the first of his works to contain the concept of God's covenant which later becomes so important for understanding his doctrine of predestination and indeed the whole of his theology.

Not a great deal is known about Arminius' theological development between 1593 and 1596. The only writings known are two letters of March and April 1595 to Drusius on Old Testament subjects. As Drusius had been his professor of Hebrew this is in a sense entirely natural, but one wonders whether, if Arminius had been left to pursue his own interests, he might have been an Old Testament scholar. Certainly the importance he attached to subjects like creation, sacrifice and especially covenants, shows a particular interest in the Old Testament roots of Christian theology.

Eventually Arminius was to meet Junius on 10 December 1596, at the wedding of his father's sister, Geertje Jacobsdr, with his former Amsterdam colleague Johannes Cuchlinus, Regent of the Statencollege of Leiden University since 1592. Arminius and Junius seem to have spent most of the time talking to each other, and failing to socialise with the other guests. Though Arminius admired Junius' provision of prolegomena for Protestant theology, the conversation was not about this, or about predestination, but about Adam's fall and whether it had happened contingently or necessarily. In his letter to Uitenbogaert of 7 February 1597,[31] our source of information for what happened, Arminius refers to a book written by Junius on the subject, without giving its title; this is supplied by Dekker as *De Peccato Primi Adami*, written in 1595 to answer four questions from Donteklok, the part-author of the pamphlet that, according to Bertius, Arminius himself had been asked to refute.[32]

---

30 The description of William Nichols, who translated it, presumably meaning 'neither very good nor very bad.'
31 *Ep.* 19.
32 Dekker, *Rijker dan Midas*, pp.33f n.79.

Arminius admitted that he had not easily followed Junius' meaning at all points, but Junius had said that

> Foreknowledge could not be sure and infallible, unless it rested on an immutable cause. But he denied that God's will was that immutable cause; it was something else, namely the divine nature, which precedes that will. I was as thrilled with this as if I had found a great treasure, which I value so cheaply in comparison with certain knowledge of those things about which I have been anxiously worrying for seven years now, that I prefer true knowledge which satisfies my mind on those articles about providence and predestination (so may God love me) than the riches of Croesus and Midas, indeed the treasures of the whole world.[33]

This is the passage from which Dekker takes the title of his book.

Arminius wanted to go on to predestination, but Junius demurred, pointing out that the winter evening was drawing on. He suggested an exchange of letters, and so began the correspondence which made Arminius into a true theologian.

After initial courtesies, Arminius begins the *Collatio* with the three opinions about predestination current among the theologians of the Dutch Reformed Church. The first is that of Calvin and Beza, according to which

> God from eternity determined to illustrate His glory by mercy and justice; (as He could only be either merciful or just towards sinners) He decreed...to make man holy and innocent...in His own image, but (mutable), so that he could fall away and sin. That He ordained moreover that...man should fall and become wicked...so that He might mercifully save some and justly condemn others.[34]

The second opinion is that of Thomas Aquinas, which Arminius initally assumes is also that of Junius himself, though Junius denies this.[35] This opinion is not stated in full, but according to Arminius differs from the preceding doctrine in three respects: election is of men considered in 'pure naturals', not as sinners; God prepared for the elect necessary, sufficient and efficacious means to obtain supernatural felicity; and God, foreseeing that those passed by would fall into sin, reprobated them. The third view, which Arminius attributes to Augustine, he accepts.[36] He discusses and rejects the first two views, and disagrees with Junius that Augustine's opinion agrees in general with the other two. Arminius considers that for Augustine the wilful sin of man is a factor which God takes into account when decreeing. Later, in the *Declaration*, he will reject

---

33 *Ep.* 19, pp.34f.
34 *Works*, III, pp.26f.
35 *Works*, III, pp.86, 88.
36 *Works*, III, pp.234f.

Augustine's position also, though he does not do so at this particular point.

It will be noted that there is no mention of Christ in all this. In the first round of his correspondence, Arminius only mentions Christ in one passage, made by Junius into the Eleventh Proposition:

> Election is *said* to have been made in Christ, who was ordained Mediator for sinners, and became Jesus, not to save some in their own pure nature, but to save His people from their sins. He is *said* to have been pre-ordained, and we in Him; and He, in the order of nature and causes, before us; He, ordained a Saviour; we, to be saved. But in Christ...as the Scripture describes Him...man could not be considered as constituted in pure naturals. Much less, then, could he be elected in Him.[37]

Arminius shows his interest in human psychology which we have noted earlier, and, trained as a philosopher rather than a theologian, he quotes theological commonplaces in a way which could suggest that he had not made them an integral part of his own thinking. We note that he says that election is said to have been made in Christ, not that it was; that Christ is said to have been pre-ordained, not that He was.

Junius, however, begins by questioning Arminius' wisdom in beginning with other people's opinions:

> If anyone [wanted] to accumulate various opinions, he might soon have several to show, but....[38]

Arminius has said that all the opinions he quotes agree that God by an eternal and immutable decree has determined to give certain men eternal and supernatural life, but Junius directs him to what the Bible says about it, citing Calvin's opinion on Ephesians 1:5:

> That eternal life is not (directly) the work of that Divine predestination, but rather secondarily and the result of adoption, (Ephesians 1:5,9; Romans 8:17)... God predestinated us to the adoption of children of God in Christ to Himself, and fixed beforehand the way and end of that adoption by His eternal decree.[39]

Junius agrees with Arminius' third proposition that, according to Calvin and Beza, God decreed within himself to create man and to make man holy and innocent, in his own image, but also decreed that man should fall into sin; but points out that, according to Beza on Ephesians 1:4,[40] this is proved by the fact that Christ is set forth to us as Mediator.

---

37 *Works*, III, pp.123f, emphasis mine in both cases in this paragraph.
38 *Works*, III, p.18.
39 *Works*, III, pp.19, 27.
40 *Works*, III, pp.26f, 45.

By this time Junius has made three important points to Arminius; first, that our basic text for understanding predestination is the New Testament; second, that predestination, like the closely-linked adoption, must be understood 'in Christ'; third, that predestination *is* based on creation and the fall, as Beza implies; all of which will reappear in Arminius' teaching, though he would continue to reject Beza's belief that God ordained the fall.

Junius goes on to argue that election was made in Christ, not in the creatures or in any condition in them. Our knowledge and understanding was originally according to the image of the first Adam, but is now according to the image of that later Adam, Christ, and of God our Creator. We have the essential image of God corrupted by sin, but have not lost it. We have lost the respective image, as Junius calls it, but Christ has restored it, so that we may be renewed in God's own image, and so that the essential image may itself be reformed, since naturals have been corrupted, supernaturals[41] lost. The image of God, preserved or renewed according to his will, God has called forth and joined to himself, to remain immutably in Christ, 'gathering together in one all things' (Ephesians 1:10).[42] Junius mentions all this in reply before Arminius has ever mentioned Christ.

A weakness in Junius' reply, however, is the very wide definition of the term 'Mediator' with which he is working. 'Election was indeed made by God the Father in Christ the Mediator, but that He was ordained Mediator only for sinners, is not true, taken simply.' He argues that mediation is attributed to Christ in creation and nature also (John 1:3f, Hebrews 1:2), and that Christ is Mediator of all to whom the Father gives him as Head to eternity, that is, (unfallen) angels and men, therefore he is Mediator of both and not of sinful men only. Head and Mediator really mean one and the same thing; he is Head of conservation and confirmation to unfallen angels, Head of redemption and conservation to fallen men. Junius distinguishes between Mediator for the standing and the fallen, Redeemer for the fallen only.[43]

When Arminius replies to Junius he does not usually accept the details of Junius' arguments, especially not on predestination and election; though some of Junius' ideas will recur in Arminius' later writings. What he does accept from Junius, and immediately, is his Christocentric bias, as in reply to Junius' comment on the 'First Proposition':

---

41 *Naturalia* and *supernaturalia*; Junius' and Arminius' terms for the gifts which belong to human nature, and the gifts of grace which transcend it; see *Works*, III, pp.94-123, Proposition 10.

42 *Works*, III, pp.90, 100, 105f, 108.

43 *Works*, III, pp.124-7.

> The justified man is adopted, not the adopted man justified, which is (shown)...by the order of obtaining those benefits effected by Christ, [and] the imputation of the same benefits effected by God in Christ. For Christ obtained remission of sins before adoption...and righteousness is imputed before sonship.[44]

Arminius continues in the same vein. The reward of a good work is of God's grace in Jesus Christ, who is made of God unto us righteousness and sanctification. The tempering of justice with the mercy which frees from misery has been effected in a marvellous manner by God, in Jesus Christ our Priest and expiatory sacrifice. The blessed are called to partake in the kingdom prepared for them by God from eternity (Matthew 25), but in and through whom?—Christ, called Jesus because he saves them from their sins (Matthew 1:21). Aquinas' and the schoolmen's doctrine of election is refuted by what they say elsewhere about Christ paying a price of redemption sufficient for the sins of all; if divine justice requires some sinners to be damned, that price is not sufficient for all. Ephesians 1 speaks of the election made in Christ, because it comes from the grace by which we have redemption in his blood. Whatever things we have from regeneration by Christ's Spirit are supernaturals. We have knowledge of God, righteousness and holiness from this source; therefore, they are supernaturals. By the blessing of Christ the curse is removed from the blessed, who are raised from the ignominy and servitude of sin to the kingdom prepared for them by Christ's blood. The wisdom of adoption is the hidden wisdom which God ordained before the ages to our glory and which none of the princes of this world knew, Christ Jesus crucified; and the grace of adoption is joined with mercy and bestowed on the sinner in Christ.[45]

Arminius is 'unmoved by Junius' answers' to his own two arguments of the Eleventh Proposition. Junius has argued that Christ is Mediator not only for sinners, but for all to whom the Father has given him as Head. This includes the angels who have not sinned and therefore do not need redemption. Arminius replies that

> 1. Christ is indeed Head of the angels, but not Mediator between God and the angels. No mediator should be inferior to those for whom he mediates, but Christ according to His human nature is [temporarily] lower than the angels (Hebrews 2:9). He does not share the nature of angels (Hebrews 2:16), nor was He taken from among them (Hebrews 5:1), but He does share human nature and was taken from among men.
>
> 2. He [Arminius] is concerned primarily with human beings, and those humans whom God has elected in Christ as Mediator have been considered as sinners; so Christ is not only their Mediator but also their Reconciler, Redeemer and Advocate.

---

44 *Works*, III, p.23.
45 *Works*, III, pp.34, 69, 74, 94, 113, 122f.

3. Christ is Mediator for men before He is their Head, and by the act of mediation He acquires the right of dominion. Thus in Philippians 2 He humbled Himself to the death of the cross, and then God highly exalted Him.

4. Christ is mediator by merit and efficacy (a contemporary theological commonplace). By merit He obtains for Himself a people, and blessings for them; by efficacy He actually communicates those blessings.

Thus Arminius rejects Junius' definition of 'Mediator', and answers Junius' reply to his one original passage about Christ.[46]

Arminius continues to introduce Christ at various points. Man was not elected in a Mediator considered generally, but in one considered specifically as a Redeemer. God has prepared merited punishment for the sins of the elect, laying them on Christ so that he might expiate them, and sometimes requiring the elect themselves to suffer punishment. Efficacious grace is bestowed on sinners, that, freed from sin by Christ, they may by him obtain life from death. God's justice is declared by exacting punishment either from sinners or from him who has offered himself according to God's will as bail and surety for sinners, and the latter is better. It shows clearly how greatly God abhors sin; it cannot be misinterpreted as revenge, as the first can; it shows the rigour of justice which could not pardon sin even to the interceding Son without full payment of the penalty; and it could not allow the intercession until the Son had shed his blood to purge sins (Hebrews 9:21). By sin man rebelled against God and other creatures were not only removed from his dominion but were also armed for his destruction, except in so far as he was restored to righteousness in Christ (Hebrews 2:6-9). Man, because he sinned freely, made himself a slave to sin, and necessarily becomes subject to sin until Christ the Mediator liberates him.[47]

These comments are made in passing, not in any organised way, and do not amount to a systematic description of the work of Christ such as would later be produced in the *Private Disputations*. Their importance is to demonstrate that, once Junius has drawn his attention to the centrality of Christ, Arminius begins to find him central here, there and everywhere. In this light he goes on to examine Junius' 1593 theses on predestination. Junius defines it as 'an act of the divine good-pleasure by which God has provided from eternity a plenitude of His blessings in Christ to those...about to be heirs of salvation'. Arminius finds the last tense wrong, because human beings are appointed heirs of salvation by the *same*[48] decree by which salvation, the fullness of blessings in Christ, is

---

46 *Works*, III, pp.128-31.
47 *Works*, III, pp.135, 174, 185, 194f, 212, 223.
48 My emphasis.

provided for them.[49] Junius rightly stresses that salvation is in Christ; as Arminius comments, Christ obtained the blessings by his death and received them from the Father to bestow on his disciples, and believers are predestinated in him to participate in them. But predestination does not, as Junius states, make these blessings communicable, but actually communicates them; they are made communicable by Christ's blood, death and resurrection. Junius interprets 'in Christ' as meaning simply 'divine in beginning and foundation', but, says Arminius, while blessing is divine in its beginning with God the Father, Christ is foundation not as God simply, but as *theanthropos*, God-Man, Mediator, Saviour and Head of the Church, which is everywhere in Scripture distinguished from the consideration of Christ as God. (John 14:1, 17:3, 1 Timothy 2:5f, 1 Peter 1:18-21, 2 Corinthians 5:19f etc.).[50]

Junius ends his Thesis VIII: 'So...Christ is the eternal Head of the predestinated.' Arminius replies that the decree by which Christ was constituted Head of those to be predestinated, precedes that by which some were destined in Christ to be saved. Christ as Mediator and Priest with God merited the good things which were to be bestowed by predestination, and at the same time the dignity of Head and the power of bestowing them. *Then* he actually received them from the Father and obtained the titles of Head, King, Prince. 'Having been made perfect, or consecrated, He became Author of eternal salvation to those who obey Him.' Lastly, believers were predestinated in him to partake of those benefits by union with him. God in Christ loves those he has appointed to eternal life. His love is the cause of predestination in Christ Jesus, born, dead, resuscitated and now constituted Head of the Church. The love of John 3:16 is distinct from and prior to the love which causes predestination; the latter cannot bestow eternal life on anyone, and could not will it until Christ had merited eternal life for us by his death. God's supernatural power is exercised in Christ, when Jews and Gentiles are called to salvation.[51]

In short, there is a great contrast between the *Dissertation*, the *Analysis* and the first letter to Junius on the one hand, and his reply to Junius on the other. In the former, Christ is mentioned comparatively rarely, often as a passive object of faith rather than an active agent of salvation. In the latter, Christ is central and everywhere, and would remain so; as would the Holy Spirit, as gracious donor of supernatural gifts. This suggests that *Epistle* 26 on predestination to Uitenbogaert, dated vaguely in 1598 with no indication of the time of year, which only mentions Christ in the final greeting, and his Spirit not at all, may antedate Junius' reply to the first

---

49 *Works*, III, p.240, Thesis II.
50 *Works*, III, pp.240ff.
51 *Works*, III, p.241.

letter. Arminius learned from Junius to apply his own convictions about Christ's work to his own doctrine of predestination, and he did so immediately in his reply. The result was not to make him reject his earlier view that predestination was of believers, but, contrary to Dekker, to subordinate this firmly to the point that predestination is in and through Christ. He remained unconvinced by the details of Junius' doctrine; he was working his way towards a view of Christ's work as central and vital for salvation, which was *not* attached to an Augustinian view of predestination. In this way Junius became, we suggest, the father of what would later be called 'evangelical Arminianism', though he himself might have been horrified by the thought!

Arminius' next major work was the *Examination of Perkins's Pamphlet*. Bangs says that he 'bought the book eagerly, for he was an admirer of Perkins, but he read it with dismay'.[52] In fact, Arminius must have had a good idea what to expect. He had Perkins' *De Praedestinatione* and *Armilla Aurea* and others of his works in his library, and had read them.[53] Arminius claimed to have seen the pamphlet first in a library. There is a letter to Uitenbogaert of July 1599[54] which deals with predestination and in which he gives the same summaries of the Calvinist and Thomist doctrines as in his first letter to Junius, and describes the Augustinian doctrine as teaching that predestination is of men considered as fallen in Adam; what would later be called 'infralapsarianism'. This letter also states that 'Drusius, when he was last in England, bought several books useful for that study in which he is engaged' and perhaps one of them was Perkins' pamphlet, which Arminius saw in someone's library—possibly Drusius' own.

The pamphlet was not a good choice. It was a slim affair and Arminius' lengthy reply seems, as Harrison said, 'heavy in comparison', the proverbial sledgehammer used to crack a nut. Arminius would have done better to answer the *De Praedestinatione* or *Armilla Aurea*. He was, however, anxious to debate predestination with someone else, now that Junius was silent, and seems to have chosen the first work that came to hand.

Arminius probably suspected, and his reading of the pamphlet would have confirmed the suspicion, that many of Junius' fellow-Calvinists needed to learn some of the lessons that he himself had learned from Junius; in particular, the fact that Christ is central for predestination. In answering Perkins, Arminius was to some extent playing the part of Junius over against his own former self, for compared with the debate with Junius, the positions are reversed. Perkins, the orthodox Reformed

---

52 Bangs, *Arminius*, p.209.

53 *Works*, III, p.266; see Dekker, *Rijker dan Midas*, p.37 and n.98, and references to Graafland and the Auction Catalogue of Arminius' books there.

54 *Ep.* 49.

theologian, begins with a comparatively Christ-less, rather abstract description of predestination, consisting of a series of 'common notions...which God has implanted in the minds of men', and proceeds to enumerate ten. In the 'notions' there is no mention of Christ, nor in his definition of predestination or its end, nor in his statements about creation or God's permission of the fall. Only when Perkins considers God's permission of sin does he quote Gregory of Nyssa: 'Doubtless, but that Adam sinned, our Redeemer would not have taken our flesh upon Him.... The Almighty did foresee that He would make of that evil...a good which should be greater.... What believer is there who doth not see how wonderfully it doth excel? Surely great are the evils which we suffer by the desert of the first fault; but what believer would not endure worse than be without so great a Redeemer? And...elsewhere he calleth the fault of Adam "a happy fault."'[55]

The importance of Christ's work comes out right at the beginning of Arminius' reply, and by this stage he has made several references to Christ. On the question of second causes mentioned by Perkins,[56] Arminius notes that God's decree for sending Christ into the world rests on foreknowledge of the Fall, for Christ is the Lamb who takes away the sins of the world (John 1:29), made a little lower than the angels for the suffering of death (Hebrews 2:9), partaking flesh and blood to destroy the devil who has the power of death (Hebrews 2:14), and constituted High Priest to offer gifts and sacrifices for sins (Hebrews 5:1). Among spiritual blessings (that is, blessings of the Holy Spirit) to which we have been predestinated in Christ, are adoption as children (Ephesians 1:5), redemption through Christ's blood and forgiveness of sins (1:7), and the revelation of the mystery of the divine will (1:9), so Paul can say that he lives his earthly life in the faith of the Son of God (Galatians 2:20). God can love no sinner to salvation unless he is reconciled to himself in Christ. Without sin there would be no room for either the martyrs' patience or Christ's sacrifice.[57] All this before Perkins has mentioned Christ! Arminius is unimpressed by the quotation from Gregory, which he considers goes against Paul's injunction not to do evil that good may come (Romans 3:8). Christ came to destroy the devil's works (1 John 3:8), so not even a little sin may be perpetrated in order that the Son of God may come as Redeemer.[58]

---

55 *Works*, III, pp.267-86, footnotes.
56 *Works*, III, pp.267f. Perkins argues that 'God is not governed of—much less doth He depend on—second causes, but doth justly order them, even when....they work unjustly.' Arminius agrees in general, but rejects the last phrase on the ground 'Shall not the judge of all the earth do right?' (Genesis 18:25).
57 *Works*, III, pp.268, 275, 278f, 285.
58 *Works*, III, pp.286f.

Apart from the quotation, Perkins first mentions Christ when he defines election: 'The decree of election is that whereby God has ordained certain men to His glorious grace in the obtaining of their salvation and heavenly life through Christ.'[59] Arminius argues that in this 'Christ does not...obtain that place which He merits and which the Apostle assigns to Him...[saying] that we have been "chosen in Christ" (Ephesians 1:4) as in the Mediator by whose blood salvation and life have been gained for us, and as in the Head from whom those benefits flow down to us...Christ...prepared it by His own blood for those who should believe in His name.... "In Christ" marks the meritorious cause by which grace and glory have been prepared.' If God can will eternal life to anyone without respect to the Mediator, he can also bestow it without the satisfaction of the Mediator. For God loves the world and gives His Son to it as Redeemer. The faith by which we are saved is faith in Christ 'concerning reconciliation, redemption and remission of sins.'[60]

Perkins goes on to discuss the 'acts' in the decree of election. In the first act, which is concerned with God's love and favour, Christ is not mentioned, which draws Arminius' criticism,[61] but the second act is at the heart of both Perkins' and Arminius' understanding. Perkins agrees with Arminius in rejecting Junius' wide definition of 'Mediator', and confining the term to Christ's work for human beings; in fact Perkins, as we shall see, in one way restricts its use more than Arminius does, to the work of Christ for the elect.

The second act is divided into five 'steps', which Perkins expresses in a decidedly clumsy style: thus the second is 'the promising of Him being ordained'. We may interpret them thus:

1) God ordains a Mediator.

2) God promises Him to men and commands them to believe in Him.

3) The Mediator 'exhibits', that is, presents Himself to God, and God 'exhibits' or offers Him to men.

4) God 'applies' the Mediator's work to men through election.

5) The application is accomplished in the salvation of the elect.

Arminius agrees that the 'steps' follow each other in this order; but the first three precede the whole predestination of men. Christ who was ordained, promised and exhibited, who also reconciled and obtained eternal redemption, is the Head of all those predestined to salvation, and they are his members. He was predestined to be Head before we were predestined to be members. He was ordained Mediator before we were

---

59 *Works*, III, pp.292f.
60 *Works*, III, pp.293, 296f.
61 *Works*, III, pp.299f.

ordained to be saved in him. Perkins' order is an inversion of Scripture. Christ gathers together in one God's children and the elect, and conducts them to salvation, but he is not only Saviour of those already elected and adopted, but also the Mediator and Head in whom election was made. Arminius seizes upon Perkins' citation of 1 Peter 2:20 to repeat to Perkins his objection to Junius that Christ has been ordained Mediator between God and sinners, not between God and men simply.[62]

Perkins discusses his third step, the exhibition of the Mediator, at greater length. The Mediator presents himself to God the Father as a sacrifice for the sins of the world, performs the office of mediation and obtains remission of sins and eternal redemption; then the Father offers him by His Word and Spirit to the world reconciled through him. So far Perkins and Arminius seem to agree. Perkins, however, says that 'the efficacy of the price as to its merit and operation is infinite', but distinguishes between 'potential efficacy' for the redemption of the whole world—a phrase, says Arminius, hitherto unknown to theologians who have distinguished between efficacy and sufficiency—and 'actual efficacy'. As Arminius understands him, the sufficiency or potential efficacy is limited, not by its actual application by faith and the sacrament of regeneration, as in Augustine and Prosper of Aquitaine, but by God's will. If so, he says, the sufficiency is taken away. If the ransom has not been offered and paid for all it is not sufficient for all, nor is it strictly speaking a *lutron*, that which has been offered and paid. In fact, the decree of predestination comes logically after the death of Christ and its efficacy, therefore it sets no bounds to its universality as the price paid for all.[63]

Perkins attempts to justify his position by introducing other aspects of Christ's work:

> 1) 'Christ does not sacrifice for those for whom He does not pray, because to make intercession and to sacrifice are conjoined, but He does not pray for all, but only for the elect and believers (John 17:9)...therefore He does not sacrifice for all.... This prayer, according to Illyricus, is expiatory and a canon of sacrifice.... Christ was destined to be the *lutron* or price, by the intercession and offering of the Son.'[64]

> 2) 'Christ is the Mediator only of those whose person He represented on the cross; But He represented on the cross the person only of the elect, therefore He is Mediator of the elect only.'[65]

> 3) 'Whatever Christ suffered and did as a Redeemer, the same have all the redeemed done and suffered in Him and with Him; But Christ as a Redeemer died, rose again,

---

62 *Works*, III, pp.304-38.
63 *Works*, III, pp.323ff.
64 *Works*, III, pp.325ff.
65 *Works*, III, p.327.

ascended, sat at the right hand of the Father; therefore in Him and with Him all the redeemed have (done these things). But the elect alone (do them); therefore they alone are redeemed.'[66]

4) 'The expiatory victim sanctifies those for whom it is a victim; for the victim and the sanctification appertain to the same persons. But Christ sanctifies only the elect and believers; therefore Christ is the victim for the elect and believers only.... Christ is the perfect Saviour of those whom He saves, not by meriting their salvation only, but by effectively working it out.... The decree of election is the cause and beginning of all saving gifts and works in men.' [67]

I will now explain how Arminius answers each of these points.

On 1), Arminius answers that sacrificing is prior to intercession. Christ could not penetrate the heavens to intercede before God for us, except through the blood of his own flesh. The sacrificing belongs to the merit, the intercession to its application. He acquired merit by sacrifice, intercedes for its application, and does both as Priest; but accomplished the application as King and Head of the Church. Christ prayed frequently for the non-elect, and Illyricus' words do not fit either with God's justice or with the infinite value of Christ's sacrifice. The words 'canon of sacrifice' occur in the popish Mass! Perkins' conclusion 'contains no right meaning; the intercession is posterior to the ransom, for the Lamb was slain from the beginning of the world.'

On 2), Arminius says that a Mediator as such does not represent anyone, but mediates between two dissident parties. Only a Mediator who is also responsible for satisfaction can represent anyone; and this is what God's justice required for reconciliation. The act is the offering accomplished by Christ on the cross, the issue is reconciliation. In his suffering he did represent our person, for we had merited death, but not in his active offering. He became a curse for us and was made a sacrifice for sin. Since all men are sinners and liable to the curse, and Christ took upon himself the fallen human nature common to all, it is likely that he represented the person of all. Nowhere does Scripture say that Christ on the cross represented the person of the elect only; frequently it says that he represented the world, or all; and nowhere in Scripture do these terms mean the elect. The proper and immediate effect of Christ's passion and death is not the actual taking away and remission of sins, justification and redemption, but reconciliation with God; Christ obtains them all from God so that God can now remit sins to sinners and bestow the Spirit of grace upon them, unhindered by a justice which has now been satisfied. Perkins does not make this distinction; he assumes that Christ has suffered punishment and performed obedience for the elect, actually taken away

---

66 *Works*, III, pp.332f.
67 *Works*, III, p.335.

their sins and transferred them to himself. But this is as if we ourselves had constituted him Mediator in our place and by him paid our debts to God, so that we can demand immunity from punishment and eternal life from God as our right. In that case God could not demand anything from us in return, for example faith or conversion. But the righteousness fulfilled by Christ is not ours as fulfilled, but as imputed to us by faith (Romans 4:5). Perkins' phrase that Christ has 'borne upon the cross the person of the elect' is simply wrong; no-one is elect, except in Christ dead, resuscitated and constituted Head of the Church and Saviour; in God's foreknowledge they were not elect while he was hanging on the cross, and he could not represent them as such.[68]

On 3), Arminius' view is that Perkins confounds the passions and actions by which redemption is accomplished, with the result itself and its application. The passions and actions of Christ come first, redemption follows, then its application, and it is from the application that the redeemed are so called. What Christ suffered and did to obtain redemption, the redeemed themselves have not suffered and done, for they were not redeemed at the time. Romans 6:3 treats of the crucifixion, death, burial and resurrection which we experience, but these are not meritorious like those of Christ, but consist of our being grafted into Christ by faith, and our communion with him—the application of redemption. Christ's death and resurrection belong to the fulfilment of the office of Redeemer (Hebrews 9:12). The sins of those for whom Christ died were so condemned in his flesh that they are not automatically delivered from condemnation, but only as they believe in Christ.[69]

To 4), Arminius replies that the expiatory victim sanctifies, not as offered, but as applied (Hebrews 9:13f), by sprinkling, just as at the first Passover; so both the ashes of the heifer and the blood of Christ are sprinkled. It was not those only who killed the lamb, but those who sprinkled the door-posts with its blood, who were passed over by the avenging angel. But this is not linked with the application of Christ as victim, but with his offering, made simply for men, human beings as sinners (Hebrews 5:1). The application was made for believers. Christ is called Saviour of other than believers in 1 Timothy 4:10, and a distinction must be made between salvation sufficient and salvation efficacious, or salvation secured and salvation applied. The decree of election is the cause and beginning of all saving gifts and works in men, not as the decree of election, but as the decree for conferring grace.[70]

At this point we are only about one third through Arminius' *Examination*, but have covered most of the relevant ground. Perkins

---

68 *Works*, III, pp.329-32.
69 *Works*, III, pp.333ff.
70 *Works*, III, pp.335f.

continues with a similar description of reprobation, then tries to answer various charges or 'criminations' brought up by his opponents; Arminius answers them also, sometimes at great length. He makes the work longer by including his own 'Treatise on Permission'. The most relevant passage is Perkins' 'Fourth Crimination', 'That we teach that the greatest part of mankind is deprived of Christ and of all saving grace'—as Arminius expands it, 'since the elect, having become sinners in Adam, cannot be (saved) unless God's justice is satisfied, and sin has been expiated, God determined to give His own Son to them as a Mediator, Reconciler and Redeemer, who should assume human nature for them alone, should die for their sins only, should merit the Holy Spirit and redemption for them alone, should of set purpose offer grace to them alone, and should call them only to faith and endow them with faith by internal vocation etc., those whom He has reprobated being excluded from all these things.'[71] Perkins in effect agrees, saying that this crimination is no crime, and argues that

> 1) They have already received in Adam saving grace, righteousness, a life of bliss, and ability to persevere in the same. But they were not willing to accept it; so it is not wonderful or unjust that they are deprived of Christ, since they repudiated the grace received in Adam.[72]

> 2) Christ may be said to have died for all (sic), but He has not died for all and each equally, not for the damned the same as for the elect, not efficiently on the part of God, arguing for this:—

> a) If Christ says to the reprobate 'I never knew you' (Matthew 7:23), He never acknowledged them for His own, therefore He did not die for them.

> b) If each and all are effectually redeemed, each and all are also reconciled to God. But all are not reconciled, nor do all receive remission of sins, therefore each and all have not been effectually redeemed.

> c) Christ gave Himself that He might obtain from the Father the right of sanctifying those who should believe on Himself.

> d) The redemption accomplished is destined for those who believe in Christ; and so is sonship.

> e) Christ's benefits are not applied to all without distinction. God has freed the elect from condemnation; yet they are not endowed with such a degree of grace that sin no longer reigns.[73]

---

71 *Works*, III, p.419.
72 *Works*, III, p.420.
73 *Works*, III, pp.420-25.

Arminius replies to 1), that the grace bestowed on Adam and on his posterity through him is not the grace of Christ, which was not then necessary. To 2), he answers that Perkins' statement that 'Christ died efficiently on God's part for the elect, not the reprobate', and the schoolmen's that 'Christ has died for all, but efficaciously only for the elect and believers', cannot be used without injury to the death of Christ and its merit, for they only attribute sufficiency, not efficacy, to it. Arguments a) and b) confuse the redemption and reconciliation with God, obtained by Christ's death and sacrifice, with their application, but these are plainly distinguished in 2 Corinthians 5:19. It is not true that remission of sins and satisfaction are joined together in every way; satisfaction, consisting in Christ's death and obedience, comes first; remission of sins is its application. On c), Christ actually executes that right by his Spirit, and by the application and sprinkling of his blood, sanctifying to himself a peculiar people, redeeming them and freeing them from its evil state of bondage; which also answers d). On e), if you grant freedom from condemnation of sin, you must also grant freedom from its dominion; you can't have one without the other.

Perkins now adduces certain objections to his doctrine and tries to answer them. First, Scripture asserts that Christ has redeemed the world. Arminius answers that redemption was obtained for all the world and for all and every human being, but is applied to believers and the elect alone.[74] Secondly, 1 Timothy 2:4 asserts that God wills all men to be saved and to come to the knowledge of the truth. Here Perkins produces a piece of what was to become typical orthodox Reformed quibbling on this text, and weakens his case by giving four different and probably incompatible explanations. These are: that 'all' does not mean all Adam's posterity, but only men in the last age of the world; that 'God wills all men to be saved who are saved'(!); that 'all' means not every one of all kinds, but the kinds of every one, that is, some of all kinds; finally, that 'Paul speaks according to the judgment of charity, not the judgment of secret and infallible certainty.' Arminius treats these weak explanations, the weakest part of Perkins' whole case, with greater seriousness than they deserve.[75]

Perkins then challenges the 'errors' which he finds in the opposing doctrine. The significant 'error' for our purpose is the fifth, that if things really are as Perkins' opponents would have them, it would mean that 'sin, Satan, the world, death and hell are more mighty than Christ the Redeemer'. Arminius distinguishes three things here: 1) the acts and sufferings of Christ; 2) the fruits and results of his acts and sufferings; 3) the communication and application of those fruits. Christ, by the sacrifice

---

74 *Works*, III, pp.425f.
75 *Works*, III, pp.426-29.

of his own body, by his obedience and passion, has reconciled us to God and obtained eternal redemption, without distinction of elect and reprobate, believers and unbelievers. Such distinction comes later, in the application, when we, having faith in the word of reconciliation, believe in Christ, are justified and accounted righteous in him, and so share in redemption. Perkins' conclusion will not follow. Sin, Satan, the world, death and hell could not stop Christ doing any of this. What they can do is to hinder many from believing in him and becoming partakers of his blessings; but God and Christ are not thereby 'overcome'.[76]

Perkins' final part concerns the doctrine of so-called 'final perseverance', and as Arminius is not sure what he himself believes about that, the *Examination* ends on an unsatisfactory note. Its weaknesses are those of trying to answer an inadequate statement of the opposing doctrine, and answering it point by point in the original order, making the reply repetitious, over-long, and lacking a proper shape of its own. Its main strength is its Christocentricity in the relevant passages, and a recognition for the first time that the opposing doctrines could be challenged as not Christocentric enough. In this way it looks forward to the statements on predestination which Arminius made in his professorial career. It has little about the Holy Spirit apart from the references to His spiritual blessings in Ephesians 1. My own judgment on the *Examination of Perkins* is that, while important in some ways, it is far less significant for the development of Arminius' Christology than the *Collation* with Junius, and it is only because many previous scholars have, in my opinion, over-stressed its importance that I have examined it in such detail.[77] Part of the reason for this may be that Perkins was an English theologian, and a better-known exponent of Reformed theology than Junius.

We have seen that from the beginning Arminius had stressed the centrality of Christ in his letter to Grynaeus. He had, however, largely failed to apply this conviction to the doctrine of regeneration in the *Dissertation*, and more importantly to the doctrine of predestination in the *Analysis* and in *Epistle* 26 and his first draft to Junius. These must, therefore, be regarded as immature works. Junius' reply had brought Christology and predestination together in Arminius' mind, in a fruitful combination that would not be broken for the rest of his career. The

---

76 *Works*, III, pp.447f.
77 See Bangs, *Arminius*, p.206, 'in many respects his most important single composition'; Kendall, *Calvin*, ch. 10; Muller, *God*, pp.22f; C. Graafland, *Van Calvijn tot Barth: Oorsprong en ontwikkeling van de leer der verkiezing in het Gereformeerde Protestantisme* ('s-Gravenhage: Uitgeverij Boekencentrum BV, 1987), Hoofdstuk [chapter] 1 section 3, 'W. Perkins', pp.71, 77, 82-83; Hoofdstuk 2, 'De reactie van Jac. Arminius', pp.85-6, 88-94, 96-105, 108-09, 111-15, 117-19; Dekker, *Rijker dan Midas*, pp.197-209.

reply to Junius is his first mature work because it brings Christology and predestination together.

Arminius sets his doctrine of election and predestination within the work of Christ, not within the work of a Father-God whose Son is merely his agent, still less within the context of the 'naked will' of the Father before creation. The weakness is that Arminius has become somewhat obsessed with the doctrine of predestination in isolation, and has not supplied anything like a complete framework of the work of Christ in which to set it. There is evidence that, perhaps even before he began to answer Perkins, he had recognised that deficiency and set himself to remedy it. To this remedy we now turn, with the final comment that the *Examination* of Perkins was the last major work in which Arminius' trumpet sounded an uncertain note. About the time of his appointment as Professor at Leiden, he gained a certain confidence which never afterwards left him. From that time, more of the story took place in the glare of theological publicity, and its pace speeded up until it reached the climax of the delivery of the *Declaration of Sentiments* in 1608, before subsiding again during the final year of his life.

CHAPTER 3

The Christology of a General Practitioner, 1599–1603

By the time Arminius was writing to Perkins he may have felt that he was in danger of becoming too much of a specialist on predestination, which was in any case influencing his views on other subjects. When Arminius left Amsterdam for Leiden in the summer of 1603 he had considered many, perhaps most subjects on which he would later express opinions, not just the one subject of predestination which had concerned him, more than any other, since 1592-93. There may be a gradual movement away from subjective issues like faith and justification, considered as aspects of human psychology, which had necessarily concerned Arminius (and Uitenbogaert) in their pastoral ministries, towards a more Christocentric approach.

The thesis of this chapter will be twofold; first, that during this period Arminius was broadening his scope, but, until he delivered his *Orations* at the commencement of his academic career in July 1603, the evidence is all contained in about six letters, which makes it difficult to summarise; secondly, that apart from three subjects, he remained surprisingly close to what even his opponents would have considered orthodox Reformed theology. These subjects were the interpretation of Romans 7 and predestination, which had already become public, and that of the relation between the persons of the Trinity, which would not become public for another seven years.

On 18 February 1599 he wrote an important letter to Uitenbogaert, which we are about to discuss, but there is a major question to be settled about dating before we can examine his theological development in this period.[1]

James Nichols claimed, in his introductory material to the *Works*, that Arminius began in 1598 *A Synopsis of Common Places in Divinity* from the Scriptures, and the following year extended it to 'all the ancient and modern divines' that he possessed or was able to consult. Nichols refers to the authority of the younger (Caspar) Brandt, who 'refers...to the ninety-eighth (letter) (February 3 1607) and a few others of the *Epistolae Praestantium Virorum* for an account of the progress Arminius made'.[2]

---

1 *Ep.* 44 of the *Epistolae Praestantium Virorum*.
2 *Works*, I, p.131.

This is taken by Bangs and Muller as a reference to the 1598-99 origin of the *Private Disputations* and as such 'surely incorrect'.[3] Muller agrees with Bangs[4] that the *Private Disputations* were written for university students and probably towards the end of his years as a professor at Leiden. More than once,[5] Muller refers to the *Private Disputations* as having been begun in 1603 and being later than the *Public Disputations*,[6] and takes a reference in the *Private Disputations* ('the divine essence is eternal...in the manner in which it has been proved by us in our public thesis on this subject'[7]) as proof of his (Muller's) point, at least for the doctrine of God.

It is unfortunate that Nichols gave no reference for his statement that Arminius' *Synopsis* was begun in 1598-99, other than Brandt's reference to the much later letter of 1607, but the evidence is in *Epistle* 44:

> I am engaged in constructing an order for a Synopsis of Common Places in Divinity (*Synopsi locorum Theologiae*); I have determined to re-read all the ancient and modern divines which are to hand and which can be obtained.... I am making a beginning with the doctrine of God, who is first in order and dignity in theology. In this I shall consider both nature and persons.[8]

It is clear that this *Synopsis* is substantially the same as the *Private Disputations*, and was begun a few years before Arminius was considered or considered himself for the post at Leiden. Nichols is right, and Bangs and Muller are wrong, about Arminius' starting point, although it is true that Arminius sometimes revised what he had written in the light of his public disputations at the university. This might seem a quibble, hardly worth mentioning, except that Muller's theological approach is considerably influenced by his belief that the *Private Disputations* do not date back earlier than 1603 in any form, and are generally later than the *Public Disputations* where the latter are on the same subject:

> Since...the *Public Disputations* almost invariably seem to have been a first draft and the *Private Disputations* a refinement, the absence of a doctrine of creation from the former...points towards the theses of the *Private Disputations* as a first attempt at doctrinal definition, perhaps lacking the polish of [the] final theses on the essence and attributes of God.[9]

---

3 Muller, *God*, p.50.
4 *Works*, I, Introduction, p.xviii.
5 Muller, *God*, pp.25, 50, 111.
6 Muller, *God*, p.50: 'at least those on the doctrine of God'; cf. pp.111, 169, 212.
7 *Private Disputation* XV.vii.
8 *Ep.Ecc.* 44, p.85; my translation.
9 Muller, *God*, p.212.

Because Arminius chose to begin his *Synopsis* with the doctrine of God, he would not concentrate for the time being on the work and person of Christ, but the doctrine of God necessarily involves the persons of the Trinity. Both Bangs and Muller discuss the *autotheos* issue (that is, the question whether Christ and the Holy Spirit derive their Godhead from the Father, or have it in themselves) in terms of a controversy of 1606 over a student and a book by Trelcatius.[10] Neither shows that he is aware that the issue presented itself to Arminius several years earlier, and that he had discussed it at length with Uitenbogaert in this same letter of 1599. Arminius says that the doctrine of God causes occasional disputes, but that of the persons (of the Trinity) is more difficult and has disturbed the Church in various ways almost from the beginning, with different opinions about the equality of, and distinction between, the persons. In his own time various heresies have been revived and challenged, but 'the Sabellian sect has not been given new shape'.[11] Nevertheless, 'those who have assumed the task of defending the truth...have said much about the unity of essence and consubstantiality of the three persons, much too little about the distinction between them.... They often seem to me to use ways of speaking which can justly be held to have affinity with the Sabellian heresy.'

He then makes specific quotations, first from Calvin:

> When we speak of the Son simply, without reference to the Father, we may well and properly say that He is from Himself (*a se esse*), and therefore we call Him the sole origin (*unicum principium*). The ancients sometimes make the Father the origin of the Son, sometimes say the Son has divinity and essence from Himself.[12]

Note the last sentence; Calvin did not claim as others, including perhaps Muller,[13] have done, that there was virtual unanimity among the Fathers that the Son was *autotheos*. Danaeus is also quoted:

> The Father is said to be the beginning and origin of all things created by Him, as Augustine thinks; but not of the Son. The Father did not give the Son His divinity.... [He] can be called the beginning (*principium*) of the Son, but not the beginning and origin of the Deity of the Son or of the Holy Spirit, lest we make them less than the Father. For the Son as He is God does not have power (*potestas*) from the Father, or the force of divinity; He has that from Himself.[14]

---

10 Bangs, *Arminius*, pp.281f; Muller, *The Christological Problem*, pp.151-4.

11 *Ep.* 44 p.85: 'Nostro vero saeculo Sabelliana factio interpolata non est.'

12 *Institutes of the Christian Religion* (1559), Book 1 Chapter 13 Section 19.

13 Muller, *The Christological Problem*, pp.153f: 'Arminius's patristic scholarship left something to be desired.'

14 *Isagoges Christianae*, Book 1 Chapter 23.

Arminius here refers to Melanchthon and Pezelius, who discuss the essence of the Son. Polanus is also quoted as follows:

> The Son is not indeed Son from Himself (*autohuios*), because He is Son of the Father; but He is God from Himself (*autotheos*), that is, the essence of the Son is not from another essence but from itself, as the essence of Father and Son is one and the same.... If [the Son] is not God from Himself, He cannot be entirely God.... He cannot be God whose essence is not from Himself.... Essence is not brought forth from essence, essence is unbegotten (*agennetos*). So also the Son as He is God is unbegotten. But the Son is engendered from the essence of the Father. Wherefore Christ as God is from Himself, as Son is from the Father.[15]

Arminius believes that such ways of speaking should be rejected as akin to the Sabellian heresy, making the persons of the Godhead more like 'modes' of the one person. He asks how Calvin can 'speak of the Son simply, without reference to the Father'; surely the very word 'Son' necessarily implies a parent? So Calvin's argument that when we speak of the Son as God we assert that he is from himself, etc., is roundly rejected; 'By no means'.[16] If the Son has essence from himself he is not Son; there is a contradiction in terms. Calvin might make the same distinction as Polanus, that he does not have essence from himself as Son, but does have it as God. No, says Arminius, he has his essence as God from the Father also. In whatever way he can be considered outside his relationship to the Father, he cannot be considered in such a way that his sonship is denied. Nor is he God in one way, Son in another; that is simply an invention. Arminius appeals to the Nicene (Constantinopolitan) Creed with its '*Deus de Deo*', God from God, more than once, and to Basil the Great, Cyril and other Greek Fathers against Arius, Eunomius, Aetius 'and similar heretics'.

It seems necessary to go back to first principles, to the New Testament. This frequently calls Christ Son of God; orthodox Christians, who include Arminius on this point, will call him God also, and will claim that the New Testament calls him this; but it must be conceded, much less frequently and less definitely, so that Unitarians can argue and have argued that the New Testament does not call him this without qualification. What the New Testament clearly does not do is to explain *how* Christ can be both truly Son and truly God. By definition God must have his essence from himself and from no-one and nothing else; by definition a son has his essence from his parent(s). Calvin, Polanus and others had tried to distinguish between what was true of Christ as God and what was true of him as Son, but this can seem a distinction without a difference, far

---

15 *Partitiones Theologicae*, Book 1.
16 *Nullo modo*; a colloquialism? Cf. Dutch geenszins; German keineswegs; American 'no way!'

removed from biblical teaching and altogether too abstract. It might seem better to modern theologians to maintain a reverent agnosticism as to the source of the Son's divine essence; but this option was not available to the late medieval or sixteenth-century Church.

To Arminius' mind another doctrine was involved, that of the Trinity:

> But where do these ways of talking come from? I don't know; I would like to say, from simple ignorance and thoughtlessness, but I fear worse. I suspect, from some distorted concept of the Trinity. (Do not marvel Uitenbogaert; for I think few have accurately considered that article [of the Trinity] as it is proposed to us in Scripture and by the Fathers...).... When three persons are called one God, they visualise individual persons with their own way of existing or subsisting and their characteristic signs (*nota*); then they form a certain common concept under the name of one God.[17]

A finite mind cannot conceive in one concept three persons in both the ways in which they differ and the ways in which they are one. So in practice they attribute what is proper to Deity, namely to be from no-one and to be unbegotten, to the three persons. Here Arminius gets bogged down in the details of his argument: 'O that I could express this as I feel it!' He eventually gets back to the point:

> If anyone should infer, that because three persons who share in a Deity which is one in number, cannot be called three Gods, but must be called one God; therefore, because this Deity lacks origin, all three persons also lack origin; for it is as appropriate for the Deity to be devoid of beginning, as to be one: I reply:— If all those persons shared in a Deity without communication (*citra communicationem*), that would be the right conclusion. [But there is such communication, and] that communication is not contrary to the unity of the Deity; but the same communication means that a person, to whom the communication is made, cannot be said to lack origin.[18]

This lack, attributed to Deity, is a lack of origin in *essence*; attributed to the person, it is a lack of origin in *subsistence*.

All these comments are made in a private letter to Uitenbogaert and so caused no trouble at the time; but from 1606 onwards such views became public and so controversial. It should, however, be noted that Arminius' rejection of the aseity of the Son and the Holy Spirit gave him no doubts as to the centrality of their work.

The next letter (*Epistle* 45) in the collection is also found in the *Opera* and has been translated by James Nichols as *A Letter on the Sin against the Holy Ghost*, and Nichols gives the date and place of writing at the end

---

17 *Ep.* 44, p.87.
18 *Ep.* 44, pp.87f; my own translation.

as 'Amsterdam, March 3rd 1599'. This date has been copied by Bangs,[19] but in fact the original text in the *Praestantium ac Eruditorum Virorum Epistolae* has no place or date given and the date is rightly omitted in Dekker's list. 3 March 1599 is in fact the date of a letter to Junius in the names of Arminius and John Taffinus, pastor of the Walloon Church at Amsterdam, concerning the English Independents who had settled there but were abusing the hospitality of the Dutch Reformed Church by criticising that Church's polity and practice.[20] It seems unlikely that Arminius would send two letters of such length on the same day. The *Letter on the Sin against the Holy Ghost* probably belongs to 1599, but its precise date is unknown. It was written in response to a letter from Uitenbogaert who intended to preach to his congregation on the subject, and wanted Arminius' opinions. Possibly the fact that Arminius had written to him on subjects other than predestination in *Epistle* 44, encouraged Uitenbogaert to seek his views on other subjects.

Bangs gives a short summary describing the letter as 'in fact a theological treatise...but important now primarily as a period piece'.[21] We may accept both comments, but it is largely concerned with the psychology of the sinner, rather than with the Christ who speaks of it or the Holy Spirit against whom it is committed. One of Uitenbogaert's questions is 'Does not the distinction between the sin against *the Son of Man*, and that against *the Holy Spirit*, contribute to the confirmation of the truth of the personality of the Holy Ghost?' Arminius agrees that it does; the Holy Spirit is not a quality of God, that is, a property, virtue or power, but something living, intelligent, willing and acting, distinct from the Father and the Son, in other words, a Person.[22] The Holy Spirit's witness to Christ and the coming of his kingdom is not only sufficient to prove that Jesus is the Christ, but efficacious, convincing the mind and conscience and leading to assured knowledge and persuasion of the truth that Jesus is the Christ, the Son of God. Those who embrace Christ even with temporary faith do so through the Holy Spirit's illumination (1 Corinthians 12:3).[23] The sin against the Holy Spirit is to crucify Christ long acknowledged by the sinner as God's Son, and to tread under foot his blood, 'by which God has redeemed the church unto Himself, which is the price of redemption, than which nothing is more precious, and by which alone the gracious covenant between God and men is confirmed and established'.[24] In contrast, renewing again to repentance proceeds from the mercy or grace of God in Christ, in response to Christ's

---

19 *Ep.* 45, pp.89-97; *Works*, II, pp.731-54; Bangs, *Arminius*, pp.204f.
20 *Ep.* 39; *Works*, I, pp.159-65.
21 Bangs, *Arminius*, pp.204f.
22 *Works*, II, pp.736, 753f.
23 *Works*, II, pp.740, 742.
24 *Works*, II, p.749.

intercession, through the operation of the Holy Spirit of grace. But this mercy, intercession and operation are not infinite; they do not operate according to the infinite omnipotence of God, Christ and the Spirit, but are circumscribed by God's will (Romans 9:18), Christ's intercession (John 17:9), and the Spirit's operation (John 14:17).[25] At this point Arminius sounds surprisingly like a Calvinist, but we have to remember that in his understanding, all these take human response into account and are partly in response to it. This is, nevertheless, a probable indication of this letter's early date. The important fact to note is that whatever Arminius' doubts about the aseity of the Son and the Spirit, he has no doubts about their divinity.

On 10 April 1599 Arminius wrote to Uitenbogaert[26] about a confession which Tako Medenblik had offered to the *conventus* (consistory or classis) of Alkmaar, in which he used the phrase '*fides iustificat acceptive*', faith justifies (the strange last word being almost untranslatable). Arminius says that the statement is ambiguous and it depends whether 'acceptive' is taken in an active or passive sense; the active is true, the passive false. He understands 'faith is imputed for righteousness' to mean that God counts faith for righteousness, as in Genesis 15:6 and quotations in Paul and James. And so justification is attributed to faith, not because it accepts, but because it is accepted (by God). If someone says that justification is attributed to faith because of the object which faith receives, Christ who is our righteousness, this does not conflict with Arminius' opinion but gives the reason why God imputes our faith to us for righteousness.

With *Epistle* 48 of 10 June 1599, Arminius sends to Uitenbogaert 'a certain arrangement and short synopsis of the first book of Theological commonplaces' for his judgment—probably a first draft of the *Private Disputations*. What this covered is not clear, but it may have been anything or everything up to *Disputation* XXIII (theological prolegomena and God). Arminius also had an argument that year with someone about the propagation and corruption of the soul, which he seems to have found amusing, as he relates in a later letter;[27] and he is very scornful of someone who uses Psalm 32:1 and Philippians 2:13 to prove that Romans 7 is to be understood of a regenerate man, on the grounds that an unregenerate man would not recognise his inner sins.[28] Between April 1599 and May 1600 the letters are short, only in passing concerned with theological issues, and rather querulous in tone, as can be seen from the translation of extracts from them by James Nichols,[29] and

---

25 *Works*, II, p.748.
26 *Ep.* 46, p.97.
27 *Ep.* 51, p.101.
28 *Ep.* 53, p.103, postscript.
29 *Works*, I, pp.132-136.

after this date they dry up completely for two years. It would seem doubtful whether Arminius had got further than the doctrine of creation in his *Synopsis*, when in 1602 he tells Uitenbogaert in a letter otherwise devoid of theological content,[30] that the circumstances of the time (the plague) have forced him recently to be much concerned with the providence of God, and that he has consulted many early and later divines without coming to a final conclusion.

The next letter[31] is concerned with Arminius' pastoral practice. It shows him as anxious to make what he regarded as necessary theological distinctions. The man and the woman concerned regarded the assurance of remission of sins and the testimony of the Holy Spirit in their hearts as identical with justifying faith, and because they could not feel this assurance and this testimony they were trying (of course unsuccessfully) to excite these feelings in themselves. Arminius turned them from such subjective considerations to the object of faith and asked them whether they believed

   1. that Jesus of Nazareth is the Christ sent by the Father into the world, and its true and only Saviour.

   2. that God the Father had in this only Saviour reconciled the world to Himself, not imputing to them their trespasses.

   3. that the same Jesus had received power from the Father to forgive even the worst sins, and to bestow the Spirit of adoption on those who believe in Him; and that Christ Himself is prepared and has promised to use this power to save believers.

They did believe all this. Arminius then said,

   1. This is the faith which is imputed for righteousness.

   2. Remission of sins is the fruit of this faith.

   3. A sense of this remission necessarily follows, perhaps at the same time, perhaps later (Romans 5:1).

   4. The Spirit is given to those who believe in Christ, and begins to operate in the way that He knows will lead to salvation.

   5. Justifying faith, remission of sins, and the sense of this remission, are all distinct in scripture.[32]

This comes in a letter in which he also speaks of the providence of God and mentions reading Ursinus, Zanchius and Gomarus on the subject, apparently without complete satisfaction, but much of the letter is taken

---

30 *Ep.* 55, dated by Dekker, *Rijker dan Midas*, p.257, after 17 August 1602.
31 *Ep.* 56 of 1 October 1602, translated in full in *Works*, I, pp.174-83.
32 *Works*, I, pp.176-9.

up with the impending appointment of a new professor of theology at Leiden and whether Arminius himself would be suitable for the post. This is naturally the subject of most of his letters written in this period; but there is one more that we must consider, the long letter of 27 March 1603,[33] which touches on a number of theological subjects.

In his previous letter, Uitenbogaert had referred to Arminius' exchange of correspondence with the now deceased Junius, in particular to *'unde nempe fides ista sit in homine'* (the origin of faith in man). Arminius says that in Scripture teaching concerning justification we are not told where justifying faith comes from, only that believers, and they alone, are justified without the works of the law. Hence he distinguishes the decree by which God resolves to justify and adopt believers, from the decree by which he resolves to bestow faith on particular individuals—which has consequences for predestination also. It means that Arminius does not disagree with some of his colleagues about predestination as a whole, but about one particular part of it, that concerned with the bestowing of faith.

As to the origin of faith, Arminius is at this time surprisingly close to the 'orthodox' Reformed position: 'I am decidedly inclined to the part of grace, and wish to make no assertion that might injure grace or even seem to do so.'[34] Indeed, he is prepared to concede, at least for the sake of argument, that

> Faith is communicated to men solely by the omnipotent act of God, which a man has neither power nor will to resist; and that faith is not communicated to those who do not have it, because God is unwilling to act in the man in this way.... Will it still be useless to teach that God justifies believers only?... 'Therefore believe so that you may be justified.' With respect, then, to this argument, faith will arise from persuasion, but with respect to the omnipotent and internal action (of God), faith will arise from irresistible efficacy. If anyone objects 'It is impossible for faith to spring at the same time from resistible persuasion and irresistible efficacy', I shall not contradict him much, but I have something else to say, that God in His omnipotent action uses this argument, and by this argument rightly understood He produces faith. Otherwise the operation would be performed on a stone or a tree-trunk, not on the intellect of a man.[35]

Note that at this stage Arminius is still more concerned to stress that justification is through faith, than that it forms part of a relationship between God and man. He is even prepared to consider that the grace

---

[33] *Ep.* 60, pp.111-116. Note that on pp.113-4 the references in the top corners are given incorrectly as '*Ep.* 63'. There are long quotations from the section on the origin of faith translated in *Works*, I, pp.746-7 in the footnotes. Translations of other parts are my own.

[34] *Ep.* 60, p.112; *Works*, I, p.746.

[35] *Ep.* 60, pp.112f; *Works*, I, pp.746f.

which confers faith is an irresistible act of God's omnipotence. What he is not prepared to accept is that God treats man, even sinful man, as a thing and not as a person, blurring the distinction between man and God's inanimate creation. This passage is in answer to Uitenbogaert's question, and Arminius asks for more time to consider. Of the link between faith and regeneration, one can say in a word that we are given life through faith. Faith is communicated to us through the Spirit of Christ, whom Christ has obtained from the Father and of whom he (Christ) is made by the Father Donor and Dispenser. The Spirit, considered absolutely, is the Author of faith, which in no way denies the previous assertion that grace is the origin of faith, for such grace is of the Holy Spirit. His projected theological system would solve all such questions. Meanwhile,

> There is nothing in that reasoning of Calvin of which I cannot heartily approve if all things (in it) are rightly understood. For I confess that that grace by which the Holy Spirit is given, is not common to all men; I also confess that the origin (*fontem*) of faith can be said to be the gratuitous election of God, but it is election to bestow faith, not to communicate salvation. For a believer is elected to participate in salvation, a sinner is elected to faith. But we must see what kind of election is so often driven home (*inculcatur*) in Scripture....[36]

On the basis of Ephesians 1:5, Romans 9:11, 11:5, 7, and particularly 2 Thessalonians 2:13 ('Because God has elected you...to salvation through the sanctification of the Spirit and belief in the truth'), Arminius argues that there is a twofold election and one cannot say that election to salvation is the same as election to faith; the former is produced through faith and sanctification of the Spirit. Arminius is arguing for careful and accurate distinctions, but even in this late stage (1603) he is prepared to concede a surprising amount to his opponents.

In this letter he also considers at some length the question of repentance (*poenitentia*) as it applies to the Ninevites in the book of Jonah, to Peter and Simon Magus, and to God himself. Bangs comments, on the fact that late in 1605 Arminius completed prelections (lectures to his students, now lost), on Jonah, 'One wonders what could detain him so long in that book',[37] but *Epistle* 60 probably gives the clue; the book of Jonah contains both human repentance and divine repentance, the latter following on the former and raising the whole question of how God can be said to change his mind in response to human acts. Arminius also cites other biblical examples; how God, having created the world, afterwards repented doing so (Genesis 6:6f), and destroyed most of it in a flood; and how he first chose Saul as king of Israel, then chose to take the kingdom from him. Arminius refers at the beginning of the passage on God's

---

36 *Ep.* 60, p.113; *Works*, I, p.747.
37 Bangs, *Arminius*, p.272.

repentance to the book (*libellum*) of F(ranciscus) G(omarus) on the subject, and to his own correspondence with Junius. He denies that he ascribes changeableness (*mutabilitas*) to God; when Scripture ascribes repentance to God, it does so 'by metaphor deduced from the creatures', and such a metaphor is not a change of will (*voluntatis*), nor even of the same volition (*volitionis eiusdem*), but one volition succeeds to another through the intervention of the act of the creature. This is not directly concerned with Christ's work, but is concerned with the attributes of God which govern it.[38]

Thus, we have established that by the time Arminius left Amsterdam in 1603 he had expressed his opinion in letters on a number of subjects, generally consistently with his statements in the *Synopsis*, sometimes closer to Reformed orthodoxy. The crowning glory of his pastoral ministry, however, came at the end when he had left Amsterdam and was just about to embark on his academic career.

The Consistory of Amsterdam, most of whom opposed Arminius' proposed appointment to Leiden, decided on 14 April 1603 to consent to his call there if Arminius would meet Gomarus and 'wipe away all suspicion of heterodoxy by a candid explanation of his opinion'.[39] This conference, at which many others were present, including Uitenbogaert, lasted two days, on 6 to 7 May in The Hague. No official report was made. Nichols and Bangs[40] follow the account in Brandt, which is naturally sympathetic to Arminius. Dekker[41] follows an account which is presumably biased on the other side by Arent Corneliszoon,[42] who, as Chairman of the Deputies of the Synods, at an extraordinary session had opposed the appointment of Arminius on the grounds that he was too young (at forty-four!) and inexperienced (after fifteen years' service in Amsterdam) and prone to quarrels (a matter of opinion), thus drawing the withering sarcasm of Uitenbogaert. Neither Gomarus nor Arminius left an account of this, and care should be taken in using either Brandt or Corneliszoon, but both agree that Arminius' interpretation of Romans 7, his correspondence with Junius and his opinion of the Roman Church were discussed. At the end, Gomarus professed himself satisfied with Arminius' explanations, and recognised that his views were not Pelagian

---

38 *Ep.* 60, pp.113ff.
39 Bangs, *Arminius*, pp.236f, quoting Brandt, *Life of Arminius*, pp.167f.
40 *Works*, I, pp.244-248; Bangs, *Arminius*, pp.238f.
41 Dekker, *Rijker dan Midas*, p.39 nn.110-11.
42 Original in the archives of the Dutch Reformed Church at Delft. Transcription published as Een Veerslag van de Conferentie tussen Gomarus en Arminius op 6 en 7 Mei 1603 by J.C.L. Starreveld in *NAKG*, 62 (1982), pp.65-76. Around 1590, Arminius had been invited to refute Corneliszoon's (and Donteklok's) attempted refutation, from an infralapsarian position, of the veteran humanist Dirck Volckertszoon Coornhert; but Arminius had produced nothing.

and did not contravene the *Catechism* or the foundations of doctrine. However, Gomarus remained suspicious.

Arminius began his academic career with a public disputation, *De Natura Dei, On the Nature of God*, on 10 July and followed it the next day with his oration to the Convocation on *The Priesthood of Christ*, now numbered *Oration* IV. Nichols describes this oration as 'charming', Bangs as 'not controversial', and Dekker as 'orthodox...as far as I can ascertain'.[43] None gives more than a brief summary of its contents. The only writer who examines the oration in any detail is Loonstra,[44] who says that although Arminius at Amsterdam had already fallen under suspicion of unorthodoxy, his doctoral speech gave no occasion to revive such suspicions, and that for the first time in the history of Reformed theology reference was made to a covenant between God and Christ concerning the salvation of sinners.

Arminius deduces the concept of priesthood from what he calls 'the very origin of the office', which he believes is the relationship between God and men, but 'God never requires, from those under obligation to Him, grateful acknowledgment of the benefit communicated...except when He has bound them to Himself by the larger and far superior benefit of a mutual covenant.'[45] Priesthood, then, is based on covenant.[46] Neither medieval scholasticism nor Lutheranism had laid much stress on covenant; the *Book of Concord* has few references, and in the treatise *On Sacrifice* of the Lutheran theologian David Chytraeus,[47] which is longer than the oration but covers much the same ground, covenant is hardly mentioned. However, contemporary and later Reformed theologians like Bullinger, Musculus, Beza, Ursinus and Zanchius made a good deal of the concept.[48]

Arminius argues that every covenant between God and men consists of two parts:

> 1. God's promise that He will be a king to men and will do for them all that a good king would do. This is the *regal* function and is of supreme authority, and includes the gift of prophecy which is the announcement of the royal pleasure, either communicated directly by God Himself, or by His human prophet.

---

43 *Works*, I, p.402; Bangs, *Arminius*, p.254; Dekker, *Rijker dan Midas*, p.41.

44 B. Loonstra, *Verkiezing-Verzoening-Verbond: Beschrieving en Beoordeling van de leer van het PACTUM SALUTIS in de gereformeerde theologie* ('s-Gravenhage: Boekencentrum BV, 1990), pp.21ff.

45 *Works*, I, pp.405f.

46 Here *'federatio'*, not *'foedus'*; *Opera*, p.11.

47 David Chytraeus, On Sacrifice: A Reformation Treatise in Biblical Theology (translated and edited by John Warwick Montgomery; St. Louis, MO: Concordia, 1962).

48 See Muller, *Christ and the Decree*, pp.40-1, 48-9, 90, 98, 120.

2. The duty required from men, that they become God's people, live according to His commands, and ask and expect all blessings from His goodness. This is the *religious* function of devoted submission, properly expressed in thanksgiving and entreaty. According to this, 'a mutual correspondence subsists between men and God.'[49]

All God's people share in a vocation to this duty, 'every one of the great body of those in covenant; and to this end they have been sanctified by the word of the covenant, and have all been constituted priests to God, to offer gifts and prayers to Him.' This is Arminius' expression of the 'priesthood of all believers'.

God loves order, being himself the only instance of perfect order. He therefore willed that some of the people should be separated to him in a special manner and by a extraordinary vocation, 'to approach His throne more intimately and with greater freedom', and in the place of others in the same covenant, should 'take charge and management of whatever affairs were to be transacted before God for them'. This separated priesthood is in effect subordinated to the priesthood of all believers, in good Protestant fashion.

The priest must be taken from among men, and must be appointed on their behalf, but the choice is not the priest's own nor that of the covenant community. As the office exists by God's good pleasure, so the choice of priest is his.[50] His practice is to choose the *paterfamilias*, father and master of the family, for example Noah, Abraham and Job; Arminius speculates with unnamed theologians 'not occupying the lowest seats in judgment' that Cain and Abel brought their sacrifices for Adam to offer. The *paterfamilias*'s successor would be the first-born. God would reveal his will and pleasure to the priest so that he might declare it on return. This included both what God required his covenant people to do, and what he would do for their benefit. It also included prophecy, according to Malachi 2:7, 'The people should seek the LAW[51] at the priest's mouth, for he is the messenger of the Lord of Hosts.' The priest was commissioned to pronounce God's blessings on the people as an expression of assured trust and confidence in His promises, and also of God's and his own goodwill to men. Thus he discharged the duties of a 'double embassy', of men to God and of God to men, and so was on both sides Mediator of the covenant. God also 'elevated [the priest] to the regal dignity, that he, bearing the image of God among his brethren, might...administer justice in God's name'.[52] The priestly and kingly offices were thereby united, and as the priest had a prophetic role also in

---

49 *Works*, I, p.406.
50 *Works*, I, p.407.
51 Arminius' emphasis in heavier type; capitals in the Nichols translation.
52 *Works*, I, p.408.

declaring the law, we find here the Reformed combination of prophet, priest and king, which 'obtained among the patriarchs after the entrance of sin', and of which Melchizedek was an example. Arminius claims that Jacob's attribution of 'excellency of dignity and power' to Reuben (Genesis 49:3) was a transfer of his own prerogatives to the one who as firstborn inherited them by right; though he admits that the kingly and priestly functions were later separated and transferred to Judah and Levi.

The priest was required to be pure and holy to approach God through 'eucharistic'[53] sacrifice and prayers, as in Leviticus 19:2, John 9.31 and Isaiah 1:15. But Adam as first priest 'did not long administer his office in a becoming manner', and by his wickedness lost his right to the priesthood, of which he was deprived when expelled from Paradise, as Eli and his sons were later to lose theirs (1 Samuel 2:30). The fall of man was not only a fall into sin, but also a fall from priesthood and covenant:

> [Adam] did not fall alone; all those he...represented and whose cause he pleaded (though they had not yet come into existence) were cast down with him...not from priesthood only, but also from the covenant, of which the priest was both Mediator and Internuncio; and God ceased to be King and God of men, and men were no longer recognised as His people. Priesthood itself was at an end, for there was no-one capable of fulfilling its duties.... Eucharistic sacrifice, invocation of God's name, and the gracious communication between God and men, all ceased together.[54]

God resolved to enter into a new covenant with men, a covenant of grace, but 'divine justice and truth could not permit this...except through an umpire and surety, who might undertake the part of Mediator between the offended God and sinners'. Eucharistic sacrifice was no longer enough; the Mediator had to offer expiatory sacrifice for the act of hostility which men had committed against God by disobedience, and to pray for their forgiveness and renewed access to the throne of God's grace.

But God would not at once bring this new covenant into effect. Men must be first educated to understand the seriousness of sin and must want to be freed from it. So there was the temporary institution of a 'typical' priesthood, in which sinful men would sacrifice beasts sanctified for the purpose. This priesthood was not restricted to that of the Old Testament; it was established in different parts of the world, and later among the Israelites, who were specially elected as a sacerdotal nation (apparently referring to Exodus 19:6). It was recognised that animal sacrifices could not remove sins; the people 'in such an act delivered to God...their own bond, sealing it in His presence with acknowledgement of their own sins'. Arminius thinks that the Israelites recognised on one hand that God was

---

53 That is, a sacrifice of thanksgiving, as in Hebrews 13:15.
54 *Works*, I, pp.409f.

pleased with the offerings (Judges 13:23), on the other, that they were looking for the final priesthood prefigured under the typical one (1 Peter 1:11).

So Arminius comes to Christ's priesthood, the greatest and final expression, yet related both to the original priesthood of Adam and to the typical priesthood of the Old Testament. He considers it under three main headings:

  I. The imposing of the office.
  II. Its execution and administration.
  III. Its results and benefits.

Each of these has sub-headings, which in the case of the first are:

  1. The person who imposes it.
  2. The person to whom it is entrusted.
  3. The manner of his appointment, and of his undertaking the charge.

I.1. Arminius was charged during his lifetime and after with not being properly trinitarian, but here he regards the 'dispensation of our salvation' as an act of 'the persons comprised under this one Divine Monarchy'. But these persons are to be considered distinctly according to the rule of the Scriptures and the orthodox Fathers. God, the Father of the Lord Jesus Christ, imposes the office on the Messiah in the words of Psalms 2:8 and 110:4.

Here Arminius launches into a debate between the different qualities of God, Justice, Mercy and Wisdom personified, previously used in the *Analysis* of Romans 9,[55] but reminiscent of classical statues depicting various virtues and their later representation in the visual arts, in a way which is not to modern taste. In his first public disputation *On the Nature of God*, given the day before, he had included these along with a number of other attributes; Mercy among the 'primary affections', along with Love, Goodness, Grace, Benignity (LXV-LXVI), Justice or Righteousness along with Patience, Long-Suffering, Readiness to Pardon and Clemency as a 'moderator of the affections'; but Wisdom had not been mentioned. Muller argues that wisdom (*sapientia*) is generally absent from Arminius' discussion of the divine attributes and where it occurs is concerned with the rule of providence.[56] The point is rather that Arminius sees Wisdom as being particularly concerned with God's relations with his rational creatures; the concept is virtually absent from the first twenty-three

---

55 *Works*, I, pp.413f; cf. *Works*, III, pp.511ff.
56 Muller, *God*, pp.144, 169, 246f.

Private Disputations on the subject of God, but occurs in the later *Private Disputations* on the subject of Christ.[57]

The result of this debate between God's attributes was to transmute the punishment due to sin into an expiatory sacrifice which would include voluntary suffering of death in a way that would satisfy both God's justice and God's mercy. A priest was needed to offer this. An angel could not do it, because a priest must be taken from men (Hebrews 5:1); nor could an angel be an expiation for human sin. As all men were now sinners, no man could offer it and no man was worthy to do so. 'Yet the priest was to be taken from among men, and the oblation was to consist of a human victim.'

The solution was for a man to be born sharing the nature of other men, so that he would be tempted as they are and sympathise with others in their suffering, yet he should have no sin. To share human nature he must be born of a human being, to be holy he must be conceived of the Holy Spirit. So God's Word, who was with God from the beginning and by whom all things were created, should himself be made flesh, undertake the office of priesthood and offer his flesh to God as a sacrifice for the life of the world. So Arminius arrives at Jesus Christ, Son of God and son of man, and refers to Augustine's *O felix culpa* with a significant difference: 'a High Priest of such great excellence, that the transgression whose demerits have obtained this mighty Redeemer, might *almost* seem to have been a happy circumstance'.[58]

This priesthood was imposed by covenant, as was the Levitical on Levi (Malachi 2:5), but the special feature of Christ's priesthood was that it was confirmed by an oath. In the covenant God required of Christ that he should lay down his soul as a victim in sacrifice for sin (Isaiah 53:11), give his flesh for the life of the world (John 6:51), and pay the price of redemption for the sins and captivity of the human race. In return, God promised that he should 'see His seed' and that he should be an everlasting priest after the order of Melchizedek (Psalm 110:4), that is, that he should, by discharging his functions as priest, be elevated to kingship. Arminius praises the omnipotent God's 'condescension' in treating with our High Priest by way of covenant rather than authority, and the High Priest's own 'pious affections', which lead him into a prayer of thanksgiving. The oath added to the covenant confirms it and demonstrates the dignity and unchangeable nature of the priesthood. Arminius digresses here to show that the original method for man to achieve righteousness before God, through the law by works, was not immutable and therefore was not confirmed by an oath; whereas the

---

57 See *Private Disputation* XXIV:iv, viii, and *Corollary* ii; XXVI:vi; XXVIII:vi, xi.
58 *Works*, I, p.415.

method of obtaining righteousness through the gospel, 'by grace and through faith', is immutable and therefore confirmed by an oath.[59]

II. The execution of the Priesthood consists of two functions:

1. Oblation of an expiatory sacrifice.
2. Prayer.

The oblation was preceded by sufferings on which Arminius does not enlarge. Oblation itself consists of two parts.

First, immolation or sacrifice of Christ's body, by shedding His blood on the altar of the cross, followed by death which paid the price of the redemption for sins by suffering the punishment due to them. This had to be performed outside the Holy of Holies, that is, on earth, because no blood can be shed in heaven; such effusion is followed by death which can have no place in heaven, any more than sin and punishment can. So Arminius interprets the 'ransom' language of Matthew 20:28 and 1 Timothy 2:6, and the words of institution at the Last Supper (Matthew 26:28). There is no suggestion, as in Aulen's *Christus Victor*,[60] that the medieval tradition from Anselm onwards had misinterpreted the New Testament or the doctrine of atonement of the first Christian millennium.

Secondly, the offering of Christ's body reanimated and sprinkled with Christ's blood as symbol of the price paid and redemption obtained. This must be accomplished in heaven, in the Holy of Holies.[61] Christ had merited this: 'that body...was entitled so to appear before the Divine Majesty'. The act is unrepeatable and perpetual in its effects (Romans 6:10), and the priesthood is unchangeable (Hebrews 6:10).

The oblation was completed in deepest humiliation, its sequel in a state of glory, but both 'out of consummate affection for God's glory and the salvation of sinners'. The former is seen as 'a kind of preparation on earth...to discharge the functions of the latter in heaven'.[62]

II.2. Prayer is defined as 'that which Christ offers for Himself', and intercession as 'what He offers for believers', and the latter depends on the oblation. Both are contained in John 17, which, though prayed by Christ on earth, 'properly belongs to His sublime state of exaltation in heaven', and contains 'a perpetual rule and exact canon' of the prayers and intercessions offered by Christ in heaven to his Father. Criticism that

---

59 *Works*, I, pp.416-7.

60 *Works*, I, pp.419f; cf. G. Aulen, *Christus Victor: An Historical Study of Three Main Types of the Idea of the Atonement* (trans. A.G. Hebert; London, SPCK, 1953), *passim*, especially chs 1 and 5.

61 The reference appears to be to Hebrews 12:22ff, which describes the heavenly Jerusalem, Jesus the Mediator of the new covenant, and the blood of sprinkling speaking something better than the blood of Abel.

62 *Works*, I, p.420.

'the common description of [John 17] as "the High-priestly prayer"...does not do justice to the full range of the material contained in it',[63] and similar comments may therefore be wide of the mark. As Arminius understands it, it would be meant proleptically as a description of how the prayer is to be used, not as a description of its contents. The prayers for himself which Christ now offers are to be distinguished from the 'supplications...in the days of His flesh' (Hebrews 5:7) which were for relief from anguish, whereas now he prays to see the result of his labours. Intercessions are made for believers (Romans 8:34, Hebrews 7:25) to the exclusion of the world, and he intercedes 'not in anguish of spirit or in a posture of humble genuflection, but' — here Arminius uses imagery which is strong meat for modern tastes — 'in the confidence of the shedding of His own blood, which, sprinkled on His sacred body, He continually presents as an object of sight before His Father, always turning it towards His sacred countenance'. The purpose is to assure us that his prayers for us will never be rejected, and that whatever we ask in his name will in the intercession be both heard and answered.[64]

The regal dignity is also given to Christ, so that he has all power and authority over everything in heaven and earth, as Christ and Lord of his whole Israel, King of Kings and Lord of Lords. This conjunction of the two supreme functions of priesthood and kingship produces 'a most intimate and inseparable union of the whole church of believers and of God Himself', and in styling Christ 'the brightness of the Father's glory, the express image of His person and the image of the invisible God', Arminius considers that he has expressed this union as fully and excellently as possible. He believes that even God's Son could not be constituted King except by discharging the priestly function; the blessings he has for us could only be asked for through the priesthood, and even when obtained could be communicated solely by his mediatorial intervention. This, says Arminius, is our certainty of obtaining salvation through Christ. There is no reference in this oration to election and predestination.

III, The fruits of the sacerdotal office administered by Christ, consist of four 'utilities':

1. Contracting and confirming a new covenant.
2. Asking, obtaining and applying all benefits necessary to those in the covenant, for the salvation of soul and body.
3. Instituting a new priesthood, both eucharistic and regal.
4. Bringing to God all the church of the faithful.

---

63 C.K. Barrett, *The Gospel according to St. John: An Introduction with Commentary and notes on the Greek Text* (London: SPCK, 2nd edition 1978), p.500.
64 *Works*, I, p.421.

III.1. The first covenant was made weak through sin and the flesh, and could not bring salvation and life; it had, therefore, to be replaced. Reconciliation between a just God and sinful men was required; Christ's death on the cross was such a reconciliation. Another covenant then became possible, and it pleased God that the same High Priest 'who had acted as Mediator and Umpire in reconciliation should...go between the two parties as middle-man or ambassador, and as a herald.' A new covenant was contracted, not of works but of faith, not of the law but of grace, and new not because it was later than the first, but because it would never be abrogated or repealed, and because its force and vigour would last, unlike the old covenant of Hebrews 8:13. The blood with which it was ratified was of the greatest possible value, and if it is rejected there remains no more sacrifice for sins (Hebrews 10:29).

III.2. There are three blessings for those in covenant:

    a. Remission of sins.
    b. Adoption as children and a right to the heavenly inheritance.
    c. The gift of the Holy Spirit.

a. Even in the time of the old covenant Jeremiah foresaw a time when God would be merciful to his people's unrighteousness and remember their sins and iniquities no more (Jeremiah 31:34, quoted in Hebrews 8:12). When Jesus spoke at the Last Supper he indicated that this time has come (Matthew 26:28), and by his blood he wins redemption for us (Hebrews 9:12, Ephesians 1:7)

b. Christ as the Father's only-begotten Son and sole heir, wanted others to share in the inheritance. Those who received redemption under the law also received adoption as children (Galatians 4:5), and God also promised his Messiah the heathen (Gentiles) for his inheritance (Psalm 2:8). Adoption is for Christ's believing people (John 1:12). Even the perfidious husbandmen of Mark 12:7 bear witness to this in a distorted way.

c. Such benefits can only be obtained in union with the High Priest himself, and the Holy Spirit is the bond of that union. The Holy Spirit could not be given till God and man were reconciled; when they were, Christ asked his Father for another Comforter for his people, and poured him out 'in a most copious manner' (Acts 2:33).

III.3. Christ placed us in his debt to offer thanksgiving for what he did for us. So he instructed us to offer sacrifices to God. Arminius explains that our souls and bodies are sanctified and consecrated by the sprinkling of his blood and by the unction of the Holy Spirit, suggesting that he had Romans 12:1 in mind. Christ has erected in heaven an altar sprinkled with his blood, for the sacrifices of his faithful people, with the eternal fire of God's immeasurable favour to reduce those sacrifices to ashes. As priests we have been consecrated by his blood (Revelation 1:6, 5:10), but he remains the Head, the first-born and the great High Priest who presides over God's whole house. Arminius also mentions the sacrifice of praise of Hebrews 13:5 and the spiritual sacrifices of 1 Peter 2:5 as offered through Christ. Our priesthood, like that of Christ, is a Melchizedek-type priesthood and therefore permanent.

III.4. Finally, all the church of the faithful, the covenant people, will be brought to God (1 Peter 3:18); they are the kingdom whom Christ delivers up at the end (1 Corinthians 15:24), and the children whom God has given to him. Christ will bring his church, his priests and kings, and God will receive the Church as the Bride, the Lamb's wife; he will receive the priests to clothe them in perfect holiness; he will receive the kings that they may reign for ever with God and the Lamb. Arminius rhetorically asks what could be better than this prospect for us sinners in our present state. He finishes with the assurance that this gives, and collects passages of praise from the Bible, concluding with the doxologies from Revelation (4:7, 5:10).

The general style of the oration is analytical, with divisions and subdivisions which suggest his Ramist background.[65] It is instructive to consider the direct quotations from biblical books; there are many from the Old Testament, as one would expect in an oration which considered priesthood in general, but when we come to the New Testament there are sixteen quotations from the Pauline books and twenty-one from the Epistle to the Hebrews, with the rest of the New Testament (Gospels, Acts and the other Epistles) contributing eighteen. Less than two years before Arminius had completed a thirteen-year exposition of Romans with his Amsterdam congregation, but Pauline theology is not the framework for this oration; he seems rather to have taken Hebrews as his framework and fitted other material, including the Pauline, into it. Perhaps the controversy aroused by his exposition of Romans made him avoid the Pauline approach in favour of what he rightly thought would be the less controversial approach of Hebrews.

In any case this oration was Arminius' first public triumph, worthy to rank with the oration *On Reconciling Religious Dissensions among Christians*, and with the *Declaration of Sentiments*, and less controversial than either. It shows that he was capable of discussing the work of Christ for men without referring to the doctrine of God, or predestination, or human psychology, and that he was happy to do so, and had indeed already given more thought to the subject that we might suppose from his earlier writings and letters. It also augured well for his career as an

---

[65] Arminius' early enthusiasm for the logic and philosophical methods of Petrus Ramus (Pierre de la Ramee, 1515-72) led to his temporary withdrawal from Geneva to Basle during his university career. See, e.g., Bangs, *Arminius*, pp.56-73.

academic teacher, but, as we shall see, the harmony of that day did not last.

We have seen that by the time he was appointed professor at Leiden, Arminius had worked out a doctrine of the work of Christ which was wide-ranging, well integrated with his other beliefs, and in some respects original; one worthy to rank with the doctrine of God set forth in his first public disputation, *On the Nature of God*; and both may have caused some surprise when delivered. He had also developed views about the Trinity and the Persons of Christ and the Holy Spirit that would prove controversial; but he at least had no problems in reconciling them with his other views.

CHAPTER 4

Synopsis:
The Roots of Arminius' Christology

In this chapter we leave the chronological treatment of Arminius' theological development, which becomes increasingly complicated as we approach his transfer from pastor in Amsterdam to professor in Leiden, and almost impossible after 1603, apart from the subject of predestination. His theology will be considered systematically before returning to later developments. The framework is provided by the *Private Disputations* which, as James Nichols recognises, are the later development of the *Synopsis* which, according to his letter,[1] Arminius undertook as 'the groundwork of a body of divinity'. The advantage of this approach is that we see individual doctrines in the framework in which Arminius himself placed them. As we have seen and will see again, scholars who have placed them in what Arminius would consider the wrong context, have misunderstood them. In the case of Christology, the root conviction is the relationship between God and man which Christ restores.

Prolegomena: Do Christ and his Work Matter Most to Arminius?

In the light of Muller's statements in *God, Creation and Providence*, we must first ask about the relative importance of the work and person of Christ in Arminius' theology. In his chapter on 'The Object and Goal of Theology', Muller uses the distinction which Arminius makes in his Oration *On the Object of Theology*, and continues to use in his next Oration *On the Author and End of Theology*, between 'legal theology', which obtained up to the time of the Fall, and 'evangelical theology', which deals with Christ and his work. Arminius does not use these precise terms and distinction in the *Private Disputations*, which may give cause for doubt whether they are as significant as Muller makes them. Muller argues for a 'logical priority of legal over evangelical theology', parallel to the 'logical priority of God as primary over Christ as secondary object of theology', and pointing towards a 'logical priority of the foundational,

---

1 *Ep.*, 44 of 18 February 1599, p.85, cf. *Works*, I, p.131; *Works*, II, p.318.

nonsoteriological topics in Arminius's system over soteriological topics'.[2]

It is hard to know how much to read into Muller's concept of 'logical priority'. If we choose to use such terms, there is certainly a *chronological* priority of legal over evangelical theology, for Arminius explained to Uitenbogaert in the same letter that he intended to study the doctrine of God before other doctrines, including that of Christ. Muller speaks of 'precedence' of this basic perception of God and God's relation to the world (legal theology), over the evangelical or saving relation, and indeed Arminius himself grants a 'claim to precedency' to legal theology,[3] but, as Muller himself acknowledges, Arminius says that when we consider that both God and Christ are its authors, we see that 'Evangelical far surpasses Legal Theology'.[4] The wisdom, goodness and power of God shown in creation (legal theology) are great, but the wisdom, goodness and power shown in the incarnation and new creation are greater, and constitute the claims by which evangelical theology asserts its right to precedence. A list of other comparisons follows. In fact, 'logical priority', as distinct from precedence, belongs neither to legal theology nor to evangelical theology; it belongs rather to God himself and his attributes, which underlie both forms of theology, and are described in some detail in the oration *On the Object of Theology*, before the distinction between legal and evangelical theology is first introduced.[5]

The Private Disputations begin with discussion of 'Theology, Religion, the Scriptures and the Christian Religion' (*Disputations* I-XIII), and follow with description of God as primary object (XIV-XXIII). Even those on the scriptures and the Christian religion offer little hint of what is to follow when he comes to discuss the work and person of Christ. If Muller had criticised Arminius for making too firm a distinction between the doctrine of God and that of Christ, he might have been on firmer ground; but it may be added that this fits in with Arminius' clear teaching about Christ's subordination to God. Arminius has described God in terms of nature, action and will, and under actions says that 'two...have been ascribed to God...CREATION and PROVIDENCE'. From this Muller takes his theme and (possibly) title, and treats these topics as 'nonchristological and nonsoteriological',[6] while admitting that it is not clear whether the whole system is regarded as 'evangelical theology'. What concerns Arminius is to show that the nature of God and his actions of creation and providence, and the underlying principles of his will, remain the same and unaffected by man's fall into sin, and therefore

---

2 Muller, *God*, p.74
3 *Works*, I, p.359.
4 *Works*, I, p.359; Muller, *God*, p.76.
5 *Works*, I, pp.325-30.
6 *Works*, I, p.329; Muller, *God*, p.74.

underlie both legal and evangelical theology, although the ways in which his providence operates and the actual decisions of his will, necessarily vary with the new situation. Muller's mistake is to take these *Orations* as chronologically prior to the *Private Disputations*, and therefore the plan of the *Orations* as determinative for the latters' interpretation, as we have demonstrated above in chapter 3.

Very God?: The Doctrines of the Trinity and the Person of Christ

Who is the God being described? The editors of the 1629 edition of the *Opera* insert after *Private Disputation* XXIII. 'On the Perfection, Blessedness and Glory of God'. a note which is dutifully translated by James Nichols: 'the candid reader will be able, in this place, to supply from the preceding Public Disputations the Theses on the Father and the Son, and those on the Holy Spirit, the Holy and undivided Trinity'.[7] No doubt; but the 'candid reader' will also want to know why, when Arminius has expressed himself freely about the Trinity in the *Public Disputations*, there should be virtually nothing on the subject in the *Private Disputations* which are supposed to be his systematic theology. Muller, in his article on 'The Christological Problem',[8] rightly bemoaning the lack of discussion of many points of Arminius' theology, says 'the sole exception known to me is Dorner's brief comment on...Arminius's concepts of Trinity and Atonement',[9] but Dorner has little to say on the former; he assumes that Arminius' rejection of the *autotheos* necessarily implies heterodoxy about the Trinity which was afterwards worked out 'more decidedly' by his followers and by Vorstius. In Arminius' *Public Disputation* V, 'On the Person of the Father and the Son', Christ is called 'the Second Person in the Holy Trinity, the Word of the Father, begotten of the Father from all eternity, proceeding from Him by the communication of the same Deity which the Father possesses without origination'. Reference is made to Matthew 28:19 and John 1:1. The Son was not created; all things were created by him (John 1:3): nor was he adopted, for we are all adopted in him (John 1:12, Ephesians 1:5f). He is Son by generation, and as Son partakes the whole divinity of his Father. He is a Person in every way that his Father is; an undivided and incommunicable subsistence, living, intelligent, willing, powerful and active (the modern sense of the word). His divinity is proved from his names in scripture, 'King of Kings and Lord of Lords' (Revelation 17:14, 19:16), and 'Lord of Glory' (1 Corinthians 2:8); if

---

7 *Works*, II, p.354.

8 R.A. Muller, 'The Christological Problem in the Thought of Jacobus Arminius', *NAKG*, 68 (1988), p.145 n.1.

9 I.A. Dorner, *A History of Protestant Thought particularly in Germany* (2 vols; trans. George Robson and Sophia Taylor; New York: AMS Press, 1970 [1871]), I, p.427.

'Son' and 'Word' are understood correctly, they also prove his divinity. Essential attributes of deity are attributed to him in scripture; immensity, eternity, immutability, omniscience, omnipotence, majesty and glory; so are divine works such as creation and preservation of all things, performing of miracles, and works relating to the salvation of the church. Lastly, parallel passages which ascribe something to God (the Father) in the Old Testament, are attributed to Christ in the New; thus Paul describes the people's speaking against God in Numbers 21:5ff as 'tempting Christ' in 1 Corinthians 10:9, and God ascending on high and leading captivity captive in Psalm 68:18 as Christ's work in Ephesians 4:8; other examples are also given.[10] There is both agreement and distinction between Father and Son in their *Persons*; agreement in sharing one and the same nature and essence, according to which the Son is in the form of God and equal with the Father (Philippians 2:6), and according to Nicene *homoousios* not *homoiousios*; distinction in the 'mode of existence or subsistence' by which each has his divinity; the Father from no-one, the Son from the Father; thus Arminius reconciles the Son's unity with the Father according to agreement in John 10:30, with his otherness in John 5:32.[11] It would seem that on the occasion this public disputation was held, no-one picked up the point that Arminius held a different view from theirs on the *autotheos* question. But so far as Christ's *work* is concerned, this chapter will argue as against Muller that the doctrines of creation and providence, and all that follow, are not only 'foundational', but also thoroughly Christological and soteriological.

In the following *Disputation*, VI 'On the Holy Spirit', Arminius says 'We may not attempt to *define* the Holy Spirit (for such an attempt is unlawful) but we may be allowed to *describe* Him according to the Scriptures...(as) "the Person subsisting in the Sacred and undivided Trinity... Third in order, emanating from the Father and sent by the Son, therefore proceeding from both and according to his Person distinct from both; infinite, eternal, illimitable, and of the same Divinity with the Father and the Son."'[12] These points are proved from scripture. Later, when Arminius was writing to Hippolytus à Collibus, he emphasised the eternity of both Word and Spirit, 'not as properties but as really existing Persons...from the Father neither by creation nor by decision, but by a most wonderful and inexplicable internal emanation, which, with respect to the Son, the Ancient Church called generation...with respect to the Holy Spirit...spiration or breathing.... But about this breathing I do not judge, whether it is from the Father and the Son, as the Latin Fathers say, or from the Father through the Son, as the Greek Fathers prefer.... This

---

10 *Works*, II, pp.139-42; *Public Disputation* V:IX-XIII.
11 *Works*, II, pp.142ff; *Public Disputation* V:XIV-XVI.
12 *Works*, II, p.145; *Public Disputation* VI:III.

matter, I confess, far surpasses my capacity. If on any subject we ought to speak and think soberly, in my opinion, it must be this.'[13]

Even the earlier *Disputation* VI ends with a caution about the Trinity which appears to be applied both to this and to *Disputation* V:

> This doctrine of the sacred and undivided Trinity contains a mystery which far surpasses...human and angelical understanding, if considered according to the internal union between the Father, the Son and the Holy Ghost, and according to the relation among them of origin and procession. But if regard be had to that economy and dispensation by which the Father and the Son, and both of them through the Holy Spirit, accomplish our salvation, the contemplation is one of admirable sweetness....[14]

This is the point taken up by the only theologian who has significant discussion about Arminius' doctrine of the Trinity, Watkin-Jones, who in *The Holy Spirit from Arminius to Wesley* includes chapters on both 'The Place of the Spirit in the Absolute Trinity' and 'The Place of the Spirit in the Redemptive Trinity'. This is precisely the distinction which Arminius is making in the last quotation. He has virtually nothing to say about the 'Absolute' Trinity; Watkin-Jones can really only quote the 'deep fear...and conscientious solicitude [with which] I [Arminius] treat that sublime doctrine of a Trinity of Persons'.[15] But if it is a question of the Redemptive Trinity, then Arminius has no such inhibitions, because there is more about the latter in the New Testament than about the former. He argues that to contemplate this produces the most exuberant fruits of the Spirit to the praise of all three Persons of the Trinity, appropriately concluding the whole with the familiar benediction of 2 Corinthians 13:14. Watkin-Jones argues that to Luther as to Arminius, 'the doctrine of the Trinity is a mystery in so far as it relates to the interior association of the three Divine Persons, [but] no mystery redemptionally or economically, since contemplation of it, as the mode of salvation whereby the Father and Son work through the Spirit, produces spiritual fruits'. He also quotes a younger contemporary of Arminius, John Donne, in his *Sermon* 32 on 1 Corinthians 12:3, where Paul is speaking of the gifts of the Spirit and the contrast between 'Jesus be cursed' and 'Jesus is Lord!':

> There are two processions of the Holy Ghost, eternal and temporal, His proceeding from the Father and the Son, and His proceeding into us. The first we shall never

---

13 *Works*, II, pp.690f.
14 *Works*, II, p.149; *Public Disputation* VI:XII.
15 *Works*, II, p.29, answering Article XXI of the *31 Defamatory Articles*, accusing him of accusing in turn those who accept the '*autotheos*' of Sabellianism.

understand, if we read all the books of the world. The other we shall not choose but understand, if we study our own consciences.[16]

This is only a partial justification of Arminius. We must say that if he felt so unsure about the 'Absolute' Trinity as he apparently did, then he should not have expressed the traditional teaching on the subject so plainly in his *Public Disputations* without disclosing any personal misgivings, while ignoring the subject completely in his systematic theology. He has often been accused of maintaining an orthodox exterior while dissembling his true opinions; the charge has usually been unjust, but on the subject of the Absolute Trinity he comes nearest to deserving it. In fact, Arminius' fault was not, as his opponents suspected, that he hid doctrines which he firmly held; with their mindset they were unable to realise that it was possible to be uncertain about any doctrine; Arminius was guilty rather of stating clearly this doctrine of which he was privately uncertain. On the other hand, what Watkin-Jones calls the 'Redemptive' Trinity and what Arminius himself calls the 'Economic' Trinity meant a great deal to him. God the Father, as Primary Efficient Cause, created everything by his Word and Spirit. The Lord Jesus Christ has the same nature as the Father and also his human nature from the Virgin Mary through the operation of the Holy Spirit. Christ was prepared as Priest by God's vocation and imposition of the office and by the sanctification and consecration of his person through the Spirit. The Father sanctified Christ to the prophetic office from the moment of his conception by the Holy Spirit, and promised him the perpetual assistance of the Spirit in the sign of the dove. One blessing communicated by Christ's regal office is the Spirit of grace witnessing in our hearts that we are God's children. The resurrection is ascribed not only to the Father through the Holy Spirit but also to Christ himself, who had the power of taking up his life again. As King, Christ's duty was to send the Word and Spirit from heaven and to administer all things in his Father's name. Not only the work of Christ in itself, but also that work as applied to man, is understood in a trinitarian way. For predestination as the decree of God's good-pleasure in Christ, the proper and peculiar means destined are the Word and Spirit; the efficient cause of the vocation of sinners is God the Father in the Son who calls by the Holy Spirit; the repentance by which men answer is caused by God by his Word and Spirit in Christ; the author of faith is the Holy Spirit, whom the Son sends from the Father as his Advocate and Substitute; believers are united with Christ, and through Christ with God, through the Spirit of Christ and of God; the Author of sanctification is God the Holy Father, in his Son the Holy of Holies, through the Spirit of holiness, and the form of holiness is conformity with God in the body of Christ through the Spirit; it is God's good-pleasure that the Head of the

---

16 Watkin-Jones, *The Holy Spirit from Arminius to Wesley*, pp.110f.

church, Jesus Christ, should be united to the church his body by the joints and bands of the Spirit and of faith. The Author of baptism is God the Father, in his Son the Mediator of the New Testament, by the eternal Spirit of both. This long but by no means exhaustive list of explicitly trinitarian statements of the work of Christ,[17] shows that it can be described in a trinitarian framework, and that whatever Arminius' misgivings about the Absolute Trinity, his soteriology depends completely on the whole Trinity being involved. For in the New Testament there is more about the 'Redemptive Trinity' than about the 'Absolute Trinity'.

The Good God and the Good Universe he Made

This note of the editors after *Disputation* XXIII is followed by *Disputation* XXIV, *On Creation*, which begins:

> We have treated [N.B. perfect tense] on GOD, who is the first object of the Christian Religion: And we would now treat on CHRIST, who, next to God is another object of the same religion.[18]

We might expect everything that follows to be concerned with Christ and his work; but, confusingly, Arminius needs first to 'premise some things, without which Christ would neither be an object of religion, nor would the necessity of the Christian religion be understood'. These are: why God has a right to require religion from any man; what religion he requires; and what has happened to make it necessary to constitute Christ as Saviour. The answer to all these, in summary, is: God's creation of the whole cosmos, of angels and men; God's lordship and dominion over his creation; God's providence over the whole world and his covenant with man; and man's failure to keep this original covenant and its effects.[19] How far Christ is involved in all this is not made so clear; what is clear is that it forms the necessary background to his saving work.

God's right to require religion from man is founded first on his creation:

> Creation is an external act of God, by which He produced all things out of nothing, for Himself, by His Word (*verbum*) and Spirit. The Primary Efficient Cause is God the Father, by His Word and Spirit.[20]

---

17 Catena of quotations taken from *Private Disputations* XL-LXIII, *passim*; *Works*, II, pp.392-441.
18 *Works*, II, p.355.
19 *Private Disputations* XXIV-XXXI; *Works*, II, pp.355-75.
20 *Private Disputation* XXIV:iii-iv; *Works*, II, p.355.

It would seem from this that Arminius emphasises the part played by both the second and third persons of the Trinity in creation, and that he sees creation not as the work of Christ strictly speaking but as the work of the eternal Word of God, the Son who later became incarnate in Christ. This is explicitly stated in *Public Disputation* V, 'On the Person of the Father and the Son', which says of the Son that 'He is not the Son by creation. For what things soever have been created, they were all created by Him. (John 1:3).... The Divine works...attributed to Him, establish the same truth. (1) *The Creation of all things.* [He quotes John 1:3 again and also Hebrews 1:2 and 1 Corinthians 8:6.] But what are these "all things"? Exactly the same as those which are said [in the same verse, i.e. 1 Corinthians 8:6], to be "of the Father".'[21] This would seem to settle the matter, but after *Private Disputation* XXIV:iv the Word is not mentioned again, and Christ is mentioned only in a question about whether angels need a Mediator and whether Christ is that Mediator, answered in the negative; until we get to *Disputation* XXXII, *On the Necessity of the Christian Religion*, where Nichols' translation appears to identify Christ and the Word:

> The Son of God...constituted by the Father CHRIST and LORD, is likewise an object of the Christian religion subordinate to God;—though He on earth, as the Word of his Father, both may be and ought to be considered as existing in the Father from all eternity.[22]

The problem is that 'Word' here is in the original not *verbum* but *sermo* and it is not clear whether to Arminius these are synonyms. *Sermo* may be the original translation in the Vulgate (though not in later recensions); a friend has suggested that Arminius used it to express the idea of God having a 'message' in creation. What is clear is the great importance which Arminius attaches to God's creation, an importance largely neglected till Muller wrote about it. Muller is fully justified in calling it a 'fundamental pivot of [Arminius'] theological system'; he is also right to see it as 'grounded in...self-diffusive divine goodness',[23] that is, God created because he is good and as *summum bonum*, the greatest good, he wished to have creatures in which he could express his goodness and, in the case of man, whom he could love and who could return his love. God's goodness is shown in the fact that he does not make a

---

21 *Public Disputation* V:vii, xii; *Works*, II, pp.140ff.

22 *Private Disputation* XXXII:viii: 'Caeterum quia visum Deo est restaurationem illam facere per filium suum Iesum Christum Mediatorem, hinc etiam filius Dei, qua constitutus a Deo Christus et Dominus obiectum est Religionis Christianae Deo subordinatum, quamquam ille in terra, ut sermo patris sui, in patre ab aeterno existens considerari et possit et debeat' , translated *Works*, II, p.377.

23 Muller, *God*, p.211.

principle of keeping oneself to oneself like a middle-class suburbanite, but seeks to share his nature in creation. Arminius also strongly links the original creation with the 're-creation' after sin, and sees God as object of the Christian religion not only as Creator but also as Re-creator, 'in which latter respect Christ also, as constituted by God to be the Saviour, is the object of the Christian religion'.[24] However, in saying that the doctrine of creation is 'set forth'[25] in the *Private Disputations* but not the *Public Disputations*, Muller fails to recognise that there is much about creation in the latter, notably in what Arminius says about the Word of God being involved—even though there is no *Public Disputation* devoted to creation. Muller links Arminius' doctrine of creation with his doctrine of God, whereas the introduction to his *Private Disputation* XXIV on creation suggests that Arminius himself linked it with re-creation and restoration through Christ as expressions of God's goodness. But Muller rightly mentions Arminius' use of the doctrine of creation in the *Declaratio Sententiae* as an element in his refutation of the supralapsarian view of predestination, which treats creation as a subordinate act of God, willed only as a necessary preparation for the greater good of redemption of some creatures through absolute predestination.[26] Whether or not redemption is a greater good than creation, still creation to Arminius is good in itself, not just a means to a greater good.

In summary, Arminius was concerned to emphasise the goodness of God's creation as an expression of his outgoing love, in contrast with a growing Reformed tendency to see creation as good only as it is one necessary preliminary to the far greater good of redemption, and even to the good of damnation, in so far as that too contributes to God's glory. But to Arminius, here very much a Thomist, creation is good as such, even when not followed by the admittedly greater good of redemption. Another more famous contemporary of Arminius, about the time that Arminius took up his professorship at Leiden, put some of his best-known words into the mouth of one of his best-known characters in perhaps his most theological play, 'To be or not to be, that is the question'.[27] It was no question to Arminius; except for rare cases like Judas, he was convinced that it was better to be than not to be.

God's Dominion, Providence and the Covenants

After the creation of angels and men, he continues with disputations on 'The Lordship and Dominion of God' (XXVII) and 'The Providence of God' (XXVIII). Neither disputation mentions Christ; indeed he does not

---

24 *Private Disputation* XXIV:ii; *Works*, II, p.355.
25 Muller, *God*, p.211.
26 Muller, *God*, pp.211f, 214.
27 W. Shakespeare, *Hamlet*, Act 3 scene 1 line 64.

mention Christ at all in relation to providence. Nevertheless, like creation these subjects are set in the context of Christ's work, and explain the principles on which God operates. God's lordship and dominion are, by his own choice, not always absolute; Arminius refers to the two Greek words for 'king', *despotes* and *basileus*,[28] and represents God as acting in a despotic way towards the perverse and recalcitrant, and in a 'kingly and patriarchal' way towards those who have not yet shown themselves unworthy of the milder approach. God does not always exact everything which he justly might; he persuades, and enters into a contract or covenant with his creature. As God's first right over his creature looks to the past, to creation, so his second right, that based on contract or covenant, looks to the future,[29] and the principle of covenant will be significant for Christ's work in establishing the new covenant.

Muller's chapter on 'The Doctrine of Providence' contains what he has to say about covenant,[30] which might give the impression that Arminius subsumes covenant under providence. In fact, Muller's chapter is concerned in its first part with God's 'lordship and dominion', or rule, which underlies both the covenant and God's providence. Concerning providence in the strict sense of the word, we may only need to add that a modern Christian will tend to think of providence as God's provision for our physical needs; food, drink, clothing, shelter, air to breathe and warmth to sustain life, and perhaps also mental stimulation; all this, to Arminius and his predecessors and contemporaries, is rather 'conservation' and 'sustentation', and a 'continuance of creation'.[31] He sees providence as God's oversight and general care over the world and individual creatures, both for their benefit and as a declaration of his own perfection.[32]

The origins of Arminius' covenant theology are typically located by Muller in late medieval scholasticism, and specifically in Arminius' 'right of the Creator' (*creatoris ius*), which, Muller says, 'embodies a covenantal principle — the concept of *potentia ordinata*', and the distinction between a 'despotic' and a 'kingly or fatherly' rule of God, which he sees as reflecting another medieval scholastic theme, the distinction between *opus proprium* in the kingly or fatherly rule, and *opus alienum* in the lordly or despotic rule. He also sees the concept of divine self-limitation in creation, linked with a doctrine of covenantal relationship, as a point of contact between Arminius and late medieval scholasticism.[33] There is no

---

28 *Private Disputation* XXVII:iv, *Works*, II, p.365.
29 *Private Disputation* XXVII:iv-viii; *Works*, II, p.366.
30 Muller, *God*, pp.241ff.
31 *Private Disputation* XX:vii, *Works*, II, p.348.
32 *Private Disputation* XXVIII:iv, *Works*, II, p.367.
33 Muller, *God*, pp.241-243; by the *potentia ordinata* God voluntarily limits his absolute right to punish his innocent creatures justly.

doubt a certain similarity, but Muller quotes no close parallels. Muller may well be right about the underlying principle of all God's covenants, and about the original covenant made with Adam, but the covenants made after the entry of sin are now of more direct concern to us, and Loonstra gives more help with the background of those.[34]

We have seen something of Arminius' doctrine of covenant in discussing the oration *On the Priesthood of Christ*. *Private Disputation* XXIX covers the same ground to some extent, but from another angle. The oration considers covenant as the origin of priesthood, the disputation as the explanation of the kind of obedience God requires from men; not prescribed obedience, but 'voluntary and free obedience, which alone is grateful to Him'.[35] This is shown in the definitions of covenant in each. Both speak of two parts in the covenant, but in the oration God's promise is mentioned first, man's duty second, whereas in the first paragraph of the disputation God's requirement of obedience is stated first and the promised reward second; and in the second paragraph the work commanded first, the reward second, and a threatened punishment, not mentioned in the oration at this point, subjoined.[36] The whole is a good example of Arminius' habit of varying his approach at different times, and not becoming hidebound by one particular form of explanation. Thus, for example, the distinction in the oration between regal and religious functions within the covenant, from the latter of which the priestly office arises, is not found in the disputation, which speaks of the whole law prescribed by the covenant being contained in the right ordering of love.[37]

The title of the disputation is 'On the Covenant into which God Entered with our First Parents'. This title is itself controversial. Muller refers to the fact that Bullinger, unlike Calvin, sees the *protoevangelion* of Genesis 3 as the beginning of the covenant and its formal beginning as 'a two-sided or duopleuric agreement' as with Noah. Altogether Bullinger, 'more than Calvin, seems to stress the mutual character of covenant and the necessity for obedience'.[38] Muller speaks of the monopleuric (one-sided) and duopleuric definitions of covenant.

To Calvin, with his Augustinian fear of suggesting any ability of man to move towards God, there is no question of God's covenant being any agreement between God and man; a covenant is simply any promise of God which is so serious that it must be confirmed with an oath. According to Punt, 'because there is no covenant apart from its being specifically expressed with an oath, Calvin is emphatic in denying that the

---

34 Loonstra, *Verkiezing-Verzoening-Verbond*.
35 *Private Disputation* XXIX:i, *Works*, II, p.369.
36 *Private Disputation* XXIX:i,ii; *Works*, II, p.369.
37 *Private Disputation* XXIX:iii..
38 Muller, *Christ and the Decree*, pp.40f.

covenant existed before it was established with Abraham and sealed with the sign of circumcision (see Gen. 17:11, Heb. 6:13 (and) commentaries on Gal. 3:17 and Hos. 6:7.) The covenant with Noah (Gen. 6:18, not 6:7; also 9:8-17) is a promise of temporal blessing for all creation and therefore distinct from the covenant of salvation'.[39]

To a large extent Reformed orthodoxy has continued to work with this definition of covenant as God's promise confirmed with an oath, and Muller himself appears to work with this definition in speaking in relation to Calvin only of covenant-*promise*. We may ask what the biblical, as possibly distinct from the Reformed, definition of covenant is, and whether 'monopleuric covenant' is a contradiction in terms. The two most important covenants in the Bible, that of God with Abraham in Genesis 15, later renewed with Moses, and the new covenant in the blood of Christ according to Hebrews 6:13, 17, were sealed with oaths, but was this of the essence of covenant? There is no suggestion of oath in the covenant with Noah in Genesis 9:8-17, but according to scripture God calls it a covenant no less than five times. Where God is not directly involved, the essence of covenant in the Old Testament appears to be an arrangement between two men or groups of men, not a promise of one to the other, however solemn. Arminius never considers the option of 'monopleuric covenant'; as we have seen, to him '*Every*[40] covenant between God and men consists of two parts'. He also goes beyond Bullinger in seeing not the *protoevangelion* of Genesis 3, but the rules which God gave man before the fall, and the promises of eternal life and of the free enjoyment of the fruits of Paradise, contained in Genesis 2-3, as the beginning of God's covenant with man. Certainly the word covenant is not used till Genesis 6, a fact which could count against Bullinger as well as Arminius; but to Arminius 'covenant' is not just a specific biblical example but also a principle on which God works with men and which underlies particular covenants. According to Arminius the oath was added in the case of Christ's priesthood not because it was strictly necessary—for 'the constant and unvarying veracity of God's nature might very properly set aside the necessity of an oath'—but to conform to human custom and to demonstrate the dignity and unchangeable nature of that priesthood.[41] He does not explain why in this case an oath was needed for the Abrahamic/Mosaic covenant, but as this established a typical priesthood prefiguring that of Christ, to that extent it was unchangeable and unchanged, unlike the covenant with Adam.

---

39 Neal Punt, *Unconditional Good News* (Grand Rapids, MI: Eerdmans, 1980), p.112 n.5.
40 My emphasis.
41 *Oration* IV; *Works*, II, II pp.415, 417.

This latter covenant, in addition to the moral law specifying man's duty to God and to his neighbour, contained another law described as 'symbolical', that is, it prescribes or forbids an act which is morally neutral but is intended to test man's willingness to obey, in this case the act of abstaining from the fruit of the tree of knowledge. Man's duty to obey this willingly is compared with a (feudal) vassal cheerfully showing willingness to obey his lord and fight the lord's enemies, by presenting the lord with a token annual gift. Obedience to the moral law would be rewarded with eternal life, obedience to the symbolical law with (otherwise) free enjoyment of the fruits of Paradise. Arminius speculates that if Adam and Eve had continued to obey, they would have received a spiritual body and enjoyed immortal life in heaven.[42]

Sin

All this was not to be. Man sinned and fell. Bangs' discussion of Arminius' doctrine of sin is the key work. He refers back to Article 14 of the *Belgic Confession* which states that man has *wilfully* submitted himself to sin and thereby to death and the curse, and points out that Arminius used this passage in the *Declaration of Sentiments* to argue that man did not sin on account of any necessity imposed by a preceding decree of predestination.[43] God hinders and permits, punishes and pardons sin; he does not necessitate it.[44] He also overcomes it. From a completely different viewpoint, Dorner argues that,

> Arminius denies the infinitude of the guilt to be atoned. Sin does not offend against God, but only against a command of God, which...stands in his view in accidental connection with the nature of God itself.[45]

This is quite false. As Arminius says, 'the proper and immediate Effect of this sin (of Adam) was the offending of the Deity', and the whole of this sin, including the offence to God, is not peculiar to our first parents but is common to the entire race and to all their posterity.[46] Arminius will sometimes distinguish between sin committed against the law and against the gospel, or sin committed against God, our neighbour, or ourselves, and he recognises the special category of sins against the Holy Ghost,[47] but there is never any implication that sin in general, or any sin, is not

---

42 *Private Disputation* XXIX:iv-x; *Works*, II, pp.369-71.
43 Bangs, *Arminius*, p.223 n.3; reference to the *Writings* is incorrect, (p.220 not p.219); *Works*, I p.622.
44 Bangs, *Arminius*, p.267; *Public Disputation* IX:vii-xxiii; *Works*, II, pp.165-177.
45 Dorner, *Protestant Theology*, I, pp.423f and p.423 n.3.
46 *Public Disputation* VII:xv-xvi; *Works*, II, pp.156f.
47 *Public Disputation* VIII:ii, iv, xi-xii; *Works*, II, pp.157f, 161f.

directly against God. So far from treating sin too lightly, Arminius believes that the result of Adam's fall was that 'man fell under God's displeasure and wrath, rendered himself subject to a double death, and deserved to be deprived of the primeval righteousness and holiness in which a great part of the image of God consisted';[48] and rightly so. Arminius may not use Dorner's concept of *infinite* guilt, but he is in no doubt about the seriousness of sin. The *form* of sin may be the transgression of the law (1 John 3:4), but it primarily and immediately strikes against the Legislator himself (Genesis 3:11), and so offends One whose express will it was that his law should not be offended.[49] Adam's sin was one of 'serious enormity' in several ways; it showed that man was unwilling to be subject to God's law; it was ingratitude after 'God had loaded man with such signal gifts'; man could easily have resisted when he had such a copious abundance of things, but allowed himself to be easily persuaded; the sin was committed in a sanctified place, a type of the heavenly Paradise, almost under God's own eyes.[50] The result was God's wrath for three just causes: disparagement of God's power and right; denial of his will; and contempt of His command.[51]

Arminius, like his contemporaries, takes the eating of the fruit literally, and under the influence of the Latin translation of Romans 5:12, argues that all have sinned in Adam and are therefore children of wrath, subject to condemnation and death in both kinds, and devoid of original righteousness and holiness. So 'with these evils they would remain oppressed for ever, unless they were liberated by Christ Jesus; to whom be glory for ever'.[52]

If Arminius treats Adam's sin so seriously, does he deny equal seriousness to the actual sins of his posterity? Bangs suggests that Arminius sees the result of Adam's sin in his posterity more in privation than in depravation, and tends to avoid use of the term 'original sin' as begging too many questions; the *Private Disputations* show that Arminius prefers to keep the term for the absence of original righteousness after the fall, as quite sufficient to produce all actual sins.[53] Certainly the Stoic doctrine that all sins are equal is rejected; a sin against God is worse than one against man (1 Samuel 2:25); deliberate sin is worse than making a mistake; to break a prohibitory law is worse than to break a mandatory one; Chorazin and Bethsaida were more sinful than Tyre and Sidon (Matthew 11:23). But 'the wages of *every* sin is death'.[54] Sins and their

---

48 Bangs, *Arminius*, p.338; *Public Disputation* VII:iii,xvi; *Works*, II, pp.151, 156f.
49 *Public Disputation* VII:xv; *Works*, II, p.156.
50 *Private Disputation* XXX:x, *Works*, II, p.373.
51 *Private Disputation* XXXI:i-ii; *Works*, II, p.374.
52 *Public Disputation* VII:xvi; *Works*, II, pp.156-157.
53 *Private Disputation* XXXI:x; *Works*, II, p.375.
54 *Public Disputation* VIII:ix, *Works*, II, p.160, my emphasis.

punishment may vary in degree but all have the same effect. What Arminius would reject is a masochistic anthropophobia which thinks that nothing is too bad to be said about sinful man and tries to go as far as possible to this extreme. Such behaviour is unnecessary; the effects of sin are damaging enough already.

Grace

After the Fall there were two possibilities. Either God could leave man in his sin without hope, to let death and damnation take their course, or he could graciously restore man to union with himself by founding a new relationship between himself as Creator and man as creature. This would mean nothing less than the foundation of a new religion; and this is in fact what God has done. Arminius says that this is 'to the praise of His own glorious grace'.[55] It should be noted here that there is no question of this grace being either resistible or irresistible by man; it is an expression of God's own nature of grace which at this point encompasses the will to restore man, the choice of Christ as Mediator, and the whole work of Christ and what it has provided for man, all before any individual man or woman has opportunity to choose or decide anything. Bangs argues that the 'keystone' of Arminius' view is that grace is God's affection to man as sinner,[56] and certainly it is shown especially as a response to man's sin, but grace or graciousness is a quality of God before it is shown in redemption. Otherwise Bangs points out that the distinction between different kinds of grace is rejected by Arminius when he asks Perkins whether it matters 'whether a man has embraced the offered blessing by the aid of common or peculiar grace, if both kinds have gained his free consent and God foreknew that they would gain it'.[57]

Dekker has a whole chapter on Arminius' doctrine of grace, but he begins by considering at some length (about a fifth of the chapter) aspects of the doctrines of Molina, Suarez and Bellarmine, apparently assuming that this is the correct background against which to see Arminius' doctrine. Arminius was certainly aware of the work of these contemporary Roman Catholic theologians and of certain similarities between his views and theirs, but this is no proof of his dependence on them. As we have seen, Dekker ignores the theological content of Arminius' 1591 letter to Grynaeus, in which Arminius speaks of our participating in salvation by grace alone through the efficacious working of the Holy Spirit (*salutem nostram...huius nos mera gratia per Spiritus*

---

55 *Private Disputation* XXXII:iii; *Works*, II, p.376.
56 Bangs, *Arminius*, p.338.
57 Bangs, *Arminius*, p.213; *Works*, III, p.445.

sancti efficaciam fide participes fieri), but this link between the Holy Spirit and grace is a constant in Arminius' theology. Dekker himself quotes passages from both the middle and the very end of Arminius' career, that is, from the *Examination of Perkins*, which Dekker regards as the most important source for Arminius' doctrine of grace,[58] and from the discussion following Arminius' last *Public Disputation* (XVI) of 25 July 1609, all concerned with grace and the Holy Spirit. These show that, for Arminius, this link between grace and the Holy Spirit remained constant throughout. The first passage is concerned with the twofold inward persuasion of the Holy Spirit, sufficient and efficacious, of which the first is administered by the decree of providence and is rejected, and the second by the decree of predestination in sure foreknowledge that it will result in faith and conversion.[59] From the *Examination* also he quotes that the Holy Spirit does not remove free will, but acts on it as he knows to be fitting and adapted for moving it, certainly and infallibly.[60] In discussion following his last public disputation, Arminius declined to specify the means (*modum*) used by the Holy Spirit in regeneration and conversion, and said that if anyone dared to do so, he should be ordered to prove it; he (Arminius) could say how it was *not* done, by irresistible power, but the only one who knew how it was done was he who searched the deep things of God, the Holy Spirit himself. This answer pleased neither the visiting Roman Catholic Smetius, nor Gomarus, but Arminius was stating the personal freedom of God the Holy Spirit in his gracious work.[61] Dekker quotes all these, but fails to bring them together, and, more importantly, fails to recognise that none of the quotations he makes from Molina, Suarez or Bellarmine link grace with the Holy Spirit! This would seem to prove that the most constant and important element in Arminius' doctrine of grace was not learned from sixteenth-century Roman Catholic sources. To be fair to Dekker, it should be added that Muller has also failed to see the importance of the Holy Spirit in Arminius' doctrine of grace, and does not mention the Holy Spirit in this context. Bangs, on the other hand, in the section on *Synergism* in his review of Arminius' theology, quotes Arminius' statement in the *Declaration of Sentiments*, 'I believe that many persons resist the Holy Spirit and reject the grace...offered', and comments, 'Grace is not a force; it is a person, the Holy Spirit, and in personal relationships there cannot be sheer overpowering of one person by another'.[62]

---

58 Dekker, *Rijker dan Midas*, p.157.
59 *Opera* p.665; *Works*, III, pp.315f; Dekker, *Rijker dan Midas*, p.164. See also Kendall, *Calvin*, p.147; but Kendall also fails to recognise the importance for Arminius of the link between the Holy Spirit and grace.
60 *Opera*, pp.770f; *Works*, III, p.474; Dekker, *Rijker dan Midas*, p.164.
61 *Ep.Ecc.* 130, p.227; Dekker, *Rijker dan Midas*, pp.169f.
62 *Works*, I, p.664; Bangs, *Arminius*, p.343; Muller, *God*, p.308 (index).

Both Roman Catholics and Reformed in the late sixteenth century were, like Dekker himself, in danger of thinking of grace as a 'thing', something belonging to God indeed, but an instrument which he uses for specific purposes. This instrument, therefore, has quasi-independent properties, of which one of the most significant is irresistibility. No doubt there are medieval precedents for such a view of grace, but with this approach it is not surprising that Dekker consistently finds *onhelderheid*, lack of clarity, in Arminius' view. Arminius thinks of grace quite differently; for him it is not an abstraction but God acting graciously, God's benevolent activity. So it has no 'qualities' of its own, neither resistibility or its opposite. It was time to get back to the persons of the Trinity and their gracious activity. Arminius wanted to see grace in what we could call, anachronistically, personal terms; therefore, he stresses that grace is of the Holy Spirit and his work. But grace is not neglected in his writings. Arminius had already called the new covenant a covenant 'not of works but of faith, not of the law but of grace',[63] and, in the *Private Disputations*, the elements of Romans 8:29-30 are all attributed to God's gracious work; predestination, vocation or calling, justification and sanctification, while evangelical faith is 'produced by the Holy Spirit, through the Gospel'.[64] The *Public Disputation on The Free Will of Man and its Powers* of 23 July 1605 has in fact more to say on the power of grace in the state of renewed righteousness, than on the free will of man:

> After...the law of God according to the covenant of grace has been inscribed upon [man's heart], he loves and embraces the good.... But this...is all begotten within him by...the Spirit of grace (Zechariah 12:10)...as the very first commencement of every good thing, so likewise the progress, continuance and confirmation, nay, even the perseverance in good, are not from ourselves, but from God through the Holy Spirit.... 'The God of all grace makes us perfect, stablishes, strengthens and settles us' (1 Peter 1:10).[65]

Arminius agreed with his Reformed opponents that God, as sovereignly free, reserved to himself the full power of bestowing unequal grace on men, but whereas they thought of the already privileged elect receiving more, he thought rather of God 'employing greater grace on those who are more wicked'![66]

Further discussion of his views on grace as irresistible or otherwise will come in the next chapter; here we are concerned with God's work through Christ. God was pleased to pardon sin and to help his creatures in

---

63 In his inaugural oration *On the Priesthood of Christ*, Works, I, p.424.
64 *Private Disputations* XL:iii; XLII:i; XLVIII:ii, iv, vi; XLIX:iv; XLIV:iii.
65 *Public Disputation* XI:xii, xiv; Works, II, pp.194f.
66 *Public Disputation* XVI:vii; Works, II, p.233.

their misery.⁶⁷ But God was pleased not to exercise this mercy without declaring his justice, by which he loves righteousness and hates sin, and has therefore appointed that the method of restoration should be through a Mediator intervening between him and sinful man, and that restoration should be performed in such a way as to make it clear that God will remit none of his right till his justice is satisfied. We find no reference in this disputation *On the Restoration of Man* to the Holy Spirit's gracious work in pardoning sins and renewing life; only the statement that we must worship not only Father and Son, but Spirit too. This may seem strange; the likely reason is that Arminius is here considering Christ's obtaining the restoration, not the actual restoring of man through the Holy Spirit. This will come in later disputations, from that on *Vocation* (XLII) onwards.

The Mediator

Here we find the person of the Lord Jesus Christ discussed. He has become incarnate so that he may be a Mediator. He is Son of God and Son of man, consisting of two natures, divine and human, inseparably united without mixture or confusion, not according to appearance or indwelling only, but by that union 'which the ancients have correctly called hypostatical'.⁶⁸ He has the same nature as the Father by internal and eternal communication; he has his human nature from the Virgin Mary through the Holy Spirit's operation. According to his human nature he has a truly 'organic' body (i.e., one which he can use as a *tool*); and a truly human soul which quickened the body with all the essential and natural properties of soul and body like other human beings. From this personal union arises a communication of forms (*communicatio idiomatum*) or properties; such communication was not real, as if some things proper to the divine nature were effused (*effusa*) into the human nature, but verbal; yet resting on the truth of this union, and signifying the closest conjunction of both natures.⁶⁹ As Muller says, Arminius' teaching about the *communicatio idiomatum* is orthodox Reformed theology;⁷⁰ the same is true of the rest of *Private Disputation* XXXIV. Where Arminius departs from 'orthodox' Reformed theology is

---

67 *Private Disputation* XXXIII:iii, ix; *Works*, II, p.378f.

68 Apparently a rejection of the heresies of Paul of Samosata, Nestorius and the Monophysites, and an assertion of the Chalcedonian definition 'in two natures without mixture, change, division or separation.' Cf. Heinrich Schmidt, *Doctrinal Theology of the Evangelical Lutheran Church* (trans. Charles E. Hay and Henry E. Jacobs; Philadelphia, PA: Augsburg Publishing House, 1961 [3rd edn, 1899]), pp.307, 316.

69 *Private Disputation* XXXIV:ii-vi; *Works*, II, pp.379f.

70 Richard A. Muller, 'The Christological Problem in the Thought of Jacob Arminius' *NAKG*, 68 (1988), pp.149f.

in the *Corollary* on the *autotheos*. It is not clear whether this is an original part of the disputation, or added later, after the dispute of 1606; nor whether Arminius saw the rejection of *autotheos* either as a corollary of what precedes, because Christ is Son of God and sonship is by nature derivative, or because his nature was communicated by the Father.

The Threefold Office: Priest, Prophet, King

As we have seen, in the inaugural oration *On the Priesthood of Christ*, Arminius argues that two functions are to be performed between God and men who have entered into covenant with him, the regal, which includes prophecy, and the religious, which requires the priesthood.[71] But in the *Private Disputations* the regal function is divided into two and the order reversed to produce the familiar *munus triplex* of Priest, Prophet and King, the threefold office which, as Muller says, was developed by Calvin and taught as normative by the Reformed, and used by Arminius before the pattern was widely accepted by Lutherans.[72] It should also be noted that Arminius puts Christ's priesthood first, rather than his prophetical office as is perhaps more usual in other writers.

The work of Christ can be summed up in the terms Saviour, which expresses its purpose and end, and Mediator, which expresses the manner in which it is carried out.[73] It is God's will that Christ should undertake offices to obtain eternal salvation for men, and that he should be given dominion over all things, and full power to save or to damn, and to receive honour from men.[74] He is Saviour of men through soliciting and acquiring salvation, which the orthodox call 'the mode of merit.'[75] Beyond this, Arminius does not use the concept of Saviour in the *Private Disputations*, but in the *Public Disputations* it is used to sum up the three offices.[76] 'Jesus' itself means Saviour. To save is to make a man secure[77] from evils, either by preventing them from attacking him, or by removing them. Two such evils are of the very worst kind: sin, and its wages, eternal death. The opposite blessings, of the greatest importance, are righteousness and eternal life. 'Christ' means anointed; oil, says Arminius, makes bodies 'not only fragrant, but agile',[78] and indicates

---

71 Works II pp.466-467.
72 Muller, 'Christological Problem', pp.149f.
73 *Private Disputation* XXXV:ii; *Works*, II, p.380.
74 *Private Disputation* XXXV:i, quoting John 5:23, Philippians 2:11.
75 *Private Disputation* XXXV:iii; *Works*, II, p.380.
76 *Public Disputation* XIV:ii, iv-v; *Works*, II, pp.211ff.
77 At this stage Arminius was still willing to use the Reformed identification of salvation with security. We shall see that he changed his mind drastically on this point at a later stage of development.
78 *Public Disputation* XIV:iv, *Works*, II, p.212.

satisfaction and consecration, and also adoption, or the conferring of necessary gifts; and the Holy Spirit is the author and giver of holiness and all endowments (Isaiah 11:2). So the Messiah was anointed with the Holy Spirit (Psalm 45:7) for all gifts (John 1:14, 3:34). He is a mediatorial Saviour, near to us not only in the nature of his humanity but also 'in the mode of saving'. There are two distinct acts in this salvation:

1) asking and obtaining redemption from sin and eternal death, and righteousness and life, as our Saviour by *merit*, as Mediator for men;

2) communication or distribution of the salvation thus obtained, as our Saviour by *efficacy*, Mediator for God in things transacted with men.

So two offices are necessary for effecting salvation, the priestly to acquire salvation, and the regal to communicate it. But since the route to salvation lies through faith, the prophetical office is also required, as the announcement must be made to the world. Jesus is called Christ because he has been anointed by God as Prophet, Priest and King.[79] In *Public Disputation* XIV, the office of Prophet is described first because chronologically our knowledge of Christ's work comes first through the exercise of that office, but in the *Private Disputations* the priestly office comes first, because Christ's actual work precedes its proclamation to us.

Public Disputation XIV includes a long series of twelve contrasts between the Levitical priesthood and the Melchizedek priesthood of Christ. The Levitical was typical and shadowy; had a different priest and victim; was instituted without an oath after the law of a carnal commandment; in the times of the Old Testament; consisted of mortal sinners from the tribe of Levi; was instituted to ratify the old covenant; was useless and inefficacious to take away sins; was to be abrogated and was in fact abrogated; had many sacrifices through years and centuries; was transmitted from father to son; had many persons of the order; and was administered at a particular place on earth.

In contrast, Christ's priesthood was real and true, containing the very body and express pattern of the things signified; had the same priest and victim; was instituted after the law of a spiritual commandment and the power of an endless life (Hebrews 7:16), with an oath; in the times of the New Testament; consisted of one sinless man from the tribe of Judah, weak in the days of his flesh, now immortal; was instituted to confirm the new covenant; was efficacious, destroying sin and obtaining eternal redemption; endures for ever; had one sacrifice to put away sin and perfect the sanctified for ever; does not pass from one person to another; had only one of his order, since Melchizedek, though a type like him, was not equal to him; was begun on earth, consummated in heaven.[80]

---

79 *Public Disputation* XIV:v, *Works*, II, pp.212-3.
80 *Public Disputation* XIV:xi-xiii, *Works*, II, pp.217-9.

Much of this public disputation reappears in *Private Disputation* XXXV, but there is the stress on the preparation of the Priest and victim; the Priest was prepared by vocation or the imposition of the office, by sanctification and consecration of his person through the Holy Spirit, and through his obedience and sufferings, even in some respects (for his heavenly priesthood) by his resuscitation from the dead. The victim was prepared by separation and obedience. Christ's priesthood was both propitiatory and eucharistic; propitiatory, in the sense that he offers his sacrifice to God the Father for his acceptance; eucharistic, in that he also offers our sacrifices: ourselves, our praise, doing good and helping each other etc., as in Romans and Hebrews. *Corollaries* are added to remove possible misunderstandings. The similarity between Melchizedek's priesthood and Christ's was not that Melchizedek offered bread and wine when he met the returning Abraham, as no doubt Roman Catholics were arguing. That the propitiatory sacrifice of Christ is bloodless, is a contradiction according to Scripture. As the living Christ is presented to the Father only in heaven, he is not offered in the Mass.[81]

Christ as the Messiah was the future Prophet promised, to Moses in Deuteronomy 18:15, and in prophecies, especially that of Isaiah, and was publicly known not only to Jews but also to Samaritans (John 4). Jesus himself confirms that these predictions were fulfilled in him in Luke 4:21 and John 18:37, as does God in Matthew 3:16.[82] God expressed approval of Christ's mission by three signs: the heavens opened; the descent of the Holy Ghost in a bodily shape (of a dove); and the voice of his Father. These are described as 'like *litterae fiduciariae,* credential letters as His Father's ambassador'.[83] Christ was instructed by the clear vision of God and by intimate intuition into the Father's secrets (John 1:18,3:32). The Holy Spirit was always available to him. The excellency of the doctrine lay not in announcing the law or the promise (Galatians 3:17ff), but the gospel, that is, grace and truth as the end of the law and the accomplishment of the promise (Romans 1:1-2, 10:4), in other words, the New Testament itself, the kingdom of heaven and its righteousness.[84]

The imposition of the office includes sanctification, Instruction or furnishing, inauguration and the promise of assistance. Sanctification commenced from the very moment of his conception by the Holy Spirit—so Arminius interprets John 18:37. Instruction includes conferring the necessary gifts, and effusion of the Holy Spirit on him and its abiding in him (Isaiah 11:2), so that he had both will and courage to

---

[81] *Private Disputation* XXXV:v, viii, and *Corollaries* i-iii; *Works*, II, pp.381-2.
[82] *Public Disputation* XIV:vi; *Works*, II, pp.213-4.
[83] *Public Disputation* XIV:vii, *Private Disputation* XXXVI:vii, *Works*, II, pp.214, 383.
[84] *Private Disputation* XXXVI:ii; *Works*, II, p.382.

teach what was needed. The instruction was imparted by a familiar knowledge of the Father's secrets (John 1:18).[85]

The functions (in the *Public Disputation*) or discharge (in the *Private Disputation*) consist of: proposing or propounding the doctrine to men; confirming it by Old Testament Scripture, holiness, miracles, predictions and finally by death; and frequent earnest prayers and devout thanksgivings.[86]

The issue or consequence (*Public Disputation*) or result (*Private Disputation*) was the conversion of a few men, who nevertheless did not know him as the doctrine required, for they thought of restoring the external kingdom to Israel; the rejection of the doctrine and its Teacher by great numbers and their rulers, as predicted in Isaiah 8:18, 49:4, Psalm 118:22; and the fulfilment of the prediction in the resurrection of Christ from the dead and his session at God's right hand.[87]

This is probably as near as Arminius gets to discussing the earthly life of Christ and its meaning. For us who live after the 'quest for the historical Jesus' one disappointing feature of medieval and early modern scholasticism, and of Reformation theology too, is the apparent lack of interest in the story of Jesus' earthly life. Even in Reformation commentaries on the Gospels, or when Gospels are quoted, it is often to illustrate a theological point drawn from philosophy or from another part of the Bible, especially the Epistles. For Arminius the life of Jesus up to his arrest in Gethsemane is summarised briefly under the *Prophetical Office*. He sees the days of Christ's flesh as a teaching of doctrine, confirmed by the holiness of his life, by miracles, predictions and the revealing of other men's thoughts, and by the rejection of his doctrine by many. But the Apostles' Creed too goes straight from birth to sufferings, and perhaps Arminius and his contemporaries would claim they were heirs to a long tradition of what they saw as most important.

Turning to the regal office, which Arminius had briefly described in his inaugural oration as of supreme authority in the communication of every needful good, in the averting of evils and in legislation,[88] he now considers Christ as King. The Messiah according to the promise was to be a king, the most eminent and famous of all kings, and was to be instructed in all things necessary to administer his kingdom. In the New Testament, God has made Jesus of Nazareth Lord and Christ, King of Kings and Lord of Lords, given him all power on heaven and on earth and authority over all flesh, that to him every knee should bow; and he has furnished

---

85 *Private Disputation* XXXVI:iii-v; *Works*, II, p.382.

86 *Public Disputation* XIV:viii; *Private Disputation* XXXVI:ix-xi; *Works*, II, pp.215, 383.

87 *Public Disputation* XIV:ix; *Private Disputation* XXXVI:x; *Works*, II, pp.215-6, 383.

88 *Works*, I, p.406.

him with his word and Spirit. He has made angels his servants to execute his command, and stands at his right hand till he makes his enemies his footstool.[89] For, as Christ was made Author of salvation to all who obey, he needed to be invested with regal dignity with full power to bestow salvation. His kingly office is a mediatorial function, by which the Father constituted him Lord over all things in heaven and earth, and peculiarly King and Head of his Church, so that he governs all things, and the Church, to her salvation and God's glory.[90]

The Messiah's kingdom is spiritual, not of this world but of that to come, not earthly but heavenly. This is proved by various examples. David and Solomon were types of the Messiah who is himself called David in Ezekiel 37:25, as their reigns are types of his kingdom, 2 Samuel 7:12-16. But earthly carnal things are types of spiritual heavenly things, not identical with them. It was predicted that Messiah should die and rise again (Psalm 16:10), see his seed (Isaiah 53:10), and rise again into a spiritual life (Psalm 110:3). As his priesthood would be spiritual, real and not typical, his kingdom by analogy must be the same (Exodus 19:6). The Mosaic law, which administered the Israelite priesthood and kingdom, was to be abrogated as carnal; another law, more excellent and therefore spiritual, would administer Messiah's kingdom according to Jeremiah's prophecy of the new covenant. Gentiles were to be called to participate in Messiah's kingdom; their kings would remain kings but serve him voluntarily (Psalm 2:10f, 110:3), whereas the Jews would be rejected for their rebellion (Isaiah 45:2f; Malachi 1:10f). The kingdom of Jesus of Nazareth is spiritual and heavenly. His subjects are born again of his Spirit, and will hereafter be spiritual in their bodies and conformed to him. The law of his kingdom is spiritual; it is the gospel of God, rational and spiritual worship (as in John 4:23f, Romans 12:8). Its blessings are spiritual; remission of sins, the Spirit of grace, eternal life, and the mode and means of administration are spiritual. While all temporal things are subject to Christ, He administers them so as to encourage spiritual, supernatural life.[91]

The acts of this office are generally included in vocation and judgment, but Arminius prefers a fourfold division:

1) *Vocation* to participate in Christ's kingdom. He calls men out of a state of animal life and sin to repent and believe the Gospel (Mark 1:15), and to share in the covenant of grace which he has confirmed with his own blood. He did not find subjects in a natural way (Isaiah 53:10), but acquired them by his priesthood, and as King calls them by his word and draws them by his Spirit (Psalm 110:1ff; Ephesians 3:17). Vocation

---

89 *Public Disputation* XIV:xvii; *Works*, II, p.222.
90 *Private Disputation* XXXVII:i-ii; *Works*, II, p.384.
91 *Public Disputation* XIV:xviii; *Works*, II, pp.222ff.

contains a command to repent and believe, a promise (Matthew 28:19f), and a threat (Titus 3:8; Mark 16:16).

2) *Legislation*, by which Christ fully prescribes, to those previously called and drawn, a rule by which they may live godly, righteously and soberly, which is a duty that as subjects they are bound to perform to him as their Head and Prince. A sanction is added through rewards and punishments, and also an act of the Holy Spirit by which believers are made fit to perform their duty.

3) *Communication of Blessings* and removal of opposite evils. These include: remission of sins; inward witness of the Spirit of grace with our hearts that we are God's children; illumination; inspiring of good thoughts and desires; strength (*corroboratio*) against temptations; inscribing of God's law on our hearts; in short, whatever blessings of this natural life Christ knows will contribute to our salvation. According to this, God sends rain on the just and the unjust, Matthew 5:45, and His judgment often begins with His own house, 1 Peter 4:7.

4) *Judgment*, as described in the parable of the sheep and the goats.[92]

The positive results of the regal office are repentance, faith, gathering together of the Church, and her association with Christ her Head; obedience to Christ's commands, participation in the blessings of this present life, for example immunity from evils; resurrection from the dead and eternal life. These come from the Holy Spirit and the word, which Christ never separates. There is a similar list of negative results.[93]

The prophetical office should be a reserve or accessory to the regal office, so those who administer the prophetical office are rightly called 'apostles and servants of Christ'.[94]

Finally, while there can be many prophets, there can be only one High Priest and only one King. So, unlike the prophetical office, but like the priestly office, the regal office is peculiar to Christ under God the Father, and the Roman pontiff, who claims to be Head of the Church, is in fact Antichrist.[95]

To sum up, we may say that, for Arminius, Christ as Priest obtains our salvation; as Prophet he proclaims it; and as King he applies it to us through his Spirit.

---

[92] This summary is of the two parallel passages from *Public Disputation* XIV:xix; *Private Disputation* XXXVII:iv-vii; *Works*, II, pp.224f, 384f.

[93] *Public Disputation* XIV:xx; *Private Disputation* XXXVII:viii-x; *Works*, II, pp.225, 385f.

[94] *Private Disputation* XXXVII:xi; *Works*, II, p.386.

[95] *Private Disputation* XXXVII:xii; *Works*, II, p.386.

Humiliation and Exaltation

Arminius follows the discussion of the *munus triplex* with a disputation *On the States of Christ's Humiliation and Exaltation*. According to Muller, the concept of the *status humiliationis* and *status exaltationis* was taken over from Lutheranism and modified to suit the Calvinist *communicatio idiomatum*.[96] He finds it less developed in Arminius than in his Reformed contemporaries, Polanus (who was brought up a Lutheran) and Perkins.

The state of humiliation began with arrest in Gethsemane. The experiences of his earthly ministry were *propatheias*, forerunners of sufferings, to test whether he would be willing obediently to endure. The crucifixion was murder, but from Deuteronomy 21:28 we understand that Christ was crucified by God's appointment rather than by human means, and that God himself reckoned Christ accursed for our sake. Christ was made a curse for us, so that through his cross we might be delivered from the curse of the law. This interpretation of the cross is found in *Private Disputation* XXXVIII;[97] an alternative interpretation is in *Oration V, On Reconciling Religious Dissensions among Christians*, based on the foolishness of the cross in 1 Corinthians 1, which Arminius finds a humbling truth; and on the demand to hate and deny oneself, despise the world and mortify the flesh with its affections and lusts, which he finds utterly opposed to human nature; yet one who does not do so cannot be Christ's disciple.[98]

In *Private Disputation* XXXVIII, Christ's death was a true separation of soul and body and would have happened in any case from crucifixion and the breaking of legs, but he himself anticipated it to prove that he had received power from the Father to lay down his soul and life (John 10:18) and to die a voluntary death. Christ's burial and remaining in the grave, show that he remained under death's dominion till the resurrection. While his body stayed in the tomb, he descended into Hades and dwelt among the dead. Arminius adduces Acts 2:27 and 31 and the Apostles' Creed in support, but is prepared to accept other interpretations of the descent into hell which agree with Scripture. Christ entered the state of humiliation as a matter of obedience, and so that he could be tempted in every way and remain sinless, sympathise with and help the tempted (Hebrews 2:18; 4:15f), and by suffering be consecrated Priest and King and enter into His glory (Luke 24:26). As Priest, Christ had to appear in heaven before the Father sprinkled with his own blood, to intercede for believers (Hebrews 9), and as King he had to send the word and Spirit from heaven,

---

96 Muller, 'Christological Problem', p.150.
97 *Private Disputation* XXXVIII:iii-iv; *Works*, II, p.387.
98 *Works*, I, p.453.

and administer all things, especially his church, from his throne of majesty in his Father's name.[99]

The state of glory and exaltation contains three degrees: resurrection, ascension, and heavenly session. It began with deliverance from the bonds of the grave, and resurrection from the dead. The effects of death were destroyed, and the body that was dead and laid in the sepulchre, was reunited with the soul and brought back, not to this natural but to a spiritual life; though from the abundant force of natural life he was able to perform its functions, as long as he needed to remain with his disciples to help them believe in the resurrection. Resurrection is not only the Father's work through the Holy Spirit, but also that of Christ himself who had power to take up his life again. We note that here Arminius ascribes equal power to Christ with his Father, and speaks both of being raised (passive), and of rising again (active), as of assumption (passive), and ascension (active).

Christ's assumption continues his exaltation. He had finished the work he was given, and had received a body, not natural, earthly, corruptible, fleshly and ignominious, but spiritual, heavenly, incorruptible and glorious. Other duties necessary to acquire man's salvation were to be performed in heaven, so it was right and proper that he should rise and be exalted to heaven and stay there till he comes to judgment. From this as a corollary Arminius refutes the papist dogma of transubstantiation and the 'ubiquitarian' (Lutheran) dogma of consubstantiation, or the bodily presence of Christ in, with and under the bread; possibly a safeguarding of his Reformed credentials after using the Lutheran concepts of the states of humiliation and exaltation.

The exaltation of Christ to the Father's right hand is the supreme degree. The Father has communicated to Christ himself consummate power and glory; glory, in being seated with the Father in the throne of majesty, because the regal office has been conferred with full command in heaven and on earth, above and over all created things; and because he received the dignity of further discharging the sacerdotal office as a more sublime High Priest constituted in heaven itself.[100]

Muller argues that Arminius' subordinationist language and his denial of Christ's aseity 'reshapes' the doctrine of these two states and the concept of kenosis; that Arminius agrees with his Reformed contemporaries that Christ's humiliation ended with the descent into hell, but that he 'defined the *status humiliationis* solely in terms of the credal articles of Christ's passion' and 'thereby excluded Christ's active

---

99 *Private Disputation* XXXVIII:iii-vii; *Works*, II, pp.386ff.
100 *Private Disputation* XXXVIII:v-xii; *Works*, II, pp.387ff.

obedience from the work of salvation and pointed to the salvific value of the passive obedience alone'.[101]

We may say that, first, while Arminius sometimes talks of Christ's obedience to the Father, he is usually more concerned with man's obedience to both. Second, Arminius does not make this distinction between active and passive obedience, as for example Piscator was doing in his time; this, rather than 'prudence', probably accounts for his avoiding the question of Piscator's soteriology in the *Declaration of Sentiments*.[102] Third, if we wish to use this distinction, it is clear from his use of the *munus triplex* that Arminius by no means excludes Christ's active obedience from the work of salvation, even if Muller thinks that certain doctrines he held logically require this. *Public Disputation* XIV:iv and *Private Disputation* XXV:ii-iii are both concerned with Christ's highly active soliciting, acquiring and consummating salvation. The distinction which Arminius makes between Christ's temporal preparation for priesthood, and the discharge of that office, does not play down active obedience. In the case of kenosis, Arminius quotes to Junius that,

> Christ is said to have received 'a name above every name', so that even heavenly things are bound to adore Him, because, when He was in the form of God, 'He humbled Himself even to the death of the cross'.[103]

He makes much of the exaltation part of this passage. Possibly he would have agreed with later Lutheranism that 'this self-renunciation...that is followed by His being in the condition of a servant, does not lie in the act of incarnation, for although it is a gracious condescension of the Logos that He assumed human nature, that cannot be the fact here referred to, as the condition of self-renunciation is designated as temporary, while the incarnation is permanent'.[104] Philippians 2:5-8 also makes the point that he himself did it, which Arminius stresses:

> The covenant...consisted, on God's part, of the demand of an action to be performed, and of the promise of an immense remuneration. On the part of Christ...of an *accepting* of the PROMISE, and a *voluntary engagement* to PERFORM the ACTION [Arminius' italics and emphases]...Christ accepted these conditions, and permitted the province to be assigned to Him of atoning for our transgressions, exclaiming 'Lo, I come to do Thy will, O God' (Psalm 40:8). But...under a stipulation, that on completion...He should for ever enjoy the honour

---

101 Muller, 'Christological Problem', p.154.
102 Muller, 'Christological Problem', p.157.
103 Philippians 2:8f; *Collation* with Junius, Reply to Answer to Eleventh Proposition, *Works*, III, p.130.
104 Schmid, *Doctrinal Theology*, p.376.

of a priesthood like Melchizedek's, and...might, as KING of RIGHTEOUSNESS and PRINCE of PEACE, rule in righteousness and...dispense peace to His people.'[105]

Ideas of subordination are very much in the background here; Christ appears to 'stipulate' to his Father as to an equal, and, whereas Muller regards Arminius in the *Declaration of Sentiments* as rejecting Barth's belief that Christ is electing God as well as elect man, this would suggest that Christ elects himself at least as Saviour and Mediator, and does not passively acquiesce in the Father's election. Arminius has a (no doubt regrettable) habit of stipulating that Christ and the Spirit are subordinate to the Father, which we have examined in the previous chapter and in the section of this chapter on the Trinity. In practice, he often shows them dealing with the Father on an equal footing.

Atonement

As there is no public or private disputation on this subject, this is the most appropriate place to treat of the atonement. Dorner claims to discuss this doctrine of Arminius, and Muller refers to Dorner as if he, albeit briefly, did so.[106] In fact, almost all that Dorner says is based on Episcopius and Grotius, that is, he confuses Arminius and the Remonstrants. For this he with others is criticised by Hicks as linking Arminius' doctrine of atonement with Remonstrant governmental theories[107]—Hicks is concerned both in his dissertation and his article to distinguish them clearly. The actual title of the article, 'Arminian versus Remonstrant Grace', indicates the line he takes. He sees Arminius as teaching the penal theory of the atonement (that Christ paid the full penalty of sin as our substitute), whereas the Remonstrants accepted the governmental theory (that Christ simply relaxed God's laws so that we could meet their requirements and be saved). However, Reformed critics argued that Arminius himself held this governmental theory; Hicks quotes H.D. McDonald's statement that 'Christ's expiatory sacrifice was not an equivalent for the punishment due to sin'.[108] As Hicks says, this is quite untenable in the light of what Arminius says to Junius:

> God's justice can be declared by the exaction of punishment from those who have sinned; the same justice can also be declared by the exaction of the *same*

---

105 *Oration* IV; *Works*, I, p.416.
106 Muller, 'Christological Problem', p.145 n.1.
107 John Mark Hicks, 'The Righteousness of Saving Faith; Arminian versus Remonstrant Grace', *Evangelical Journal* 9 (1991), pp.27-39; in fact the article deals with the atonement and with faith rather than with grace directly. For Reformed and 'Arminian' misinterpretations, see p.36 nn.6-7, 9-11.
108 Hicks, 'Righteousness', pp.28f.

punishment [my emphasis] from Him who has offered Himself...for sinners.... In this way the rigour of inflexible justice was declared, which could not pardon sin, even to the interceding Son, except the penalty were *fully* paid [my emphasis].... It would have been free for God to impose on His Son the punishment due from sinners, and taken away from them, to be borne and paid in full by Him.[109]

Similarly, Arminius argues against Perkins that the *lutron*, ransom, was 'equivalent to the guilt of all men universally'.[110]

We see that Hicks is correct in his argument that Arminius regards Christ's death as a full and complete satisfaction according to the rigour of an unrelaxed and unmodified divine justice; that it was an act of penal substitution, and that Christ suffered both temporal and eternal penalties of sin in full in our place. As Hicks says, Arminius' doctrine of atonement is fundamentally the same as that of the (Zwinglian and Calvinist school of) Reformers, except for his belief in the universal potential of Christ's death.[111]

Twentieth-century Christians have found both moral and exegetical difficulties in the concept of penal substitution, and Gustaf Aulen has argued that Luther's doctrine of the atonement is not one of penal substitution.[112] However, Arminius is an orthodox Reformed theologian of his time in his understanding of the nature of atonement, if not of its scope.

The subject of *Private Disputation XXXIX, On the Will and Command of God the Father and of Christ...that Religion be performed to them by Sinful Man*, is the new covenant, testament or will. This is based on Christ's death and he, as Mediator, intervenes between God and man; on the part of God proposing the covenant, confirming the promise with his blood, bringing believers to faith and sealing it as the witness that the promise of forgiveness of sins and eternal life will be ratified; on the part of man promising that by his Spirit he will cause man to perform his promises to God. The sacraments, which are not discussed till much later in the *Private Disputations*, are both God's seal to his own promises and men's binding themselves to their obligations. To Arminius this is the reason why the Christian religion is excellent above every other, that all things are transacted by the intervention of Christ our Mediator, Priest and King; and why Christ is said to be God's Wisdom and Power, manifested in the gospel for the salvation of believers.

---

109 *Works*, III, pp.194f.
110 *Works*, III, p.329.
111 Hicks, 'Righteousness', p.35.
112 Aulen, *Christus Victor*, pp.117-38. See also a critique in the Appendix to John Warwick Montgomery, *Chytraeus on Sacrifice: A Reformation Treatise in Biblical Theology* (St. Louis, MO: Concordia, 1962), pp.139-46.

Predestination in its Proper Setting

Dekker dismisses *Private Disputation* XL, *On Predestination*, as 'an edited and shortened version of *Public Disputation* XV...wholly identical in content to the *Public Disputation*.... A few explanations and pedagogical omissions and additions make the difference.'[113] This is the result of Dekker's confining his attention to what one may call the vertical plane of development, seeing how the doctrine changed and developed over a period of time. This is a legitimate way to approach it, provided we also see the doctrine in what we may call the horizontal plane, recognising the position of predestination in Arminius' thought relative to other doctrines. Dekker completely ignores the first paragraph of *Private Disputation* XL, which is quite different from the opening paragraph of *Public Disputation* XV.[114] The latter begins with the definition of predestination, which is proper at the beginning of a public disputation. The former, however, speaks of 'the object of the Christian religion, Christ and God' (note the order!), and 'why religion should be performed to them', the last reason being 'God's will and command that prescribes religion by the conditions of a covenant'. It thus refers back directly to the previous disputation, and by inference to the whole work of Christ as Priest, Prophet and King in restoring man to God's favour, on which that new covenant is based. This work, therefore, is in Arminius' understanding prior to Christ's work of predestination, which in turn comes before the predestination, call, justification and sanctification of individuals. For him, predestination comes not at the very beginning of God's work, as it did for Calvin and for later Reformed orthodoxy, but after the new covenant, and before vocation, as in Romans 8:30.

Public Disputation XV, in spite of its irenic manner and intention, brought about the renewal of controversy in 1604, this time between Arminius and Gomarus, and therefore is more suitably considered in the next chapter.

We return to *Private Disputation* XL, which at several points makes clear that predestination is God's work *in Christ*. Predestination is the decree of the good pleasure of God in Christ, and gracious according to his benevolent inclination in Christ. Christ is the foundation of predestination, and the meritorious cause of the blessings destined for believers. God's love, by which he 'loves men absolutely to salvation, and absolutely intends to bestow eternal life on them', does not exist except in Jesus Christ, the Son of his love, who solicits, merits, obtains, brings back and dispenses the salvation that was lost. In short,

---

113 Dekker, *Rijker dan Midas*, p.211 n.125.
114 See *Works*, II, pp.226, 392.

sufficient is not attributed to Christ, when He is called the *executor of the decree* which had been previously made, and without consideration of Him as the one on Whom that decree is founded.[115]

The believers predestined, believe in God who justifies the ungodly, and in Christ raised from the dead and Mediator between God and men. God's internal act fore-ordains to believers union with Christ their Head and participation in his benefits. Without this Mediator, God neither willed to show mercy nor to save men without faith in him (the Mediator). Such predestination is the foundation of Christianity, of salvation, and of the certainty of salvation.[116] Arminius' doctrine of predestination is not Dekker's *eigenschappen-predestinatie* so much as a covenant-predestination.

Dekker, however, prefers to stress *Private Disputation* XLI, *On the Predestination of Means to the End*, as representing Arminius' fundamental view of the subject.[117] It may be conceded that this disputation does not mention Christ except in the first paragraph, which refers back to the preceding disputation's statements about the necessity of faith in God and Christ for the obtaining of salvation and as man's bounden duty to God and Christ. What Arminius stresses is that a natural, carnal, sensual, sinful man cannot perform an act of faith; no-one can perform it except through God's grace. The question is whether this grace is not only that of God the Father, but also of the Lord Jesus Christ. Arminius had made it clear in his inaugural oration that the covenant in Christ's blood is a covenant of grace, and referred to Ephesians 1:7 with its reference to redemption in Christ and through his blood, the forgiveness of sins according to the riches of his grace. One of the works of Christ as High Priest was to ask and obtain the gift of the Holy Spirit, the Spirit of grace, for his people.[118] Arminius was to use the actual phrase 'the grace of Christ...which belongs to regeneration' in his *Letter to Hippolytus à Collibus*, and the means of grace are the word and the Spirit[119] (of Christ).

The Call to Repentance

Private Disputation XLII, *On the Vocation of Sinful Men to Christ and to a Participation of Salvation in Him*, is almost identical to the last *Public Disputation* XVI, *On the Vocation of Men to Salvation*. We know many

---

115 *Private Disputation* XL:ii-iv; *Works*, II, p.392, italics original. 'Previously made', that is, by God the Father in a hidden depth to which Christ is not admitted.
116 *Private Disputation* XL:v,vi,ix; *Works*, II, pp.392f.
117 Dekker, *Rijker dan Midas*, Hoofdstuk 8:8, pp.212ff.
118 *Works*, I, pp.424ff.
119 *Works*, I, p.700; *Private Disputation* XLI:ii,viii, pp.394f.

details of how this latter was received from a letter of Borrius, who was present, to Episcopius.[120] It is an expansion of the earlier private disputation (*Private Disputation* XLII), perhaps the only one to have such an origin.

Arminius begins the public disputation by defining terms. 'Vocation' includes whatever enables men to answer the call; 'salvation' includes whatever God appoints as necessary for eternal life. Vocation is God's gracious act to call through his word and Spirit, men under sin and liable to condemnation, from natural life and the world's defilements and corruptions, to supernatural life in Christ through repentance and faith, to union in him as their Head destined and ordained by God, and to the enjoyment of his benefits to God's glory and their own salvation. Its efficient cause is God the Father in the Son. The Son, appointed by the Father Mediator and King of His Church, calls men by the Holy Spirit of both, and by whom both work. The Spirit appoints bishops and teachers, furnishes them with gifts, helps them and makes their word forceful and authoritative. The internal cause is God's grace, mercy and love towards man, which lead him to relieve the sinner's misery and bless him with eternal happiness. The external cause which outwardly moves God is Jesus Christ's obedience and intercession. The instrumental cause is God's word, normally preached or written, exceptionally proposed by God directly to the human mind and will without human assistance, but always the word of both law and gospel.

The object of vocation is mankind in the sensual life, worldly, natural, carnal, alienated from the life of God and dead in sins, therefore unworthy to be called and unfit to answer, unless accounted worthy by his grace and made fit by his powerful operation. The form of vocation is the administration of the word and of the Holy Spirit in a way that conforms to his justice tempered with mercy in Christ. God remains free not to use all possible methods to convert man and free to bestow unequal grace on men otherwise equal, and to use greater grace on those who are more wicked. Men are called from animal life, sin and misery, guilt and condemnation, and the bondage and dominion of sin, to share in Christ supernatural good and every spiritual blessing in this present life, and afterwards, in the state of glory, the perfect fruition of God himself.

The proximate end of vocation is for men to answer by faith to God and Christ and to become God's covenant people through Christ, to love, fear, honour and worship God and Christ, obey God who calls them, and thus make their calling and election sure. The remote end is the salvation of the elect, the glory of God and Christ, and the union of God and man. As God declares his willingness to unite himself to man and actually does

---

120 See *Works*, II, pp.230f note for a translation; and *Works*, I, pp.302f, for Episcopius' reply. Original in *Ep.Ecc.* CXXX, pp.226ff, 30 July 1609.

so, he makes his glory illustrious; as man is united to God, he obtains salvation.

Vocation is both internal and external; external through men who preach the law and gospel, and therefore are called workers together with God, planters, waterers, builders and ministers; internal by the Holy Spirit illuminating the mind and affecting the heart, that man may attend to what is said and believe it. These concur to produce one result, obedience to the call. The company of those who answer is called 'Church' and is distinguished into the visible church that confesses with the mouth and the invisible that believes with the heart, just as man is distinguished into the outward and inward man (here Arminius draws a parallel between Romans 10:10 and 2 Corinthians 4:16). We should avoid the error of mystics and enthusiasts (*spiritualibus*) who regard the human word as only preparatory and the inward word as perfective, that is, that the Spirit convinces the believer of another truth or another knowledge of God and Christ, than that contained in the outward word.

The accidental consequence of vocation, not intended by God, is rejection of the call. Its cause is the wickedness and hardness of the human heart, and God's just judgment avenging this contempt. God knows all his works from the beginning of the world (Acts 15:18), so this vocation is instituted according to his eternal decree and the result of each call was destined from all eternity.[121] This is a remarkably Calvinistic-sounding end to the disputation, but states the divine side of what was to Arminius a two-sided relationship; God does this in full foreknowledge of the human response. The issue of human free-will and its relationship to grace, brought up by the Jesuit, Adrian Smetius, at the public disputation, is not considered in the disputation itself.

Repentance, like vocation, is considered in both a public and a private disputation, which overlap to some extent, though not as closely as those on vocation. The title of *Private Disputation XLIII, On the Repentance by which Men answer to the Divine Vocation*, shows the link between the two. Repentance is man's act as distinct from regeneration, which is God's act.[122]

In the matter of salvation God is pleased to treat with man by a covenant, and vocation is to participation in that covenant. Vocation is accepted by faith—not faith in Christ, but that by which a man believes that if he obeys God's command he will enjoy the promise, and this faith is the foundation of obedience. But here Arminius adopts a definition of obedience which he attributes to 'divines generally', as consisting of three parts: repentance; faith in Christ and in God through Christ; and the

---

[121] *Public Disputation* XVI:i-xv; *Works*, II, pp.230-5; cf. *Private Disputation* XLII:i-xii, pp.395ff.
[122] *Public Disputation* XVII:iii; *Works*, II, p.237.

observance of God's commands. The third is only possible after the first two are accepted.[123]

The primary efficient cause of repentance is God, and Christ as Mediator between God and man through the Spirit. The internal cause is the goodness, grace and philanthropy of God our Creator and Redeemer who loves the salvation of his miserable creatures and desires to show the riches of his mercy in salvation. The outwardly moving cause is Christ's obedience, death and intercession, and mercy shown to sinners whom the devil holds captive in the snares of iniquity, who will perish by their own demerits unless they repent. The proximate, but subsidiary cause, is man himself, converted and converting himself by the power and efficacy of God's grace and Christ's Spirit. The instrumental causes God ordinarily uses for our conversion are the law and gospel; the more excellent part is assigned to the gospel, the law being servant and attendant. The very command to repent is evangelical, and the promise of pardon and threat of destruction belong peculiarly to the gospel; but the law proves repentance necessary, by convincing men of sin and creating fear of punishment. At first this is servile or slavish, but it develops into filial fear when the gospel comes into view. The services of the gospel are necessary to administer the Spirit, by whose illumination, inspiration and strengthening, repentance is completed and perfected. Conviction of sin itself belongs to the gospel, since sin is committed against the command both to believe and to repent.

The penitence of Saul, Ahab and Judas lacked assured faith and hope of the divine mercy, and so was unworthy to be called repentance. The fruits of repentance are, on God's part, remission of sins according to Christ's obedience and the covenant of grace, and, on our part, good works which are 'meet for repentance', which God foreordained for those recreated in Jesus Christ to walk in. The ultimate end is the glory of God the Redeemer, who is both just and merciful in Jesus Christ our Lord.

Repentance has two parts: aversion, turning away from the devil and sin; and conversion, turning to God and righteousness. Papists make three parts: contrition of the heart; confession of the mouth; and satisfaction of the work. But no contrition can be great enough; no outward confession, even to God, is necessary if the 'confession of the heart' is present; and there is no satisfaction except the obedience of the passion of our Lord Jesus Christ which satisfies God's justice either for sin or for its punishment.[124] A real penitent, however, will try to make restitution both to the injured party and to the Church.[125] Impenitence brings about

---

123 *Private Disputation* XLIII:i-iii; *Works*, II, pp.397f.
124 *Public Disputation* XVII:v-xi; *Works*, II, pp.238-41.
125 *Private Disputation* XLIII:ix; *Works*, II, p.399.

certain eternal destruction, even according to God's most merciful will revealed in Christ and the gospel; by the habit of sinning man can be made unable to feel, (*anaisthetos*), and his conscience becomes seared with a hot iron (1 Timothy 4:2); when God's just judgment closes the gate, the Spirit, the only author of repentance, cannot enter. But a corollary is added that those who refuse to forgive their brother unless he confesses and earnestly begs pardon, on the grounds that God pardons only the penitent, act harshly.[126]

Because God by his word and Spirit in Christ is the cause of repentance, it tends not to despair but to salvation, but only in Christ, in whom alone a sinner can find deliverance from sin's condemnation and dominion. The Spirit of Christ the Mediator urges by the word of the law, then shows the grace of the gospel, and removes self-security and despair, the twin pests of religion and of souls. Repentance is not a sacrament: presumably because only Roman Catholics treat it as one (penance).[127]

Faith

Here Arminius introduces a subject on which two modern theologians have made comments. According to Kendall, Calvin regards faith as knowledge given by God, intellectual, passive and assuring, whereas Beza, the Heidelberg theologians and Perkins have a 'seed of voluntarism' in their doctrine of faith — it requires experimental knowledge to prove its presence.[128] Kendall also argues that Arminius shared his view of the nature of faith with Beza and the Heidelberg theologians and that is why his opponents, who also shared this view, found it hard to answer him, and why Perkins would have found it so if he had lived to read Arminius' criticisms. Kendall is not particularly interested in Arminius himself; he is trying to prove a point about 'orthodox' Reformed theology after Calvin, so his views on Arminius should be treated with caution. Muller challenges the idea that 'Calvin's thought is substantially different from later Reformed orthodoxy' on the subject of the infinite sufficiency of Christ's death at least,[129] and is generally critical of Kendall. Kendall understands Arminius to mean that faith is a gracious gift of God which only needs to be accepted, but can also be rejected, and that God predestines believers, those who choose to accept and not reject the proferred gift.[130] Bangs, on the other hand, refers to Arminius' letter of 31 December 1605 to Uitenbogaert[131] with its distinction made by earlier

---

126 *Public Disputation* XVII:xii; *Works*, II, p.242.
127 *Private Disputation* XLIII:viii, and *Corollary, Works*, II, p.399.
128 Kendall, *Calvin*, pp.19,29-41, 51-66.
129 Muller, *Christ and the Decree*, pp.132 and 194 n.130.
130 Kendall, *Calvin*, pp.142f.
131 *Ep.Ecc.* .81, in *Works*, I, pp.179f note; Bangs, *Arminius*, pp.271f.

Reformers between historical and saving faith, and the distinction between Christ as Saviour and actual salvation through him. He argues that no-one need be left, in Arminius' understanding, with mere historical faith; historical faith passes over into saving faith *when exercised*.[132]

There is an element of truth in Kendall's view of Arminius' doctrine of faith, for he recognises that Arminius believes that faith is a gift of grace, but that grace is not irresistible; hence, neither is faith. But this applies to faith in saving grace in Christ, and Kendall does not recognise that Arminius distinguishes between different types of faith, nor that even in the case of saving grace the faith by which this is appropriated is only made possible through grace; as, for example in Arminius' reply to Article XXVIII of the *31 Defamatory Articles*, that 'the grace sufficient for salvation is conferred on the Elect and on the Non-elect; that, if they will, they may believe or not believe, be saved or not saved'.[133] Bangs does not consider the origin of historical faith, or the fact that in the *Private Disputations* Arminius uses a parallel distinction between legal faith and evangelical faith. Faith generally, he says, is assent given to truth, and divine faith is that given to truth divinely revealed. The external foundation of faith is the truth of God, but its internal foundation is the general idea (*notio*) by which we know that God is true, and the knowledge (*notitia*) by which we know that it is God's word. In other words, legal faith is based on revelation, not grace (although revelation expresses the goodness to man of a God who had no obligation to reveal himself or his truth). But legal faith has no power to save. On the other hand, 'Evangelical faith is an assent of the mind, produced by the Holy Spirit, through the Gospel, in sinners, who through the law know and acknowledge their sins, and are penitent', and is certainly the product of grace and powerful to save.[134]

We should here recall that Arminius' first theological statement, in his letter to Grynaeus, includes faith: 'we obtain this salvation by grace alone (*mera gratia*, ablative), through (*per*) the efficacious working of the Holy Spirit by faith (*fide*, also ablative)'. The point is that the Holy Spirit is author of both grace and faith and uses both in saving humankind. This is explicitly restated in this private disputation:

> The Author of faith is the Holy Spirit, whom the Son sends from the Father, as His Advocate and Substitute, to manage His cause in and against the world. The Instrument is the Gospel, or word of faith...concerning God and Christ, which the Spirit proposes to the understanding and of which He brings conviction.[135]

---

132 Bangs, *Arminius*, pp.271f, italics original.
133 *Works*, II, pp.51f.
134 *Private Disputation* XLIV:iii; *Works*, II, p.400.
135 *Private Disputation* XLIV:vi; *Works*, II, p.401.

That is, they are fully persuaded that Jesus Christ has been made author of salvation to those who obey him, and that he is their Saviour if they believe in him; and they do believe in him as such, and through him on God as their Benevolent Father. Through faith, trust (*fiducia*) is placed in Christ, and through him in God. The end of faith is salvation; its chief end, the glory of God through Jesus Christ. The faith of the Patriarchs under the covenants of promise was in substance the same as ours under the New Testament.[136] In view of this, it is pointless to argue whether faith or grace comes first; the Holy Spirit is author of both, but faith should be seen as a (resistible) gift of the grace of the Spirit. Kendall in particular fails to see the importance of the Holy Spirit to Arminius for both.

Union with Christ

Believers are united with Christ, who is exalted in heaven to the Father's right hand and communicates to them all the blessings he has asked for from the Father and obtained by his obedience and actions. But this can only be done through an ordained and suitable union between the communicator and his people. This union of Christ with us is the primary and immediate effect of our faith in him as only Saviour. His names, 'Head', 'Spouse', 'Foundation', 'Vine' etc., express this, as do descriptions of believers as members of the body, spouse of Christ, lively stones built on him, young shoots or branches etc.; all signifying the closest, most intimate union between Christ and believers. The union is spiritual, strict and essential; by it believers are intimately connected by God the Father and Jesus Christ, through the Spirit of both, with Christ himself and with the Father through him. They become one with both, and share in all his blessings, to their own salvation and the glory of Christ and God. That is, the author of this union is not only God the Father but also Christ himself. The administrators are Prophets, Apostles, and others, who lay Christ as the foundation and bring his spouse to him. The bond of unity for believers is faith in Christ and God, by which Christ is given to dwell in our hearts; for God and Christ it is the Spirit of both, who flows from Christ as Head into believers, that he may unite them to Christ as members. The form of union is a compacting and joining together by joints fitly supplied according to the measure of Christ's gift. There are various biblical illustrations of this, such as a foundation and a house built on it, or a married couple's participation of flesh and bones, or an ingrafting and implanting of a vine and its branches, or an olive and its boughs. The immediate end is the communion of the parts united among themselves, which flows from Christ into believers and is received by them. The whole relationship is an

---

136 *Private Disputation* XLIV:ii-v, viii and Corollary, Works II pp.400f.

unequal one. Christ the foundation possesses all things and needs nothing. The believer lacks everything. But because of this most close and intimate union, Christ considers good things bestowed on believers, and evils inflicted on them, as done to himself, producing anger against their enemies which remains unless they repent, but pity and certain succour for his children, and reward for those who give even the cup of cold water in Christ's name to his followers.[137]

All this may sound rather abstract. In his *Oration II, On the Author and End of Theology*,[138] Arminius shows what this union will lead to in heaven. Man's salvation consists ultimately in the love, sight and fruition of Christ, to the glory of Christ himself. But there is a passage in 1 Corinthians 15 (verse 24), which might seem to exclude Christ from this and make God the Father all in all. However, Christ's kingdom embraces both the mediatorial function of the regal office, and the regal glory. The former will be delivered up and laid aside as no longer needed; the latter, which was obtained by the Mediator's acts and conferred on him by the Father according to covenant, will remain. Christ promises union with himself; Paul desires to depart and be with Christ; John's letter conditionally promises that we shall continue in the Son and in the Father.[139] 'What! Shall the union of Christ and His church cease when He places before [God's] glorious sight His spouse, sanctified to Himself by His own blood? God forbid. The union commenced here on earth will then be consummated and perfected.' The vision of Christ is not for this world, as is shown by the imagery of the marriage supper of the Lamb. As Christ is King, the Church is Queen (Psalm 45:9); in heaven the glory of God will be concentrated in Christ, as in the sun of the fourth day of creation (Revelation 21:23). We shall be delighted by the contemplation of such excellent properties, and by God's immeasurable condescension; and the body of our humiliation will be changed into the likeness of Christ's glorious body.

Communion and Redemption

In the *Private Disputations* Arminius goes on to speak of the communion of believers with Christ, in both his death and his (risen) life. The title may not give the average modern reader much idea of the content; 'communion with Christ's death' largely coincides with redemption, which, like much else in Christ's work, has already been touched on in the *Examination of Perkins*, where Perkins argues that whatever Christ suffered and did as a Redeemer, all the redeemed have done and suffered

---

137 Private Disputation XLV:i-ix; *Works*, II, pp.401ff.
138 *Works*, I, pp.365-9.
139 John 14:23, 17:24, 20:31; Philippians 1:23; 1 John 1:3, 2:24.

with him and in him; as this is true only of the elect, they alone are redeemed.[140] This, says Arminius, confounds the sufferings and actions by which redemption has been accomplished and obtained, with the result and application of redemption. Redemption is not any passion or action of Christ, but its result, issue or fruit. The passions and actions precede redemption, and redemption precedes application. It is from the application that the redeemed are so called, and they have not suffered and done what Christ suffered and did, for they were not redeemed at the time. Otherwise they would have been redeemed before the Redeemer performed the act of redemption.[141]

In Arminius' understanding, communion with Christ flows immediately from union. By communion believers united to Christ share all things which belong to him, but the distinction between Head and members is preserved. Communion is first with the body of his death, crucified, dead and buried. We are planted together in the likeness of His death and participate in his power and in all the benefits which flow from his death. Such 'planting' is the crucifixion, mortifying and burial of our 'old man' or 'body of sin', in and with the body of Christ's flesh, which itself may be called the 'body of sin' in so far as God has made Christ to be sin for us, and given him to bear our sins in his own body on the tree. As the strength and force of sin is what kills us, the strength and efficacy of Christ's death consist in abolishing sin, death and the law, the 'handwriting against us'. The benefits of Christ's death are: first, removal of the curse which we deserved through our sin, which brings reconciliation with God, perpetual redemption, remission of sins and justification; second, deliverance from sin's dominion and slavery, that sin may no longer exercise its power in our crucified, dead and buried body of sin, nor obtain its desires by our obedience to it; third, deliverance from the law as the handwriting against us, with its ceremonial institutions and its rigid exaction of what we owe; such law has been abused by sin to seduce and kill us and is now useless and inefficacious.[142]

Gomarus later indirectly brought up the subject in his *Theses on Predestination*. He argued that the means of election for the elect angels was their perpetual obedience in holiness, and grace preserving them in the upright state of original righteousness. Arminius questions whether the election of angels was according to grace, since Scripture says nothing about this, but in any case communion with Christ was prepared by election for men, not angels, and consists of faith in Christ, justification or remission of sins according to faith, gracious imputation of righteousness,

---

140 *Works*, III, pp.332f.
141 *Works*, III, pp.333ff.
142 *Private Disputation* XLV:i-ix; *Works*, II, pp.403f.

sanctification from impurity, and finally conformity with Christ; of these angels have no need and have not been predestined to them.[143]

But communion with Christ is also in his glorious state and in the new life of his resurrection. We are ingrafted into Christ by conformity with his life, partaking the whole power of his life, and all the benefits which flow from it. These blessings fall partly within our present life, partly within the life to come. In the present, we are raised to a new life, and sealed spiritually in the heavenly places in Christ our Head. In the future, we are resurrected bodily and the entire man is elevated to heaven. In this age we have a new spiritual life and spiritual conversation in heaven; after this life we have conformity to Christ's glorious body and enjoyment of heavenly blessedness.[144]

In more detail, blessings in this life consist of adoption as God's children, and the communication of the Holy Spirit, who perpetually helps us by stirring us up and co-operating with us. The subject of adoption had been raised by Junius in answer to Arminius' *First Proposition*, 'that God by an eternal and immutable decree determined to give to certain men life eternal and supernatural'. Junius argued that eternal life is not the primary work of the decree, but secondary and the result of adoption, as in Ephesians 1:5, 9-10.[145] Arminius replied that adoption in Christ requires not only sin as a condition, but also faith in Christ, without which God's predestination prepares adoption for no-one and no-one is actually adopted, just as later, in the *Private Disputations*, he would consider both human sin (*Private Disputations* XXX-XXXII) and faith (*Private Disputation* XLIV) before adoption. He objected to Junius' statement that 'the way [of adoption]...is that of grace, leading us in the path of duty, by our call and justification'. To Arminius at the time, both call and justification came before adoption,[146] but when he came to write the *Private Disputations* he took the call (*Private Disputation* XLII) before adoption (*Private Disputation* XLVII), but adoption before justification (*Private Disputation* XLVIII), on the grounds that adoption is in the present life, but justification belongs to our preservation from wrath which, though begun and continued in this world, is consummated only at the last judgment.[147] Over the years he had come to accept Junius' view in part; as against Perkins who defined predestination as God's counsel 'touching the last end...of man out of this temporal or natural life', Arminius argued that the effects of predestination—adoption, redemption and forgiveness through Christ's blood, and revelation of the mystery of God's will—are for the

---

143 Gomarus' *Thesis* xxx in *Works*, III, p.635, and Arminius' reply p.637.
144 *Private Disputation* XLVII:i-iv; *Works*, II, pp.404f.
145 Collation with Junius, *Works*, III, p.18f.
146 Collation with Junius, *Works*, III, p.22f.
147 *Private Disputation* XLVII:vi-viii; *Works*, II, p.405.

predestined in this life, a thoroughly Junian touch.[148] The Holy Spirit is called the Spirit of adoption because he testifies with our hearts that we are God's children.[149]

Regeneration

We have seen the distinction in *Public Disputation* XVII:iii between repentance as man's work (though caused by God and Christ), and regeneration as wholly God's work. The only work of Arminius dealing with regeneration as such is the *Articuli Nonnulli*, which say that it is effected in the present life by the Spirit of Christ. The *Private Disputations* state, more fully, that it is a blessing of this life that flows from the life of Christ, and is communicated by the Holy Spirit through the illumination of the mind and renewal of the heart, and continued through his perpetual aid.[150] Regeneration makes a man spiritual and able to resist sin by God's grace, but he still has within him the flesh lusting against the Spirit. The regenerate can do more good than they actually do and omit more evil than they actually omit, and this is not the result of any decree of God or any weakness of his grace, but of the negligence of the regenerate themselves. They can commit deliberate sin against their consciences, and in effect destroy their consciences so that they only hear the sentence of condemnation. They can grieve the Holy Spirit and quench him, till they let themselves be brought back to repentance. God truly hates their sins, all the more because they have received greater benefits from him and greater power to resist sin. Popular distinctions about the amount of will with which a man sins or overrules his conscience, or 'sins according to his unregenerate part', are rejected as 'noxious to piety and good morals'—here Arminius the ex-pastor speaks. It appears that he would have affirmed most of this section XX of the *Articuli* 'in a decisive manner'. On the other hand, he claims that it is not Pelagian to say that 'the regenerate, through Christ's grace, can perfectly fulfil the law in the present life'.[151] In the *Declaration of Sentiments*, he defines the opinion of Pelagius, following Augustine, as being 'that man could fulfil God's law *by his own strength and ability*, but with greater facility *by means of the grace of Christ*', which he counters with '*Without me you can do nothing*'.[152]

---

148 Examination of Perkins' title and definition, *Works*, III, pp.274ff.
149 *Private Disputation* XLVII:v; *Works*, II, p.405.
150 *Private Disputation* XLVII:iv-v; *Works*, II, p.405.
151 *Articuli Nonnulli (Certain Articles)*, section XX:i-x; *Works*, II, pp.724f, and see introduction, p.706.
152 *Works*, I, pp.685-688; G.J. Hoenderdaal (ed.), *Verklaring van Jacobus Arminius* (Lochem: De Tijdstroom, 1960), pp.117f; John 15:5 (italics original).

Assurance

Assurance, the testimony of the Spirit of adoption in our hearts, was brought up as a controverted subject later, in the *Declaration of Sentiments*. Arminius believes that a believer in Christ can be certain and persuaded, and, if his heart does not condemn him (1 John 3:21), be assured that he is a son of God and stands in the grace of Jesus Christ. Such certainty has a threefold origin: first, the action of the Holy Spirit inwardly moving him; second, the fruits of faith; third, his own conscience and the testimony of God's Spirit witnessing together with it. Arminius also believes that such a person with an assured confidence in God's grace and mercy in Christ can leave this life and appear before the throne of grace without anxious fear or terrific dread; but he should constantly pray, 'Lord, do not enter into judgment with thy servant' (Psalm 143:2). But since God is greater than our hearts and knows all things (1 John 3:10), and since God is his Judge, not himself (1 Corinthians 4:3), Arminius does not put this assurance on an equal footing with that by which we know that God exists or that Jesus Christ is Saviour of the world. He suggests 'the extent of this assurance' as one subject for discussion in the forthcoming convention.[153]

References to assurance in the *Articuli Nonnulli* are not surprisingly more polemical. Arminius questions Reformed views that a believer without a special revelation can be assured that he will not decline or fall away from the faith, or that believers are bound to believe that they will not so decline (so-called final perseverance). He rejects the claim that these are Catholic doctrines and that their denial is heresy. To him, what such views lead to, is not so much consolation against despair, or against the kind of doubt that destroys faith and hope, as to *security* (his emphasis), which he finds 'directly opposed to that most salutary fear with which we are commanded to work out our own salvation, and which is exceedingly necessary in this scene of temptations'. Arminius' dislike of *securitas* may, it is suggested, owe something to its classical use as 'unconcern, carelessness'. He denies that one who rejects this kind of assurance lacks necessary consolation, or is tormented with anxiety; the knowledge that neither Satan, sin nor the world, and no weakness of his own flesh, can make him decline from the faith, unless he willingly and of his own accord yield to temptation and neglect to work out his own salvation, is enough to inspire consolation and exclude anxiety.[154]

Such are the blessings flowing from Christ's life to us in our present life.

---

153 *Declaration of Sentiments* VI; *Works*, I, pp.667-71.
154 Articuli Nonnulli section XXII:i-v, Works II p.726.

Justification

There are also blessings in the life to come: preservation from wrath and eternal life, and continued justification from sins through Christ's intercession.[155] Here Arminius returns to the terminology of the *armilla aurea*, or 'golden chain', of Romans 8:30.

Justification is one of the doctrines which became controversial during Arminius' lifetime, and has continued so since; indeed, the criticisms made at the time are still repeated by Reformed critics today. Article XXVI of the *31 Defamatory Articles* reads, 'Faith is not the instrument of justification',[156] and Kendall claims that Arminius asks whether the term 'instrument' is the correct one to use about justifying faith, and that he sees that there is no good reason to retain it as it is simply a remnant of Calvin's theology. Praamsma claims that Arminius taught that man is justified before God not on the basis of the imputed righteousness of Christ, but by the human act of believing, which constitutes his righteousness before God, and that this contradicts the *Heidelberg Catechism*.[157] These criticisms are based on Arminius' reply to the aforesaid Article XXVI, but Arminius calls the article 'another proof of desperate and profligate negligence' and asks who is so utterly senseless as to deny that faith is in any sense an instrument, since it receives God's promises, including that of justification. On the other hand, he rejects the idea that in the business of justification, faith acts only as an instrument. God is the primary cause of justification, but faith is not his instrument to justify us. It is a gift of God which the sinner uses to accept justification, and such acceptance is an act of obedience to the gospel. The question is, when faith is imputed for righteousness, is that faith an instrument or an act, and Arminius considers that Paul's quotation of Genesis 15:6 in Romans 4:9 proves that in this context it is considered an act. Arminius accepts his (Reformed) brethren's explanation that 'Faith is imputed for righteousness on account of Christ, the object which it apprehends', but this immediate apprehending of Christ is nearer to justification than is the mediate instrument by which he is apprehended.[158]

It is Arminius' use of the word 'act' upon which modern Reformed critics seize, but we should examine Arminius' own description of justification in a non-controversial setting. The whole promise of the new covenant is contained in justification and sanctification: God promises

---

155 *Private Disputation* XLVII:vi-vii; *Works*, II, p.405.
156 *Works*, II, pp.49ff.
157 Kendall, *Calvin*, pp.147f; Louis Praamsma, 'The Background of the Arminian Controversy 1586-1618', in Peter Y. DeJong, ed., *Crisis in the Reformed Churches* (Grand Rapids, MI: Reformed Fellowship, 1968), p.55, quoted by Hicks, 'Righteousness', p.37 n.26.
158 *Works*, II, pp.47ff.

that he will pardon sins and write his laws in the hearts of believers. Justification is God's just and gracious act as Judge, by which he absolves a sinner who is a believer (not on account of his faith, but) on account of Christ and his obedience and righteousness, and considers the sinner righteous, to his salvation and the glory of God's righteousness and grace. There are two conditions, and the order is significant. God would not justify unless reconciliation and satisfaction had already been made through Christ's blood; and he will only justify those who acknowledge their sins and believe in Christ. Justification is a gracious and merciful act, *not with respect to Christ*, as if the Father, through grace as distinct from strict and rigid justice, had accepted Christ's obedience for righteousness—the later Remonstrant view of Limborch and others, which Arminius specifically rejects. Justification is a gracious, merciful act *with respect to us*, because God has made Christ sin for us and righteousness to us, that we might become the righteousness of God in him, and because he has placed communion with Christ in the faith of the gospel and has set him forth as a propitiation through faith. In fact, in Arminius' analysis, Christ is the meritorious, principal, outwardly-moving and material cause of justification. Faith is the instrumental cause, but not the formal cause, as some divines would make it; the form of justification is God's gracious reckoning by which he imputes Christ's righteousness to us and imputes faith for righteousness, remits our sins on account of Christ, accounts us righteous in him, adopts us as children and confers the right to eternal life. What this means is that God does everything, including supplying faith as an instrument, except using the instrument himself; we, not God, use it—or not. The external seal of justification is baptism, and the internal seal the Holy Spirit. Justification begins with conversion; is continued throughout life, as sinful believers repent and flee to Christ; and is completed at the end of life when God grants believers absolution from all sins. Justification is declared and manifested at the Last Judgment. Works are excluded from justification, and Christ has not obtained by his merits that we should be justified by the merit of faith, still less by the merit of works.[159]

Critics like Praamsma may consider that Arminius contravened the teaching of the *Heidelberg Catechism*, but at the meeting of the States of Holland and West Friesland on 30 May 1608, when Arminius was challenged by Gomarus on justification, he replied by quoting Articles 60 and 61 of that *Catechism* as his own opinion.[160] Moreover, when he delivered the *Declaration of Sentiments* he claimed that his opinion on justification was not so different from Calvin's that it would prevent him

---

159 *Private Disputation* XLVIII:i-xii, and *Corollaries*; *Works*, II, pp.405-408.
160 See Bangs, *Arminius*, pp.297f, and Hicks, 'Righteousness', pp.30 and p.37 n.27.

from subscribing to all Calvin had said on the subject in Book 3 of the *Institutes*, if this were required;[161] an undertaking he certainly could not have given on the subject of predestination. There seems to be nothing in the *Catechism* which he could not have accepted whole-heartedly. Probably he could have accepted all that Calvin said about the work of God and Christ in providing justification and about man's need of it as a sinner; the question remains about Calvin's and Arminius' own understanding of how faith is an instrument.

Writing to Hippolytus à Collibus, Arminius agreed that he said that the act of faith is imputed for righteousness, as Paul had said the same in Romans 4. But when his critics then charged him with believing 'that Christ and His righteousness are excluded from our justification, which is thus attributed to the worthiness of our faith', he would not accept that at all. To impute means to account something for what, strictly speaking, it is not; faith is not righteousness itself and has no value unless God graciously condescends to account it worthy; which he will only do in reference to Christ, in Christ and on account of Christ and his righteousness.[162] The righteousness of Christ cannot be imputed for righteousness, for it is that already; but it can be imputed to us because we are not righteous.

As Hicks says,[163] the misunderstanding is due to failure to appreciate that for Arminius faith is both an act of the human will which is graciously enabled by God's Holy Spirit, and, at the same time, an instrument, because the act of faith is never the work of man alone, but also of God's grace preceding, accompanying and following any good that man accomplishes. Faith is the instrumental cause of justification which receives the gift of righteousness, but itself contains no righteousness. The righteousness of justification is that of Christ, who earned it through his life and death, and gives it to the believer as if the latter were personally righteous.

Holiness

Sanctification is also a benefit enjoyed by believers in the present life. It first occurs in the *Examination of Perkins*, who argues that the expiatory victim sanctifies those for whom it is offered, but Christ sanctifies only the elect and believers, therefore he is victim for them only—a form of Perkins' standard assumption that what does not happen in the end was never God's will in the first place.[164]

---

161 *The Justification of Man before God*, Section IX, *Works*, I, p.700.
162 *Works*, I, pp.701f.
163 Hicks, 'Righteousness', p.30 nn.33-34.
164 *Works*, III, p.335.

Arminius replies that the expiatory victim sanctifies, not by being offered, but by being applied. Later he replies to Perkins' argument that 'Christ gave Himself that He might obtain from the Father the right of sanctifying those that should believe on Himself', that Christ actually obtained that right and executes it in the Spirit. He applies and sprinkles his blood, and thus sanctifies to himself a peculiar people, redeeming it and freeing it from its evil state of bondage. But it does not follow that, because not all actually partake of that sanctification, Christ did not give himself a ransom-price for them, as Perkins would have it. This is to confound Christ's action with its results, and the obtaining of benefits with their application.[165]

Private Disputation XLIX gives Arminius' own approach. Sanctification means separating anything from common use and consecrating it to God's use. Common use is either according to nature, by which man lives a natural animal life, or according to corruption, by which he lives to sin and obeys it in its lusts and desires. God's use is according to the holiness and righteousness in which man was created. In sum, sanctification is from a natural or sinful use, to supernatural divine use. It is God's gracious act by which he re-purifies (the prefix suggests restoration to primeval innocence) a sinner who is yet a believer, from the darkness of ignorance and indwelling sin with its lusts and desires, and imbues him with the Spirit of knowledge, righteousness and holiness. The purpose is that man may be separated from the life of the world and may live the life of God, to the praise of God's righteousness and glorious grace, and his own salvation. Sanctification consists of, first, the mortification of the old man; second, the quickening and enlivening of the new man, created after God in righteousness and holiness. The Author is God the Holy Father himself, in his Son who is the Holy of holies, through the Spirit of holiness or sanctification. The external instrument is God's word; the internal, faith. The word preached does not sanctify, unless faith is added to purify man's heart. This happens in man's soul, which Arminius calls 'the subject'. First the mind is illuminated and the dark clouds of ignorance driven away; then the will is delivered from the dominion of indwelling sin and thoroughly filled with the Spirit of holiness; then the body is removed from sinful uses, by the sanctified soul indwelling it, and admitted to and employed in God's service (1 Thessalonians 5:23). The form is conformity with God in Christ's body through his Spirit. The end is that the believer be consecrated to God as a priest and king, and serve him in newness of life to the glory of God's name and his own salvation.

Old Testament priests, approaching to worship God, were sprinkled with blood, and the blood of Jesus sprinkles us whom he makes priests to

---

165 *Works*, III, pp.335f, 424.

serve the living God. This sprinkling principally serves for the expiation of sins in justification, but it belongs also to sanctification. In justification it washes away sins already committed, in sanctification it makes holy those men whose sins have been remitted, that they may be further enabled to offer worship and sacrifices to God through Christ. Sanctification is not completed in a single moment, but sin, from whose dominion we are delivered by Christ's cross and death, is daily weakened. While we carry about Christ's death in our bodies, and the outward man is perishing, the inner man is daily renewed more and more.[166]

How far can the process go in this life? This is not made clear in the *Private Disputations*, but came up as an issue in the final round of controversy. Article XXIX of the *31 Defamatory Articles* states that 'believers can perfectly fulfil the law, and live in this world without sin'.[167] As usual, Arminius denies having said it, but agrees that he was challenged in a public disputation (apparently not one of his own) on the subject of infant baptism, and refused to answer other than by quoting Augustine's *De Peccatorum Meritis et Remissione*.[168] Augustine, when asked 'Is it possible for a man to exist in this present life without sin?', allowed the possibility 'through God's grace and the man's own free will'. Augustine even agreed with Pelagius that those who ask the question 'Who would not want to be without sin, if it were placed in human power?', thereby acknowledge that this is not impossible. But, said Augustine, let Pelagius only confess the means by which it is possible—the grace of God through our Lord Jesus Christ—and that finishes our controversy.[169] Arminius also quotes from Augustine, 'It is an open question...whether there ever has been, is now, or ever can be, anyone who lives so righteously as to have no sin at all—except Christ Himself. Anyone who doubts the possibility after this life is foolish, but I do not wish to dispute the point concerning this life.'[170] And again, 'By the very fact...that a just and good God could not have commanded impossibilities, we are admonished what to do in easy things and what to ask for in hard things; because all things are easy for love to do.'[171] Like Augustine, Arminius does not want to argue about the matter, and thinks praying for our needs would be a better use of time. Question 114 of the

---

166 *Private Disputation* XLIX:i-xii; *Works*, II, pp.408ff.

167 *Works*, II, p.55.

168 Augustine, *De Peccatorum Meritis et Remissione*, Book II Chapter 7 (vi).

169 Augustine, *De Natura et Gratia contra Pelagianos*, Chapters LIX-LX, (69-70), using the translation by P. Schaff in *The Nicene and Post-Nicene Fathers: 1st Series, Volume 5: St Augustine: Writings Against the Pelagians* (Grand Rapids, MI: Eerdmans, 1973).

170 Augustine, *De Natura et Gratia*, LX (70).

171 Augustine, *De Natura et Gratia*, LXIX (83), translation slightly amended from that by Schaff, *Nicene and Post-Nicene Fathers*, Series 1, Volume V, pp.150-51.

Heidelberg Catechism, 'Can those...converted to God perfectly observe the Divine Commands? By no means', is more of a problem for him; his reply that the question is about the possibility, the answer about the act, is unconvincing.[172]

He returns to the issue in the *Declaration of Sentiments*,[173] and again appeals to Augustine 'whose words I have frequently quoted in the University, usually with the corollary that I had no addition to make'. Augustine asks four questions which Arminius rearranges as:

1) Was there ever a sinless man? Answer: No, except Jesus Christ.

2) Is there such a man now, or can there be in the future? Answer: No, except Jesus Christ.

3) Is it possible for a man to exist without sin? Answer: Yes, through God's grace and the man's own free will.

4) Then why has such an individual never been found? Answer: Because men are unwilling.[174]

Arminius finishes by repeating what Augustine had said, 'Let Pelagius confess that it is possible for man to be without sin only by the grace of Christ, and we will be at peace with each other.' He rejects what he says seemed to Augustine to be Pelagius' opinion—that man could fulfil God's law by his own strength and ability but more easily by Christ's grace—as heresy, because Christ said 'Without me you can do nothing' (John 15:5).[175] It was shrewd of him to lean so heavily on Augustine at this point, because the Reformed hated to contradict Augustine.

Christ and the Church

Arminius delivered a public disputation on the Church as early as 29 May 1604, though Bangs points out that the title of the disputation we have, *On the Church and its Head*, differs from that given by Brandt.[176]

Arminius recognises that the word *ecclesia* has no necessary religious connotation, and means those who are called out and assemble in response. Sometimes it means a great multitude, as at Pentecost, at other times only a few persons in a single family (Romans 16:5; he assumes, probably mistakenly, that the church was restricted to Priscilla and Aquila's family). He visualises a church of men in the primeval state, whom God would adopt as children, because they would observe the law he gave them, and promise them a life of blessedness through the sacrament of the tree of life. They were not redeemed by Christ's blood,

---

172 *31 Defamatory Articles*, Article XXIX, *Works*, II, pp.55f.

173 Section VII, *Works*, I, pp.672-89.

174 Augustine, *De Peccatorum Meritis et Remissione*, c.34 (xx), c.8 (vii), c.7 (vi), c.26 (xvii).

175 Section VII, *Works*, I, pp.683-689.

176 Bangs, *Arminius*, p.263.

regenerated by the Spirit, or born again, but they were God's church, called according to the legal covenant. That is, Adam and Eve formed a church, which was catholic because it embraced the whole human race in their loins, and which God included in that covenant, provided the parents continued in it. But the covenant had no provision for remission of sins, so at the Fall humankind ceased to be God's Church. A new Church had to be called from the state of sin and misery, through the decree of God's gracious mercy, instituting a new and gracious covenant, ratifying remission of sins by the blood of Christ the Mediator, and by the Spirit of grace through faith in Christ. The call came first by the solemn promise of the Blessed Seed, when the heir-Church was an infant (Genesis 3:15), detained for a time under the preparatory discipline of the law; later the call came by the full manifestation of the gospel when the heir reached maturity. This difference in call does not make a double, and substantially different, Church. As one and the same person is an infant, and later an adult, only distinguished by age, so the Church is one and the same in infancy and maturity. The whole Church, Jews and Gentiles, is called 'one new man' (Ephesians 2:15). The Church is one city, the heavenly Jerusalem, mother of all who are blessed with Abraham and are children of promise like Isaac (Galatians 4:26ff), and one house of God founded on Christ as chief cornerstone through the preaching of apostles and prophets (Ephesians 2:20f). The Church is 'catholic', called from those of every period and age, from the first promise of the woman's seed to the end of the world. This is catholicity of time; he mentions also, and in the corresponding *Private Disputations* will enlarge on, catholicity of place. *God's* Church is 'a congregation called...into the supernatural dignity of adoption as God's children...who answer God's call'. Arminius, like other theologians of his time and like present-day evangelicals, does not regard God's human creatures made in his image, as automatically his children, in spite of Acts 17:28 and a few other texts. Adam was God's son (Luke 3:38) not by being created in God's image, but by calling and adoption like later Christians. The definition of the *Christian* Church is that part of God's Church 'called by God's saving vocation from the state of corruption to the dignity of God's children through the Gospel, and by a true faith ingrafted into Christ as living members to the Head, to the praise of God's glorious grace'.[177]

But the definition in the *Private Disputations* is different and more Christocentric: 'called...by God and Christ through the Spirit of both, to a supernatural life to be spent according to God and Christ in the knowledge and worship of both, that...they may be eternally blessed, to the glory of God through Christ, and of Christ in God'.[178] Christ is given

---

177 *Public Disputation* XVIII:i-viii; *Works*, II, pp.243-6.
178 *Private Disputation* L:v; *Works*, II, p.411.

an altogether greater part in the calling. This difference is maintained in other ways. The efficient cause in the *Public Disputation* is 'God the Father in His well-beloved Son Jesus Christ, by the Spirit of Christ who is Redeemer and Head of the Church';[179] the *Private Disputation* substitutes for the second phrase 'and Christ Himself through the Spirit of both Father and Son, as He is Mediator and Head of the Church, sanctifying and regenerating her to new life', and adds as impulsive cause 'the gracious good-pleasure of God the Father in Christ, and the love of Christ towards those whom He has acquired for Himself by His own blood'.[180] Where the *Public Disputation* speaks of the gospel as described in 1 Peter 1:23ff, and the work of gospel ministers, the *Private Disputation* speaks of the Spirit of God and Christ and their word, which outwardly requires a life according to God and Christ, and inwardly illumines the mind to a knowledge of this life.[181] If the *Public Disputation* came early in Arminius' career at Leiden, the *Private Disputation* was probably later and suggests a greater readiness to emphasise Christ's work in calling, regenerating and sanctifying the Church, which throws doubt on Muller's argument that in the *Declaration of Sentiments* Arminius excludes Christ from a share in predestination.[182] If in the *Public Disputations* Christ is both efficient and impulsive cause of salvation, this, in other words, comes near to Barth's description of Christ as 'electing God'.

The remote matter of the call are sinners; the nearer matter, sinners acknowledging their sins through the law, deploring them and expecting redemption; the proximate matter, believers—the same threefold distinction found in the *Dissertation* as (those with) 'no sense of God', 'under the law' and 'under grace'. Heretics who do not recognise Christ as Head are not part of the Church. We know the form of the Church by her names: Body, Bride, City or Kingdom (Hebrews 1:8), House (1 Timothy 3:15), all in relation to the Head, Bridegroom, King and Master of the family. Her relationship is, first, union with the Head through his Spirit and the Church's faith; second, subordination under the Head, required by the Head's perfection and the needs of the Church herself; third, life received from the Head which the Church gladly accepts.[183] Again, the definition in the *Private Disputation* is more Christocentric: 'The Form of the church resides in the mutual relation of God and Christ who call, and the church who obeys...God in Christ, by the Spirit of both, infuses into her supernatural life, feeling and motion...and she...begins to

---

179 *Public Disputation* XVIII:ix; *Works*, II, p.246.
180 *Private Disputation* L:vi; *Works*, II, p.411.
181 *Public Disputation* XVIII:ix; *Works*, II, p.247; *Private Disputation* L:vi, p.411.
182 Muller, 'Christological Problem', p.159.
183 *Public Disputation* XVIII:xii; *Works*, II, p.248, cf. *Dissertation, Works*, II, pp.492-8.

live and walk according to godliness, and in expectation of the promised blessings.'[184]

The chief end of the Church in the *Public Disputation* is the glory of God which he completes in his gracious acts, by creating, preserving, increasing and perfecting her (Ephesians 1:12). She is commanded to ascribe to him still greater glory for her perfecting throughout all ages. As the salvation of the Church is the gift of her Head and King (which certainly means Christ), he is clearly given the glory.[185] The *Private Disputation* regards the end and chief good of the Church as 'blessedness perfected and consummated through union with God in Christ'.[186] This results in the glory of God, who unites the Church to himself and beatifies her in an act which declares this glory, as does the Church when in her triumphant songs she ascribes to him praise, glory and honour for ever and ever.

Jesus Christ is the same yesterday, today and for ever, the cornerstone on which the Church's superstructure is raised by (Old and New Testament) Prophets and Apostles, and Head of all who will partake of salvation; so in a sense the whole Church can be called Christian. This term, however, belongs peculiarly to the Church as she began to be called together after the ascension. The Church is one in foundation and substance, but it has pleased God to govern her by different methods, so she may be distinguished as the Church in Old Testament times, before Christ, and the Church in New Testament times, after Christ was revealed.[187]

The Yoke of Bondage and the Freedom of the Christian

The public disputation, *On Christian Liberty*, gives the background to Arminius' theology of freedom. God created the first man free. Having abused his liberty, he lost it and was made slave to the one whom he obeyed, that is, sin, with its guilt of condemnation and its dominion of real bondage and consummate misery. This was followed by what Arminius calls 'economical bondage', the dispensation of Moses, which God introduced by repeating the moral law and imposing the ceremonial law. The bondage of the moral law was its rigid demands which reduced man to despair of fulfilling it, so that he might acknowledge the tyranny of sin over him. The bondage of the ceremonial law was its testifying to condemnation, so that man might be convinced of guilt and flee to Christ who could deliver him.[188] The moral law demonstrates the necessity of

---

184 *Private Disputation* L:ix; *Works*, II, pp.411f.
185 *Public Disputation* XVIII:xiii; *Works*, II, p.248.
186 *Private Disputation* L:x; *Works*, II, p.412.
187 *Private Disputation* LI:i-ii; *Works*, II, p.412.
188 *Public Disputation* XX:v; *Works*, II, p.260.

the gracious promise, and it required observance from the parties to the covenant of promise. The Church of the time was called out by the word of promise concerning the seed of Abraham and the coming Messiah, and by the word of the law to worship God in confidence of obtaining mercy. The word of promise was first propounded obscurely and in a very general way, later more distinctly as the time of Messiah's coming approached. Observance of the ceremonial law was not in itself pleasing to God, but was prescribed for two purposes: to convince men of the guilt and curse of sins, and the necessity of the promise; and to sustain believers by the hope of the promise. In the first case it was the seal of sin, in the second case, the seal of grace and remission.[189]

The Church of those times was, according to dispensation, under the law, an infant heir 'differing in nothing from a servant' (Galatians 4:1), so that her people are called servile or in bondage. But according to substance she was under the covenant of promise, free, born of a free woman like Isaac, counted as the seed. In this paradoxical state the people were carnal, heir of earthly blessings, especially the land of Canaan, but also of spiritual blessings. The Spirit of adoption was mixed with the spirit of bondage as long as the promise continued.[190] Believers under the Old Testament possessed, through the promise of the blessed seed and through faith in him, deliverance from real bondage, the privilege of being God's children, and the Spirit of adoption, but these were mixed with the spirit of economical bondage and could not be enjoyed in a pure form.[191]

There are important corollaries. First, the Old Testament was always due to be abrogated, so it was confirmed not by the blood of a mediator but by that of brute animals. Second, the 'Old Testament' never means the covenant of grace. Third, as a book the Old Testament contains both the law and the covenant of promise; these must not be confounded, but compared and in some respects contrasted; failure to do so produces obscurity and error.[192]

When the New Testament was confirmed by the blood of Christ its Mediator, the Church began to be called out from a state of sin to participate in the righteousness of faith, and in salvation, through faith in the gospel, and to worship God and Christ in the unity of the Spirit. This will continue to the end of the world, to the praise of the glory of the grace of God and of Christ. The efficient cause is the God who manifested himself first as Jehovah, and now as Father of Jesus Christ; and Christ himself, elevated to the Father's right hand, invested with full power in heaven and on earth, endowed with the gospel word and Spirit

---

189 *Private Disputation* LI:iii-vii; *Works*, II, p.413.
190 *Private Disputation* LI:viii-ix; *Works*, II, pp.413f.
191 *Public Disputation* XX:vi; *Works*, II, p.260.
192 *Private Disputation* LI:x, and *Corollaries*; *Works*, II, p.414.

beyond measure. The inner motivation is the grace and mercy of God the Father and of Christ, and God's justice, now fully satisfied through Christ Jesus. The Spirit of Christ is the administering cause as Christ's 'vicar' or substitute, who receives power from him to glorify him by calling out his Church, and to administer all things as he wills. The Spirit uses the word of the gospel in his servants' mouths, and the word of the law, written or implanted in the mind. The object of the calling is not only Jews, but Gentiles also, as Christ's flesh and blood have removed the middle wall of partition which once separated them; that is, all people generally without any difference, since all are sinners, whether they recognise it or whether they must still be brought to acknowledge their sins. As this Church is adult, and no longer needs a tutor or governor, she is free from economical bondage and is governed by the Spirit of full liberty.[193]

Christian liberty is so called from its author Christ and from its Christian subjects. As it was not necessary except for those 'who through fear of death were all their life subject to bondage', it presupposes earlier servitude. It is the fullness of grace and truth in which believers are placed by God through Christ and sealed by the Holy Spirit. Its internal cause is God's grace and love for man in Christ Jesus; its external cause the ransom-price of redemption and satisfaction, paid by Christ. The sealing and preserving cause is the Holy Spirit, the earnest and witness in believers' hearts. God's instrument is the saving doctrine of his mercy in Christ; man's instrument is faith in Christ. The effects or fruits are consolation, and admonition that being free from sin, we should become servants of righteousness.[194]

In detail, Christian liberty consists of:

1) Freedom from the guilt and condemnation of sin, which has been expiated by Christ's blood; remission of sins by faith in his blood, and justification from all that we could not be absolved from by the Mosaic law.

2) Deliverance from the dominion of indwelling sin, whose power is weakened and mortified by Christ's Spirit dwelling in us. Both of these spring from the fact that sin was condemned in Christ's flesh, and therefore possesses no power now either to condemn or command.

3) Softening of the rigour by which God demanded observance of the moral law in the primeval state, and in the Old Testament, as shown in the literally 'terrific' (terror-inspiring) legislation on Mount Sinai. 'But we are come to Mount Sion, and to Jesus the Mediator of the New Covenant' (Hebrews 12:22f) 'whose yoke is easy and whose burden is light' (Matthew 11:30). Christ has broken the former yoke, and God is now pleased to treat man with clemency.

---

193 *Private Disputation* LII:i-v; *Works*, II, pp.414f.
194 *Public Disputation* XX:i-iv; *Works*, II, pp.258f.

4) Freedom from the economical bondage of the ceremonial law, which was: first, the seal of condemnation and the handwritten bond of our debt; second, a symbol or token to distinguish Jews from other nations till Christ came; third, a typical shadowing forth of Christ and prefiguration of his benefits; fourth, a sentinel or guard, or a schoolmaster or tutor, to keep the infant Church safe in a hostile world and maintain faith and hope in the promised approaching Messiah. The first was removed when the condemnation of sin was taken away and abolished by Christ. It has attained its end or purpose; Christ sprinkled the handwriting over with his own blood and obliterated it. There is no place for the second now; Jews and other nations are now one in Christ. The third consisted of types and shadows which cannot continue now after the body and substance has been displayed. The last is now useless, for when the heir arrives at maturity, he no longer needs a governor, but is capable of managing his inheritance, being his own adviser, consulting his own judgment. So when the Church has passed through years of infancy, and has entered on the age of maturity in Christ, she is no longer held under Mosaic worship, 'the beggarly elements of this world', but is guided by God's Spirit. So the Pharisees and Ebionites were badly wrong to maintain that even Christians who had previously been Gentiles must add observance of the ceremonial law to the gospel.

Christian liberty also includes free use and exercise of things indifferent (the Lutheran concept of adiaphora). But God, consulting his own glory and the salvation of his Church, wills to circumscribe this liberty by two laws, those of faith and charity. That of faith says you must be rightly instructed about the legitimate use of things indifferent, and sufficiently confirmed, fully persuaded in your own mind. That of charity commands you to build up your neighbour, whether he is a weak brother or one confirmed (in the sense just used). It is part of this law to abide by the Church's ceremonies, lest by outrageous or unseasonable change you produce trouble or even schism; in other words, in the original sense used by Ambrose of Milan, 'when in Rome, do as Rome does'. Those persons err greatly who prefer their own private advantage and happiness to the edification of their neighbour; they err still more who abuse this liberty to satiate the lusts of the flesh, or by unseaonable zeal despise or offend their weak brethren; they err most of all who call indifferent things necessary, or *vice versa*.

5) Immunity from the judicial laws of the Jewish courts. The laws of Moses contain: first, the common law of nature; second, a particular law suited to the Jewish nation. The first embraces universal notions of justice, equity and honesty, appointed for the general good; these are immutable and not affected by Christian liberty. The second is mutable, therefore Christians are not bound by these laws. Some laws are of a mixed kind, and here we must distinguish between the moral and the political.

Whatever is moral is binding and remains; whatever is political is not binding. 'Therefore we disapprove of the ridiculous imitation adopted by Monetarius [Müntzer] and Carolostadius [Carlstadt], who obliged Christian magistrates to observe the peculiar forensic laws of Moses in administering justice.' The right to be God's children, heirs of God and joint-heirs with Christ, and the sending of the Spirit of adoption into believers' hearts, follow this liberty from the bondage of sin and the law. So do peace of conscience, immortality, and deliverance of the body from vanity and the bondage of corruption—the 'redemption of our bodies' (Romans 8:15-23). So God's children are also 'children of the resurrection' (Luke 20:36). The Spirit of adoption is seal, earnest and firstfruits of this inheritance, and by this we are assured that our life is hidden with Christ in God and that when Christ appears we too shall appear with him in glory. Thus, the liberty of glory that will last for ever, will succeed to the liberty of grace which we have in this world through faith in Christ's blood; and the public disputation ends with doxology.[195]

The Head and the Body

Meanwhile the Church with unveiled or open face, beholds the Lord's glory as in a mirror, and in Christ has the image of the invisible God, the express image of the Father's person, the brightness of his glory, and the 'very body of things to come'. She has not experienced, does not now experience and never will, any change in the word itself or the Spirit, for God has spoken to us in his Son 'in these last times' (Hebrews 1:2). We may call the state of the Church from the time of John the Baptist till the ascension a temporary or intermediate one, between the states of the promise and the gospel. John's ministry is placed between that of the prophets and that of the apostles, and is not like either in every respect; Jesus called John more than a prophet, but less than the least in the kingdom of heaven. John's baptism, so Arminius believes, was the same as that of Christ, and therefore does not need to be restored.[196]

The head and body of a being are of one nature and constitute one substance. According to nature, God is Head of his body the Church. But he cannot have communion with her, for she is his creature. So it is his good-pleasure to bestow on his Church his incarnate Son Jesus Christ as her Head, and to create his Church by him, as a new creature, thus making the union between the Church and her Head closer, and the communication freer.[197]

---

195 *Public Disputation* XX:viii-xiii; *Works*, II, pp.260-4.
196 *Private Disputation* LII:vi-vii, ix-x, and *Corollary*; *Works*, II, p.416.
197 *Private Disputation* LIII:i-ii; *Works*, II, p.417.

What should a Head of the Church be? Arminius lays down three conditions: a Head should contain within itself, in a most perfect manner, all things necessary to the Church's life and salvation; it should have a due symmetry to the Church—apparently meaning that the Head should not be so large as to overwhelm the body; it should supply to her life, sensation and motion. All these conditions agree with Christ alone.[198] He is fitly united to the Church his body by the joints and bands of the Spirit and of faith; he can infuse his own perfection into her and she can receive it from him. And not one of the three agrees with any person or thing except Christ. She immediately coheres to him according to her internal and real essence.[199] He bestows salvation on her, and by his Spirit the Church is animated, sees and moves. He sends out his word and Spirit, institutes ministry in the Church and appoints apostles, evangelists, pastors and teachers; for which he is called Chief Pastor or Shepherd (1 Peter 5:4), who helps and works with his ministers with signs, wonders, miracles and gifts of the Holy Ghost, and defends his church from her enemies and procures her temporal good, as far as he considers it appropriate.[200]

All this has anti-Roman Catholic implications. Arminius argues at length against the Petrine primacy and the Pope's claim to be head of the Church,[201] and against anyone, even St Peter, being vicar or substitute of Christ. Christ cannot have a universal minister, though his ministers do perform functions which belong to the Head. But only her Head knows the Church's internal essence; others know her from signs and indications emanating from her internal essence, if these are real, not counterfeit or deceptive.[202] Such signs are profession of a true faith and conduct of life according to the Spirit's instigation and direction. But public preaching and hearing of the word, the sacraments, prayers and thanksgivings may produce a mere profession of faith, and in her life the Church may degenerate and deny in her deeds the Christ she professes to know. She does not cease to be a Church as long as it is the pleasure of God and Christ to bear with her ill manners, and not to divorce her. But if she become heretical and idolatrous those who desert her are not the cause of dissension, but the Church herself is justly deserted, because she declined from Christ, to whom all believers must adhere inseparably.[203]

---

198 *Public Disputation* XVIII:xviii; *Works*, II, p.250; cf. *Private Disputation* LIII:ii-iv, p.417.
199 *Private Disputation* LIII:iv; *Works*, II, p.417.
200 *Public Disputation* XVIII:xviii; *Works*, II, pp.250f.
201 *Public Disputation* XVIII:xix-xx; *Works*, II, pp.251f.
202 *Private Disputation* LIII:v-vii; *Works*, II, pp.417f.
203 *Private Disputation* LIII:viii-xi; *Works*, II, p.418.

One, Holy and Catholic

Arminius has already used the word 'Catholic' to describe the New Testament Church as opposed to that of the Old Testament. The Catholic Church is so called as diffused throughout the world and embracing all nations, tribes, peoples and languages. This universality is not hindered because most of the Jews are at present unbelievers; they also will be added at some time, 'in a great multitude and like an army formed into columns'.[204]

Private Disputation LIV, *On the Catholic Church, her Parts and Relations*, follows quite closely the relevant parts of *Public Disputation* XVIII. The catholic Church is the company of believers called out from every language, tribe, people, nation and occupation, who have been, are now or will be called by the saving vocation of God from a state of corruption to the dignity of God's children, through the gospel, the word of the covenant of grace. They are ingrafted into Christ as living members to their Head through true faith, to the praise of God's glory. Here the *Public Disputation* adds, 'This, as a general definition, belongs to every congregation, small or large; it also applies to the Catholic Church which contains the entire number of believers, from the time when Christ came into His kingdom, to the consummation of all things.' So the catholic Church differs from particular churches in nothing which belongs to the substance of a church, but solely in size.[205]

She is also called 'holy' from her relation to Christ, whom she embraces by faith as her Head and Spouse, and who so closely unites her to himself as body, by his Spirit, that the Church lives by the life of Christ himself and shares in all his benefits: and 'one' because under one God and Father, who is above all and through all things and in all of us (Ephesians 4:6), she has been united as one body to one Head through one Spirit; and through one faith in the same word, through one hope of the one inheritance, and through mutual charity, she has been built into a holy temple, God's habitation through the Spirit (Ephesians 2:22). The whole of this unity is spiritual, though those thus united consist partly of body and partly of spirit. By the blessing of the Holy of Holies she has been separated from the unclean world, washed from sin by his blood, beautified (*decorata*) with the presence of God, and adorned with true holiness by the sanctification of the Holy Spirit.[206]

The church is one, but distinguished as follows:

1) The Church that has only been created and preserved by God is said to be 'in the way' (*in via*) and is called 'militant' because she must still

---

[204] *Private Disputation* LII:viii; *Works*, II, p.416.

[205] *Private Disputation* LIV:i; *Works*, II, p.419; *Public Disputation* XVIII:viii, p.246.

[206] *Private Disputation* LIV:ii-iv; *Works*, II, p.419.

contend with sin, the flesh, the world and Satan (Ephesians 6:11f, Hebrews 12:1-4).

2) The Church that has received all God's blessings is said to be in her native land and is called 'triumphant'. Having conquered all enemies she rests from her labours and reigns with Christ in heaven (Revelation 3:21, 14:13).

The Church militant is also called Catholic or Universal as embracing all particular militant churches and 'soldiers'. The *Public Disputation* adds, 'We place neither any church, nor anything belonging to her, in Purgatory. That is a real Utopia' (the title of a book in Arminius' library, by the Roman Catholic Sir Thomas More, used to challenge More's own doctrine!).[207]

The question 'Can the Catholic Church err?' is confused and preposterous. It should be 'Can the assembly that errs, be the Church?' Faith is prior to the Church, so the name of 'church' is removed from any assembly so far as it errs from the faith. The question means 'Can it happen at any time, that there is no assembly in the whole world who have a right faith in God?' The answer is no, otherwise Christ would have no kingdom on earth and could not rule among his enemies till they are made his footstool (Psalm 110:2).[208] Single particular churches may err, but the Church Universal cannot.[209] The Church on earth will never totally fail, but must continue to be collected together without interruption to the end of the earth, though not always from the same places and nations (Matthew 28:20; Revelation 2:5).[210] But no congregation, however large, is exempt from error, unless it has one or more persons so guided into all truth that they cannot err.[211] Since the Church is called inwardly by the Spirit, outwardly by the word preached (Acts 16:14), and since those called answer inwardly by faith and outwardly by profession of faith, so the Church is distinguished into the visible and the invisible Church; invisible, as believing with the heart for righteousness; visible, as making confession with the mouth for salvation (Romans 10:9).[212]

What is called the 'Catholic Invisible Church' does not belong here, because it cannot come together in one place and be exposed to view. As more are called than are chosen or elected (Matthew 20:16), and as many called profess to know God with their mouths, while in works they deny

---

207 *Private Disputation* LIV:v-vi; *Works*, II, pp.419f; *Public Disputation* XVIII:xiv, pp.248f.
208 *Public Disputation* XVIII:xvii; *Works*, II, p.250.
209 *Private Disputation* LIV:vi; *Works*, II, p.420.
210 *Public Disputation* XVIII:xvii.
211 *Private Disputation* LIV:vi.
212 *Public Disputation* XVIII:xv; *Works*, II, p.249; *Private Disputation* LIV:vii, p.420.

him (Titus 1:16); and since God, who alone knows who are his (2 Timothy 2:19), is the sole judge of such hearts, they are judged, on account of the promise, to belong to the visible Church, though they may not belong to the invisible Church or have inward communion with the Head.[213]

The Church is collected out of a world 'under the rule of the Evil One' (1 John 5:19), often by ministers who preach another word beside or instead of the word of God; and she is composed of men exposed to deception and falling; so with respect to doctrine, she is distinguished into orthodox and heretical; with respect to worship, into idolatrous and right-worshipping; with respect to morals, into purer and impurer. All these are matters of degree rather than absolute distinctions. The word 'Catholic' is also used for churches which are not idolatrous nor afflicted with destructive heresy.[214]

Sacraments

Other private disputations on the Church (LV-LIX) are concerned with discipline and ministry and less directly linked with the work of Christ. We take up the subject again with the sacraments.

Bangs claims that in defining a sacrament, Arminius follows Calvin precisely.[215] Arminius introduces *Private Disputation* LX, *On Sacraments in General*, with 'we now discuss those signs or marks which God appends to His word'. He wishes to link sacrament with word as well as with Church. By such signs or marks God seals and confirms the faith in the minds of his covenant people.[216] Sacrament is thus linked with covenant also; and as Arminius believed in a prelapsarian covenant with Adam, while Calvin did not, we may expect disagreement about the origin of sacraments, if not about their definition.

The word 'sacrament' is not used in Scripture, but is necessary because of 'agreement about it in the Church'; thus Arminius dismisses any Christian who rejects sacraments. It is derived from the oath sworn by Roman soldiers to their general, and so is appropriate for those bound in covenant to Christ by their reception of these signs. The phrase 'sign and seal' (*signum ac sigillum*) is taken by Arminius, as he mentions, from the sign of covenant, i.e. circumcision of Genesis 17:11, as quoted by Paul in Romans 4:11 (σημεῖον καὶ σφραγίς). Sacraments according to Arminius are not a New Testament invention. 'They have been either instituted before the Fall, and are of the covenant of works; or after the Fall, and are

---

213 *Public Disputation* XVIII:xv.
214 *Private Disputation* LIV:viii; *Works*, II, pp.420f; *Public Disputation* XVIII:xvi, pp.249f.
215 Bangs, *Arminius*, p.334.
216 *Private Disputation* LX (Introduction); *Works*, II, p.435.

of the covenant of grace.' The only sacrament of the first covenant was the Tree of Life. Those of the covenant of grace are either of the promised covenant, circumcision and the paschal lamb; or of the covenant of grace confirmed, that is, Christian sacraments. God is the author of all. The proximate purpose of sacraments is the sealing of the covenant promise; their remote purpose, the salvation of the church and the glory of God. Some sacraments are sacrifices, but the terms do not mean the same.[217]

Arminius points out that females were not circumcised in Israel (he may not have known of the practice of female circumcision in various parts of the world), but 'they were reckoned among the men, and considered by God as circumcised'. He does not directly link circumcision and baptism, but states that the paschal lamb adumbrated Christ the true Lamb. The paschal lamb was made obsolete by the sacrifice of the cross, and abrogated by the destruction of the city and temple. Whereas the Tree of Life was bloodless, there was bloodshed in circumcision and the paschal lamb, because sin had entered the world and sin is only expiated by blood.[218]

New Testament sacraments were instituted to testify to the covenant or New Testament, confirmed by the blood and death of its Mediator and Testator. They declare that the blood has been shed and expiation made; no further shedding of blood is necessary. But they had to be instituted before the death of the Testator, because as Mediator he had himself to partake of them in order to consecrate them in his own person and to seal the covenant between his people and himself more strongly. These sacraments do not profit adults who use them without faith and repentance, but the infant offspring of believing parents may be reckoned in the covenant.[219]

In baptism, sprinkling with water signifies and testifies the spiritual ablution effected by the blood and Spirit of Christ. Through it the baptised have communion with the Father and Son. Its first administrator was John. Christ confirmed it both by receiving it and by afterwards administering it through his disciples. The external sign is water, the internal thing signified is of blood and the Spirit. The primary end is to confirm and seal the communication of grace in Christ; the secondary end is to symbolise our initiation into the visible Church. In the case of infants at least one parent must be within God's covenant people. As an initiatory sacrament, it must not be repeated. Grace is not immediately conferred through the water, but through the promise of which water is a sign.[220]

---

217 *Private Disputation* LX (Introduction); i, iii, v, viii, and *Corollary*.
218 *Private Disputation* LXI:iv, vii-viii, and *Corollaries*.
219 *Private Disputation* LXII:iv-vi, viii; *Works*, II, pp.439f.
220 *Private Disputation* LXIII:i-iii, vi-viii; *Works*, II, pp.440ff.

As baptism is the sacrament of initiation, the Lord's Supper is the sacrament of confirmation. The Lord's death is announced, the inward receiving and enjoyment of his body and blood are signified, and our union with Christ our Head is sealed and confirmed. Christ is the author of this sacrament, for he alone is constituted by the Father Lord and Head of the Church.[221]

The matter is bread and wine:

> which, with regard to their essence, are not changed, but remain what they precisely were; neither are they, with regard to place, joined together with the body or blood, so that the body is either in, under or with the bread etc.[222]

Communion in one kind only is of course rejected. The signs represent Christ, but seal Christ to us with his benefits. The end is twofold, the strengthening of our faith and the certainty of our being ingrafted into Christ, so that believers may:

1) by remembering the death of Christ, testify their gratitude and obligation towards God.
2) cultivate charity among themselves.
3) be distinguished by this mark from unbelievers.[223]

The Mass is rejected because Christ instituted not a sacrifice but a sacrament, in which we are not commanded to offer anything external to God; but as in all acts there should be the internal sacrifice by which believers offer to God prayer, praise and thanksgiving; so the Lord's Supper is a Eucharist.[224] The five false (Roman Catholic) sacraments are rejected.

Summary

Arminius' letter to Uitenbogaert of 15 March 1609 shows that by then he had reached, in the *Private Disputations*, what he calls 'the second part of Theology or Religion', worship and 'the observance of the Divine commands', or ethics, which were never finished because of his illness and death in October.[225] The 'first part' on theological prolegomena and the doctrine of God, and the work and person of Christ, was therefore completed by early 1609. It remains to summarise our findings.

To take more negative criticisms first, Arminius is not particularly easy to read, either in Latin, Dutch or English. This may in part account for his having been 'one of the most neglected of the major Protestant

---

221 *Private Disputation* LXIV:i-iii; *Works*, II, pp.442f.
222 *Private Disputation* LXIV:iv.
223 *Private Disputation* LXIV:iv, vi; *Works*, II, pp.442f.
224 *Private Disputations* LXV:i-ii; *Works*, II, p.443, and LXVI, *passim*, pp.444f.
225 *Ep.Ecc.* 125, p.220; *Works*, II, pp.446 note.

theologians', as Muller puts it.[226] His early training in, and enthusiasm for, philosophy, and perhaps his Ramism, produced an inelegant and very analytical style. As well as producing repetition, this becomes monotonous, particularly when he proceeds by a series of (for example), 'functions', 'matters', 'ends' and particularly 'causes'. I have tried to smooth out to some extent the jerky effect this produces, but certainly enough is left to give a flavour of the original. In addition, the analysis will seem to the average modern reader over-confident; Arminius may seem too sure of the inner workings of the will of God or the work of Christ or the Holy Spirit. In part this is because he is a man of his time. The sixteenth and seventeenth centuries liked confident faith, not reverent agnosticism. Concerning his philosophical position, Muller points out that his theology, in spite of nominalist tendencies like his conception of the divine transcendence, leant towards Thomism (realism in the philosophical sense), although nominalism had influenced Reformed epistemology and definitions of theology, and appeared a powerful and attractive alternative to some in the early Reformation.[227] 'Certainly Arminius rejected 'the concept of a divine *potentia absoluta*, ...inherited from the nominalism of Augustinians like Gregory of Rimini and represented in his own day by Perkins and Gomarus'.[228] The reason, I suggest, lies in his strong sense of the Scriptures as a real revelation of God to man. We may take as an example the concept which has caused most difficulty for later Christians in classical orthodox Reformed theology, the (apparent absence of) love of God for the world. A nominalist would be content to leave this as an unresolved difficulty, for God's thoughts are not like man's, nor are his ways like man's; God's thoughts and ways are infinitely higher. Therefore, if God is revealed as love, then we must say that he is love but must not expect to understand *how* he is so, and must accept that, for example, he chooses to do apparently unloving things like reprobating some humans absolutely and unconditionally. Such names for God as 'love' have, from a human standpoint, no cash value. But to take such principles as Isaiah 55:8f so far is, to Arminius, to make the revelation of God in Scripture into an anti-revelation which leaves the unfortunate recipient of it more confused than he was before. If God reveals himself to his creatures as love, justice etc., then they, or at least Christians, should be able to recognise, up to a point, how God is so. Here Arminius deliberately 'bucks the trend' of the increasingly nominalist tendencies of Reformed theology in his day.

Second, the modern Reformed study of Arminius has shown the (hitherto neglected) importance of his links with both late medieval

---

226 Muller, *God*, Preface, p.ix.
227 Muller, *God*, pp.34, 227.
228 Muller, *God*, p.228.

scholasticism and with its sixteenth-century continuation in the Roman Catholic Church, particularly with the theology of Luis de Molina (1535-1600) and the concept of 'middle knowledge'. Both Muller and Dekker make much of this in discussing Arminius' views of the divine knowledge and will, and Muller sees a continuation of Molinism in his view of providence,[229] as does Dekker in his views of grace and predestination.[230] Undoubtedly, Arminius was aware of Molina's work and saw certain similarities between Molina's views and his own. But when he held public disputations, or expressed his theology of the work of Christ in the *Private Disputations*, there is precious little sign of input from scholastic sources, whether medieval or sixteenth-century Roman Catholic. The patterns he follows are either what were becoming traditionally Protestant, like the threefold office of Priest, Prophet and King, the states of Christ's humiliation and exaltation, or the concept of union and communion; or biblical concepts like that of covenant, and the 'golden chain' of Romans 8:30 of predestination, call, justification and glorification (sanctification), which underlies *Private Disputations* XL-XLIX. That is, in dealing with the doctrines of Christ's work and person, Arminius shows himself perhaps less of a traditional scholastic, and certainly much more a man of the Reformation than one would gather from the work of Muller and Dekker, whose viewpoint, though needed for a full picture, is as one-sided as the view it seeks to correct.

Third, Arminius' doctrine of Christ's work is tightly constructed and belongs together as a unit, which is why I have kept it as one in this chapter, at the disadvantage of making it inordinately long. His doctrine of Christ's, and the Holy Spirit's, Persons as subordinate to the Father, though less satisfactory, is to his mind demanded by the parts all three play in human salvation.

Fourthly, we have shown how important a place the doctrines of Christ's work and person played in Arminius' whole theology. He had more to say about them than about theological prolegomena or about the doctrine of God. Muller is right to stress the importance of the two latter subjects, but not at the expense of what Christ has done. Even the doctrine of God may be regarded, from the viewpoint of human need, as a prolegomenon to the work of Christ.

Fifthly, we have seen how the details of Arminius' doctrine of Christ's work all contribute to illustrate the convictions he expressed as early as 1591, that our salvation rests on Christ alone, and that more fundamental than our faith, or even God's grace, is the Holy Spirit of God who produces faith and administers grace, all so that we may share in this

---

229 Muller, *God*, p.255.
230 Dekker, *Rijker dan Midas*, Hoofdstukken 7 en 8, especially pp.157-161, 178-182.

salvation in which our sins are forgiven and our lives renewed. As a generalisation, we may perhaps summarise that Arminius saw Christ himself as particularly concerned with the objective securing of salvation, and his Spirit as particularly concerned with the subjective outworking of that salvation in our lives; but this should not be over-pressed.

Sixthly, I have tried to discuss other views expressed about the various subjects of which Arminius treats, whether by his contemporaries or by later theologians. I have also tried to show whether I agree or disagree with them, and why. But many of these subjects, particularly those discussed in this section, seem to have provoked no scholarly discussion at all! In such cases I have tried to let Arminius speak for himself as far as possible, and to compare his views where appropriate with earlier or contemporary statements on these subjects.

Finally, the disputations were composed during a period of increasing controversy. They, particularly the *Private Disputations*, were among other things a refuge for Arminius to find the peace he craved for both himself and the Dutch Church; they represent his own beliefs and approach to theology without the possible distorting effect of such controversy. But there was to be no peace. We return to chart the controversy's development.

CHAPTER 5

The Return of Controversy, 1604–1608

Arminius' career in academic teaching was not long, as he suffered from ill-health (Bangs says tubercolosis), and died a little over six years after his appointment. His career may be divided into two parts. The first ends with the close of his term as Rector Magnificus on 8 February 1606, when he delivered the rectoral oration *On Reconciling Religious Dissensions among Christians*. During this period controversy continued, but generally at a level with which he could cope, and in the latter part of 1605 he seemed to be settling down into a tolerable if not entirely cordial relationship with his fellow-professors, students, university authorities and the Church generally. But the final three to four years were a period of increasing trouble and misery that it becomes tedious to recount in detail, and the best part of it was that opposition from many sides helped to sharpen and clarify his views.

For some months after his appointment to Leiden, controversy was muted. He began teaching in September 1603 with the three orations, *The Object of Theology*, *The Author and End of Theology* and *The Certainty of Sacred Theology*, which Bangs calls 'noncontroversial and widely applauded', and whose importance Muller rightly recognises in providing prolegomena on the nature of theology and its subject, God, for the Reformed churches. The first hint of trouble came early in 1604 with Gomarus' objection that Arminius was 'invading his professorship', infringing on his prerogative to expound the New Testament, by referring to the New Testament in expounding the book of Jonah. Arminius defended his right as a professor of *Christian* theology to refer to the New Testament so long as he did not mention the particular topic Gomarus was currently teaching.[1]

Arminius' first public disputation as professor was held on 7 February 1604. Its subject, predestination, had come up briefly in the oration *On the Object of Theology*. Christ's subordination to his Father means that every saving communication between God and man, is performed through Christ as Mediator; so when God is pleased to make, of his goodness and mercy, some gracious decree (of salvation), he interposes Christ between the purpose and its accomplishment; so Arminius

---

1 Bangs, *Arminius*, p.261.

understands 'predestinating us in Christ to the adoption of children' (Ephesians 1:5).[2]

The public disputation was never intended to include every detail of what he believed on the subject. It is the shortest of all the twenty-five extant public disputations, just over four pages in Nichols's translation, compared with an average of about nine and a half. As Bangs says, 'no one is (explicitly) attacked; no opposing positions are defined and rejected; no mention is made of Calvin, Beza, Confession or Catechism; the appeal is entirely to Scripture.'[3] But this is clearly deliberate. The purpose of the whole is to maximise understanding and agreement, and to discover how far a form of words acceptable to all the warring parties could be found, even if they would interpret them differently. Arminius was deliberately seeking to find common ground with those of different views, and so laid himself open to the charge that he was deceitfully suppressing his own opinions. He had published nothing on the subject, but would later argue that his views on it were readily available:

> Of this distinction [between negative and affirmative reprobation, used by Gomarus] I have treated...at length in the *Conference* with Doctor Francis Junius of pious memory; and any one that likes can there read about it.[4]

In *Public Disputation* XV, Arminius was prepared to say things that have caused surprise, as for instance the definition of predestination as 'the decree of God's good-pleasure in Christ, by which in Himself He resolved from eternity to justify, adopt, and endow with eternal life, to the praise of His glorious grace, believers *on whom He had decreed to bestow faith*'[5]—which Dekker finds the only element that goes further than the *eigenschappen-predestinatie*, which he regularly finds the main theme in all Arminius' work on the subject.[6] But if election is based on God's foreknowledge, as the fourth decree in the *Declaration of Sentiments* claims, then Arminius was prepared to concede that God would not bother to bestow faith on those he knew would reject it; hence he could accept these words, in a different sense from his opponents, granted, but he was seeking as much agreement as possible, and was not trying to impose his views on others in detail.

At its widest, he says, predestination can be interpreted as God's decree for the governance of all things, that is, providence, but it is usually used in Scripture, for example in Romans 8:29, for God's decree about the

---

2 *Works*, I, pp.338f.

3 Bangs, *Arminius*, p.262.

4 *Examination of Gomarus*, reply to Thesis XXIV, *Works*, III, p.596; cf. Dekker, *Rijker dan Midas*, p.142 n.84.

5 'Fideles quos fide donare decrevit'; my italics.

6 Dekker, *Rijker dan Midas*, p.210.

salvation or damnation of men, and is so defined in this disputation. The decree is not legal, based on gaining life by doing things, but evangelical, based on seeing the Son, believing on him and so having everlasting life (Romans 10:5, 9; John 6:40). As the whole counsel of God concerning our salvation is contained in the gospel, the decree is irrevocable. It is based on God's good-pleasure, and therefore excludes every cause, positive or negative, that could be found in man. Jesus Christ as Mediator is the foundation of the decree, and also the Head of all those who will by God's predestination share in the blessings of salvation. This is confirmed by Ephesians 1:4, which also confirms that this predestination was decreed from eternity. There is a double object: the spiritual blessings predestined, and the persons (believers) for whom they are predestined. Belief presupposes sin, for none can believe in Christ except a sinner, and believers are such, not by their own desire, merits or strength, but by the gratuitous and *peculiar*[7] kindness of God. The form is the communication of blessings to believers, and the end is the praise of the glorious grace of God, that is, his gratuitous love in Christ. Election, however, necessarily implies reprobation, which is based on unbelief. The use of the doctrine of predestination is to establish God's glory, by ascribing the whole praise of the process to God's grace and mercy alone, and taking it entirely from our own strength, works and merits; it assures those struggling with temptation of the gracious and inalienable love of God in Christ, and it terrifies the ungodly and drives away their security.[8] However, nothing should be taught about it beyond what the Scriptures say, and only in the way they say it,[9] and this is reinforced by a sort of corollary in which Arminius quotes from Ecclesiasticus about avoiding things which are secret, unprofitable, unnecessary or beyond our understanding.[10] Unfortunately, just before this quotation and after the requirement to be scriptural in all things, Arminius is betrayed into saying, 'This, by God's gracious assistance, we think we have done',[11] which strikes a wrong note; it could seem complacent, and to Gomarus it probably did.

For some months nothing further happened to create outward controversy, although, as Bangs says, Arminius' frequent letters to Uitenbogaert during the summer show that he was aware of simmering opposition.[12] He delivered other public disputations on other subjects, but the first proof that his olive branch on predestination had been rejected

---

7 My italics.
8 *Opera*, p.285: 'securitati illorum excutiendae'.
9 *Public Disputation* XV; *Works*, II. pp.226-9.
10 Ecclesiasticus 3:20-23.
11 *Public Disputation* XV:xv; *Works*, II, p.229.
12 Bangs, *Arminius*, p.263; *Ep.Ecc.* 69-72, pp.125-41.

came with Gomarus' public disputation on that subject on 31 October 1604.

At this point something must be said about Gomarus.[13] He had been a pupil of Junius, and ministered to him in his final illness, and Gomarus had made it clear that he did not want Arminius appointed to the university and stated that the dying Junius had expressed the same opinion. This is likely enough, but may not mean that Junius thought Arminius unfit for the post. It may rather mean that, knowing both Arminius and Gomarus as he did, he realised that they were both temperamentally and theologically quite unsuited to be colleagues in a small faculty. Gomarus may not have been such a ogre as later 'Arminianism' has represented him (e.g., the works of Brandt and Nichols), and Bangs, for an 'Arminian', gives a surprisingly sympathetic account of him.[14] But even for a Reformed theologian of the sixteenth and seventeenth centuries, Gomarus was an abnormally aggressive man, and his behaviour at the Synod of Dort, when he is said to have challenged a fellow-Calvinist to a duel (this a week before his fifty-sixth birthday!), suggests that Arminius never had a chance of placating him.

Gomarus' disputation was not part of the schedule agreed between the three professors, and views differ about its morality. Perhaps Arminius could have made a counter-accusation that Gomarus was invading *his* field! Dekker argues that it need not be criticised negatively, and that such unscheduled disputations were held; for example, two students had held such disputations under Arminius on 28 October and 5 November 1603.[15] However, it was less than nine months since Arminius had held a disputation on the same subject, and such an excuse for a man who had made a fuss over his rival quoting from the New Testament, sounds rather hollow. The whole affair was a 'demarcation dispute' of the kind found in industrial relations. Gomarus' methods were entirely different from those of Arminius; he stated his own supralapsarian views in as extreme a form as he could, and threw them down as a challenge. Arminius found such behaviour objectionable and interpreted it as a direct attack upon himself, as he made clear in a letter of the following day to

---

13 The following is based largely on the short accounts of Gomarus in Bangs, *Arminius*, pp.245-8, 252ff, 261-4; and Dekker, *Rijker dan Midas*, pp.38ff, 43ff and *passim*. Both these appear to depend largely on G.P. van Itterzon, *Franciscus Gomarus* ('s-Gravenhage: Martinus Nijhoff, 1930). For Gomarus's behaviour at the Synod of Dort, not mentioned by Bangs or Dekker, see van Itterzon, *Gomarus*, pp.231-8; although van Itterzon is highly favourable to Gomarus he records his challenge to a duel made to Martinius of Bremen, and quarrels with other Bremen theologians and with an English bishop.

14 Bangs, *Arminius*, pp.245-8 and *passim*.

15 Dekker, *Rijker dan Midas*, p.44 n.141; cf. Bangs, *Arminius*, p.261.

Uitenbogaert.[16] The fact that he was ill and in pain at the time did not help. Bangs gives only a short summary of Gomarus' *Theses* and occasional references to Arminius' reply. Dekker concentrates on what he finds in Arminius' reply concerning Arminius' own doctrine, and says of Gomarus' *Theses* only that they are very clear (zeer duidelijke) and 'geheel (entirely) supralapsarich'.[17]

This is very unsatisfactory. No-one will quarrel with the 'wholly supralapsarian' description, but it is one of the objections Arminius raises, that the apparently self-evident 'clarity', which others beside Dekker have found in supralapsarian Calvinism, is largely illusory and disappears under close examination. Thus, for example, the definition of predestination in Gomarus' *Thesis* VII is of rational creatures; that is, it includes angels as well as men, yet in *Thesis* I it is called a 'principal part of the subject-matter of the Gospel', a gospel with which angels are not concerned (1 Peter 1:12). These rational creatures are described as 'indefinitely foreknown'; how, asks Arminius, can foreknowledge be indefinite and still be a form of knowledge? Gomarus describes them as 'creatures' when in fact they are creables, still to be 'preordained to creation'. God does this 'of His own right and good-pleasure', but, says Arminius, as creables they are only non-entities or at best possible creatures, and God's right over such can be no more than a metaphor and a 'borrowed meaning', for a right is a relation between two existences; and so on.[18] Close scrutiny shows that Gomarus' argument cannot be sustained. Dekker is of course examining the theology of Arminius, not Gomarus, but when Arminius is himself examining someone else's theology, he can only be judged fairly if the text he is examining is also subjected to judgment and not merely described, as Dekker does, as 'very clear'. Otherwise the implication is that that text is above criticism. Gomarus' text will certainly not be treated here in that way, but will be subjected to criticism in the same way as Arminius' reply.

The first comment on Gomarus' *Theses* must be that their purpose was entirely different from that of Arminius', indeed the opposite. If Arminius wanted to find common ground with his opponents, Gomarus wanted to present a complete and watertight argument with which others, especially Arminius, were in effect ordered to agree. He seems to have enjoyed his task hugely. It is recorded that before his death, even the mild Junius had said that Gomarus 'pleases himself most wonderfully by his own remarks'.[19]

Gomarus begins from a quite different starting-point; predestination is 'the difference between those who are to be saved and those who are to

---

16 *Ep.Ecc.* 74, p.141; Bangs, *Arminius*, p.264; *Works*, I, p.261.
17 Dekker, *Rijker dan Midas*, p.44.
18 *Examination of Gomarus, Thesis* VII; *Works*, III, pp.533-7; cf. *Thesis* I, p.527.
19 Quoted *Works*, I, p.171; Bangs, *Arminius*, p.248.

be damned'.[20] That is, the predestination of individuals is primary. It must be taught with reverence and we must not 'carp' at what we do not understand. This is preliminary skirmishing and Arminius replies that no such 'difference' is set forth in Scripture which does not encourage the reader to seek salvation and avoid damnation. While he agrees with teaching with reverence, it is permissible to 'carp' at the views of those who bring forward things *beyond* the Scriptures, as for example that God ordains the causes of damnation and yet is not to blame, which Beza himself admitted he could not explain.[21] He finds little to argue with in Gomarus' *Theses* III-VI, but the battle is joined over *Thesis* VII, the definition of predestination:

> the purpose of God, whereby, out of rational creatures indefinitely foreknown, He preordained certain ones, of His own right and good-pleasure, to their own supernatural ends, and to creation in the upright state of original righteousness, and His other means, to the glory of His saving grace, wisdom, and most free power.[22]

This is supralapsarianism. In *Thesis* VIII, God's purpose makes predestination eternal, immutable and certain. God's intellect knows all things possible, whether they will or will not be, and all rational creatures that can be saved and created, but he only chooses to create and predestine some of them.[23] But all this happened not only before the Fall, but before creation; predestination is of creables (creabilitarianism). Creation in the upright state of original righteousness is simply the first of the means by which creatures are preordained to their supernatural ends; the next means is the fall into sin. The end of predestination is the glory of divine and saving power, wisdom and grace; not internal glory, of which God has no need; but external glory to be seen by his creatures.[24] From *Thesis* VIII through to *Thesis* XV Gomarus is expounding at fuller length the definition of *Thesis* VII. We may note, however, that in *Thesis* VII all this is done not only to the glory of God's grace and wisdom, but also to the glory of 'His most free power', which he wanted to make known (Romans 9:22). God foreknows definitely future things, because he has foreordained them by decree.[25]

Gomarus now distinguishes between two species of predestination: election to eternal life and glory; and reprobation to eternal death and ignominy.[26] This is worked out in detail in the following *Theses* up to

---

20 *Thesis* I; *Works*, III, p.527.
21 *Theses* I-II, and Arminius' *Consideration*, *Works*, III, pp.527-30.
22 *Thesis* VII; *Works*, III, pp.533-4.
23 *Theses* VIII, X; *Works*, III, pp.543, 553.
24 *Theses* XII, XIII, XV; *Works*, III, pp.559, 564, 569.
25 *Thesis* XVI; *Works*, III, p.572.
26 *Thesis* XVII; *Works*, III, pp.573-4.

Thesis XXVIII. God chooses and calls some to temporal office, but others to inherit eternal life, which is efficacious calling. God has foreordained certain individuals to this by his own right, good-pleasure and gratuitous love. The good-pleasure is twofold, towards the thing, election, and the elect persons; although the latter are without merit, God approves of both. As the obedience of holiness due to God is one of the means, Augustine can call it the predestination of the saints. The end of such predestination is God's glory and (eternal) life for the elect.[27]

Interestingly, Gomarus spends five theses on the predestination of the elect and six on that of the reprobate. God has from eternity rejected the latter for eternal life and condemned them to death and eternal ignominy, by creating them in an upright state of original righteousness, permitting them to fall into sin and to lose righteousness, and forsaking them in sin. Although Gomarus speaks of 'permission' of falling into sin, he also makes it clear that rejection from life to eternal death is pre-ordained. The impulsive cause is God's good-pleasure towards the thing (reprobation) which he approves, not towards the person; for reprobation is hatred, the reprobate are called 'never known' and 'cursed', and this is just, because God is the heavenly Potter, supreme Lord of all and debtor to none. It is also right and wise because the world should have a variety of vessels to honour and dishonour. Gomarus here refers to 2 Timothy 2:20, 'A great house contains not only gold and silver vessels, but also vessels of wood and clay; and some for honour and others for dishonour', but ignores the next verse with its implication that a man can actually cleanse himself from wrongdoing and *become* a vessel for honour! Finally, God does not lead the reprobate down to their destined destruction except by permitting their (evil) desert as a subordinate means; so the efficient and sufficient cause and matter of their perdition may be found in the reprobate themselves. Here Gomarus, in typical Reformed fashion, contrives to make man take the full blame for his damnation while attributing all the action to God. In Gomarus' view, God cannot be accused of injustice if he has destined and created any for destruction, because he has a twofold right, the absolute right of dominion, and the subordinate right of judgment for sins. Gomarus goes on to say that Roman Catholics and Lutherans contend with 'our' (Reformed) churches about the will and the deed (whether God actually willed to do this and actually has done it) but acknowledge his freedom to do so, quoting from the Catholics Javellus and Viguerius, and the Lutherans Andreae (at the 1586 Colloquy of Montbeliard with Beza), Rungius and Major. The subordinate end of reprobation is the glory of God's power, wrath and dominion over the reprobate, but the preordained end is the glory of God's grace towards the elect, illumined

---

27 *Theses* XVIII-XXII; *Works*, III, pp.575ff, 580f, 586, 588.

by the foil and dark shadow of reprobation. Here Gomarus associates himself and his fellow-elect with Moses and Paul in desiring the (impossible) salvation of the reprobate, but this is not genuine compassion, but only designed to render the reprobate more inexcusable if they do not humbly and passively 'acquiesce' in what he takes to be God's decision.[28]

If Arminius was self-satisfied to *think* that he had explained predestination, Gomarus had no such uncertainty. He begins *Thesis* XXIX, 'And so we have explained the nature of predestination and its species', that is, both election and reprobation of both angels and men; although, he says, they are strictly not species but circumstances, 'because they are not of contrary form'. This and the following two theses are concerned with the difference between the predestination of angels and of men, which is concerned with the means; and here at long last Gomarus introduces Christ as something more than a witness to one of his theological points. In the case of angels the means is the perpetual obedience of holiness, and so Christ is not offered to them; but (some) men are said to be elect in Christ to holiness and predestinated to adoption by Jesus Christ and to be conformed to his image (Ephesians 1:4f; Romans 8:29) 'just as Christ also was foreknown (as Mediator, and as the destined *subordinate* [my italics] cause for salvation) before the world's foundations were laid (1 Peter 1:20)'. Consequently Christ is offered to them, even to the reprobate; but only so that they may be convicted of unbelief and stubbornness and become the more inexcusable.[29]

The final *Thesis* XXXII has caused disagreement between Bangs and Dekker. Bangs argues that in it Gomarus gives his case away, by making the kind of men God has chosen to life logically prior to the election itself, and that Arminius recognised this and was 'gleeful' to seize upon it. It seems unlikely that Arminius felt any 'glee' in composing his answer, but Dekker is not surprisingly unhappy with the implication that Gomarus has slipped into *eigenschappen-predestinatie*, and accuses Bangs of being unfair (*onjuist*) to Gomarus. Certainly Gomarus has been at pains in his previous theses to deny that anything in men is the cause of their predestination, but in *Thesis* XXXII he is trying to explain how someone can know that he is elect, and argues that the gospel teaches what kind of men God has chosen to life, that is, believers, and there can be no doubt that he has, carelessly, made faith and penitence logically prior to election, and Arminius was right to notice it. Gomarus was not the

---

28 *Theses* XXIII-XXVIII; *Works*, III, pp.588, 596, 612, 626, 632.
29 *Theses* XXIX-XXXI; *Works*, III, 633ff, 643.

first or last supralapsarian to get into problems when he tried to work out the pastoral implications of his beliefs.[30]

In the *Corollary* Gomarus considers just one objection to his doctrine; whether the blasphemy follows that God is the author of sin. Instead of arguing that this does not follow, he impugns the motives of those (Castellio, Coornhert and the Lutherans) who say it does, and claims Calvin and Beza for his own supralapsarian position. He ends on a note of typical Reformed triumphalism:

> We, with the Reformed Churches, with justice deny that, and do not in the least doubt that the truth and sanctity of this opinion will endure, in spite of the gates of hell.[31]

As in the case of Perkins, Arminius was commenting point by point on another's text and this again makes his work rather long and disjointed, and sometimes difficult to read. However, of the three long works of Arminius which are direct replies to other theologians — the *Collatio*, or *Conference with Junius*, and the *Examinations* of Perkins and Gomarus — the reply to Perkins is the most obscure and this reply to Gomarus is the clearest. Perhaps Arminius, through his university work, was becoming more practised at theological argument, and also, perhaps, the resentment he felt sharpened his ideas. We shall see that the long attack on supralapsarianism in the *Declaration of Sentiments* was directed in the first instance against Gomarus and his doctrine, when Arminius had had four more years to consider his reply and to put it into his own order, not Gomarus'. It is unlikely that he had developed his views significantly between the public disputation and the *Examination of Gomarus*, although Dekker claims to find an 'order in the decrees' which was not made clear before.[32] Probably Arminius had been hoping that the public disputation would have laid the subject to rest, and he had had other things to think about.

In the *Examination* we find many of the points we would expect. Arminius balances Acts 13:48, a difficult text for one of his views, with John 1:12 in which receiving Christ and believing in him precedes the power to become God's children.[33] Creation is an act of God which stands in its own right and is not merely a means of carrying out a decree

---

30 *Thesis* XXXII; *Works*, III, pp.649-50; Bangs, *Arminius*, p.353; Dekker, *Rijker dan Midas*, p.215 n.137; cf. Kendall, *Calvin*, on Beza pp.33-4, the Heidelberg theologians pp.39ff, and Perkins chs 4-5.

31 *Corollary of Gomarus*; *Works*, III, p.654.

32 Dekker, *Rijker dan Midas*, pp.216ff, Hoofdstuk 8.9.2. It is true that Arminius has more to say about creation than in previous discussions of predestination, and is more concerned to stress that creation comes logically before election and reprobation.

33 *Consideration of Thesis* XII; *Works*, III, p.560.

of election. As Arminius puts it in a very Thomist statement, 'So far from creation being a way of election, it is rather the foundation on which election can be built up, just as grace also is founded on nature, elevating nature above its own mode to the supernaturals.'[34] So predestination is not of creables, but of creatures. A creable is a non-entity until it is created and becomes a creature, and a non-entity cannot be an object of either election or reprobation, unless it is foreknown as a creature.[35] In saying that it is of creables, Gomarus is going against the definitions in Article 13 of the *Belgic Confession* and Question 27 of the *Heidelberg Catechism*.[36] Moreover, there is always something else about objects of predestination in God's mind, apart from the bare fact that they are creables or creatures, whether that they are believers (according to Arminius' interpretation of Ephesians 1), babes (Matthew 11:25-6), or subjects of mercy or hardening, which presuppose misery and sin (Romans 9:15, 18).[37] But a weightier objection is one that Arminius makes at the beginning and returns to at the end:

> If predestination be the matter of the Gospel, it cannot be that Jesus Christ is excluded from its definition and essence, since He is the principal object and matter of the Gospel. But in this whole treatise no mention is made of Jesus Christ, except where an exposition is given of the means appertaining to its execution.[38]

Gomarus' answer would probably be that predestination is of angels as well as men, and he assumes that Christ is not involved in the former, so he is not mentioned until the difference between the two is stated, as the means by which God's decree is carried out.[39] Arminius will not accept this excuse; Christ is not the means of election but its foundation, as Ephesians 1 makes clear. We are said to be elected in him before the foundations of the world were laid, from eternity. The decree was made

---

34 *Consideration of Thesis* XIX; *Works*, III, p.579.
35 *Consideration of Thesis* XIII, pp.565-6.
36 *Consideration of Thesis* I; *Works*, III, p.529. According to the *Heidelberg Catechism*, Question 27, the providence of God upholds and governs 'heaven, earth and all *creatures*'—not creables; see G.I. Williamson, *The Heidelberg Catechism: A Study Guide* (Phillipsburg, NJ: Puritan and Reformed Publishing, 1993), p.48; similarly in the *Belgic Confession*.
37 *Consideration of Thesis* VII; *Works*, III, p.536.
38 *Consideration of Thesis* I; *Works*, III, p.529; *Examen Thesium D. Francisci Gomari De Praedestinatione* (n.p., 1645), p.5: 'Si praedestinatio Evangelii materia sit, fieri nequit ut ab illius definitione et essentia Jesus Christus excluditur, qui objectum et materia Evangelii est praecipua.... Hoc vero toto tractatu nulla Jesu Christi fit mentio, nisi quum de mediis ad executionem pertinentibus exponitur.'
39 *Thesis* XXX; *Works*, III, p.635. The contemporary assumption was that Christ's death only redeemed humans; but which God predestined angels, the Father, or the whole Trinity?

from eternity; therefore it was made in Christ; and grace was founded and given in Christ before the world began (2 Timothy 1:9; Ephesians 1:6); and predestination proceeds from grace before the intervention of power. Removal of sin precedes predestination to salvation, and this was achieved by Christ (John 1:29), who is, therefore, the foundation of election. Predestination to adoption is not *by* Christ as a means, but *in* Christ, into sonship to God, as in Romans 8:29; and this is true also of conformity to Christ's image. The predestination of the Head is prior to that of the members. Christ is Saviour not only because he applies salvation, but because he acquires it. But the predestination of believers to salvation belongs to application, not acquisition, so, in logical order, it happens after God in his foreknowledge takes account of Calvary. Here Arminius charges Gomarus with the heresy of Paul of Samosata (and indirectly, as Nichols points out, Arius and Socinus also), that Christ has not obtained salvation for us, but only imparts it according to the Father's will and command. Reconciliation, too, precedes predestination, and proceeds from love.[40]

The great difference between the *Examination of Gomarus* and any preceding work of Arminius, is in its tone. Previously, Arminius had treated those who disagreed with him, Plancius, Junius, Perkins and Gomarus himself, with Christian charity, as men who might be mistaken but who were brothers in Christ, to be reasoned with mildly and corrected in friendly fashion from Scripture and sound theology. Almost from the start the spirit of this *Examination* is changed; it is full of revulsion and anger, and the reason is not only that it dishonours Christ, but that it paints an utterly unacceptable picture of God. If Gomarus is right,

> will not the first act of the Lord...be the volition of damnation, who is, and is called, the Highest Good, and is communicative of Himself, who is both supremely good and the cause of all good!... Does not that doctrine mark out God to us as being not more supremely good than supremely bad, nay, more inclined to will evil to men than good, since He wills damnation to more than He wills salvation. Let us so beware of falling into Pelagianism as not to slip into a doctrine worse than the Manichaean.[41]

Here he charges supralapsarianism not simply with being false, as he has done before; he charges that it is bad, and that not because of anything it says about man, but because of what it says about God. If anyone says that it is good for the reprobate creature to serve God for the illustration of his wrath, this is contrary to Christ's clear word, 'It would have been good for that man (Judas) if he had not been born'.[42]

---

40 *Consideration of Thesis* XXX; *Works*, III, pp.639-642.
41 *Consideration of Thesis* VII; *Works*, III, p.537.
42 *Consideration of Thesis* VII; *Works*, III, p.539.

There is more to come, especially when Gomarus turns to the subject of reprobation. According to Gomarus, God by his own first volition about rational creatures, wished to make 'a nation of light and a nation of darkness' and was delighted with this; he willed some to be damned at the same moment and point of time as he willed others to be saved. Arminius replies, 'What baser charge can be brought against the good God?'[43] The decree of creation, in an upright state of original righteousness, was a means to the execution of the decree, not only of election, but also of reprobation; this is 'something new and unheard of in God's church, contrary to the Scriptures, most alien to God's truth, not to say blasphemous'.[44] Creation for the purpose of damnation is an evil intention for the donor and the greatest evil for the recipient. He receives a brief existence so that he may eternally suffer infinite misery; animal good that he may receive everlasting spiritual ill. 'It is horrible even to think such a thing of the Creator.'[45] If creation be an act of reprobation, it is done from hatred towards the reprobate.

The answer could be that God did not create anyone to damn him as a creature, but that having become wicked he could be condemned. To Arminius this is worse:

> This, according to them, is the order of reprobation: In the first moment, God willed to reprobate rational creatures; in the second moment, because they could not be damned while non-existent, He determined to create them; in the third moment, because He must damn them justly, they had to sin and become wicked; He therefore ordained [all this]...for His glory. In this process they ascribe far baser things to God than if they simply said that He created creatures in order to damn them.[46]

This is 'worse than the devil himself could conceive in his most wicked mind'.

Arminius objects strongly to Gomarus' methods of arguing, in his calling of 'papal adversaries and Lutheran Doctors' to support his view in *Thesis* XXVII, that the truth of his view is so plain that even heretics must acknowledge it; while citing the same heretics in the *Corollary* to prove the truth of his view because in this instance they reject it! As Arminius says:

> The Samosatenians will say that it is so plain that Jesus Christ is a mere man, and that there are not three persons in one Deity, that the truth of this doctrine compels

---

43 *Consideration of Thesis* XXIII; *Works*, III, pp.590-1.
44 *Consideration of Thesis* XXV; *Works*, III, p.598.
45 *Consideration of Thesis* XXV; *Works*, III, p.600.
46 *Consideration of Thesis* XXV; *Works*, III, pp.602-03.

even Jews and Turks to confess the same; but that its contrary cannot be true, since even Antichrist entertains that opinion.[47]

So after the attack on Gomarus' view of Christ as the subordinate cause for salvation, Arminius makes the strongest attack yet on supralapsarianism:

> This treatise on God's predestination is an inversion of the whole Divine decree, an injustice to His gracious mercy, and to Jesus Christ our Saviour: *wherefore it must be exploded and ejected from the Church of Christ.*[48]

Was Arminius proposing what would have amounted to a Synod of Dort in reverse? Possibly, in the heat of the moment before he had cooled down. But he had still one final objection to the *Corollary*. He agrees that to say that God is the author of sin is the worst possible blasphemy against him; even the Manichaeans, whom he considers the worst of heretics, would not do that, so postulated another evil god whom they could blame. Gomarus' mention of Calvin, Beza and the Reformed churches generally, is a red herring. Theologians like Calvin and Beza may, as Gomarus puts it, 'deserve very well of the Church' for their defence of truth and refutation of heresy, and yet, in Arminius' view, make mistakes. The 'illustrious restorers of the Church' (the Reformers) may not have identified all the errors in the Church as they found her, and may have built 'a superstructure of some errors upon a true foundation'. Many opponents of Pelagianism, including Augustine himself, would have rejected many things in these *Theses*. But as for Arminius himself,

> I freely and openly affirm, that *it seems to me to follow certainly from these Theses, that God is the author of sin; that God really sins; that God alone sins; finally that sin is not sin*, because God (by definition) cannot sin.[49]

If the doctrine of these *Theses* is indeed pure and holy, certainly it will endure against all that the kingdom of Satan can do. But Arminius is certain from the word of God and of his Christ, that the doctrine is false and profane, not contrary to that kingdom, but very well adapted for establishing and confirming it. He does not hesitate to say that the doctrine has crept into the hearts of good men by the subtlety and craft of Satan himself, and that for what they have done for the kingdom of darkness they will find it hard to repent sufficiently.[50]

---

47 *Consideration of Thesis* XXVII; *Works*, III, pp.630ff.
48 *Consideration of Thesis* XXX; *Works*, III, p.642, italics added.
49 *Consideration of Corollary*; *Works*, III, pp.654-7, italics original.
50 *Consideration of Corollary*; *Works*, III, p.658.

The basic objection is moral. Arminius is claiming that the very nature of God is simply not like what Gomarus is describing. This tone of moral revulsion is found in all that Arminius said later about opposing doctrines of predestination, except for the *Answers to Nine Questions* drawn up by the Synod of South Holland and sent by the university curators to each of the theology professors for their answers, in 1605-06. Such revulsion is found in the *Declaration of Sentiments*, and particularly strongly in the *Apology Against Thirty-One Defamatory Articles*, and links Arminius with similar moral revulsion felt by later 'Arminians' like John and Charles Wesley. As Bangs says, there were weaknesses in both Gomarus' *Theses* and in Arminius' reply in the *Examination*, which had been a hasty reaction.[51] Arminius' reply was not published till 1645, but the original (1604) disputations of both Arminius and Gomarus were published together early in 1609 by order of the curators and burgomasters, to quash inaccurate rumours.

There was no immediate response from Gomarus. According to Dekker, his *Disputation IX, De Decretis Dei (On the Decrees of God)* shows that he took Arminius' criticisms seriously,[52] but they did not affect the general structure of his thought. Arminius himself calmed down, and was able to write to Uitenbogaert some months later that there was peace between him and Gomarus and he thought that it would continue sufficiently firm unless others made trouble; in any case he wanted to make his own modesty and equanimity conspicuous to all, and to outdo his opponents in both the goodness of his cause and his way of acting.[53] Bangs points out that the three professors of theology at Leiden responded to a complaint from the Classis of Dordrecht unanimously on 10 August 1605, that they could have wished that the Classis had acted in a better and more orderly way, and that while there was more disputation among the students than they liked, there was no disagreement between the professors themselves on the essentials of doctrine. Gomarus is said to have remarked that he could easily be induced to cultivate peace with Arminius, but the churches and their deputies were making it difficult for him. Bangs concludes that there was in mid-1605 some degree of peace between Gomarus and Arminius.[54]

If so, it did not last. The *Nine Questions* from the Synod of South Holland were answered by Arminius, but did not contribute towards the ongoing controversy. The next significant action was taken by Arminius himself, in his rectoral oration to mark the end of his term as Rector Magnificus. His public disputation on predestination had misfired as an

---

51 Bangs, *Arminius*, pp.353-4.
52 Dekker, *Rijker dan Midas*, p.44 n.140. See also Curcellaeus's Preface to Arminius' *Examination*; *Works*, III, pp.522-5.
53 *Ep.Ecc.* 77, p.147, translated in part in *Works*, I, p.286.
54 Bangs, *Arminius*, p.270; cf. *Works*, I, p.286, Brandt, *Life*, p.235.

attempt to bring peace two years previously, and he now tried another method, widening the scope of the discussion. Division into parties, he says, is in direct contradiction to the nature and genius of Christianity, whose Author is called 'Prince of Peace', its doctrine the 'Gospel of Peace', and its followers the 'Sons of Peace'. Its very foundation is an act of pacification, concluded between God and men, and ratified by the blood of the Prince of Peace. Its fruits are righteousness, peace and joy in the Holy Spirit, and its end is peace and tranquility with God in heaven. Clearer light shines among the Churches that profess to have been *reformed from popery* (Arminius' emphasis), but not greater peace, and this causes deep regret to Arminius and, he believes, to all who love Christ and his Church.[55]

The title of this oration should be noted; it is not just about reconciling dissensions generally, but *On Reconciling Religious Dissensions among Christians* (emphasis added), and it begins from this position. Certainly Christ said that he came not to bring peace but a sword, but these words do not indicate the end and purpose of Christ's coming, but the result of it.[56] The Christian Religion is founded in *the Cross of Christ*, and claims that *Jesus, the Crucified, is the Saviour of the world*, and these appear absurd, a stumbling-block to the Jews and foolishness to the Greeks,[57] so dissension between Christians and the natural world is inevitable; but such dissensions should not occur between Christians themselves. Popish and other remedies are considered and dismissed. Finally, Arminius makes his own proposals which are intended to be practical. What he wants is an assembly or council, and he argues that the presidency of it belongs to *him* alone who is *Head* and *Husband* of the Church, Christ by his Holy Spirit, that the rule in all the transactions should be the *word of God*, and that this should be signified as it was in the ancient councils, by placing a *copy of the Gospels* in the first and most honourable seat. Christ is provoked by our manifold trespasses and offences, but he will not neglect his Church, and will lead her into general unanimity and agreement. But if mutual consent and agreement cannot be obtained on some articles, a fraternal concord in Christ should be sought, or at least the right hand of friendship extended, and future preaching of truths and confutation of errors should be free of bitterness, evil-speaking and railing. Anyone who will not accept this should be punished by the magistrates, and the imprecations of an incensed God and of his Christ should be invoked on him.[58]

---

55 *Oration* V; *Works*, I, p.436.
56 *Oration* V; *Works*, I, p.445.
57 *Oration* V; *Works*, I, p.453. In the original Latin of the *Opera*, the words or phrases here in italics are in small, but heavier type. This is replaced by capitals in Nichols's translation.
58 *Oration* V; *Works*, I, pp.473-526 and *passim*.

In a sense the proposal for such a national synod was not controversial, for both sides wanted it; but Arminius' view that everything should be judged by the word of God alone caused him to recommend that the members should 'be absolved from all other oaths, either immediately or indirectly contrary to this, by which they have been bound either to Churches and their confessions, or to schools and their masters...'.[59]

This was dangerous stuff. As Bangs points out, 'schools and their masters' could mean Geneva, Calvin and Beza; more immediately important 'churches and their confessions' could mean, and were taken to mean, the *Belgic Confession* and *Heidelberg Catechism*; and there already had been a proposal from the States of Holland in 1597 to revise these. Bangs asks and considers how serious Arminius was in making his proposals.[60] It is impossible to be sure; but while his opponents felt threatened by any suggestion of revision, Arminius could at least point to the fact that the *Confession* and *Catechism* were signally failing to keep such a Christian peace as he had described and advocated.

The oration has in the long run made Arminius a minor early hero of the ecumenical movement, but his practical proposals were quite unrealistic in the atmosphere of the Reformed churches at the beginning of the seventeenth century. Up to the time of the *Second Helvetic Confession* in 1675, the movement of thought was quite the other way, towards greater rigidity and intolerance, and it remains uncertain whether Arminius was naive enough to think that his proposals were a practical possibility, or whether he was ignoring that and setting out his vision of what the Church should really be.

During 1606, Arminius' public disputation *On the Divinity of the Son* (not extant) revealed that he had misgivings about the application of the term *autotheos* to the Son (and Spirit). As we have seen, these misgivings date back at least to early 1599 when he wrote on the subject to Uitenbogaert, but one of his colleagues, Trelcatius, held the doctrine and had taught it to his students, one of whom proposed it stubbornly in the debate following the disputation. The subject never attained quite the same importance as predestination, or as the revision of *Confession* and *Catechism*, as an article of controversy, but it strengthened the feeling among Arminius' opponents that he was unreliable in a variety of ways.

Political developments early in 1607, with the overtures for a truce between the United Provinces and Spain, caused further trouble. Arminius was accused of advising his students to read the works of the Jesuits and of Coornhert—which, as Bangs points out, were poles apart theologically.[61] Certainly, Arminius had personally studied works by

---

59 *Oration* V; *Works*, I, p.522.
60 Bangs, *Arminius*, pp.278ff.
61 Bangs, *Arminius*, p.287.

Jesuits and Coornhert, and, as Muller and Dekker have shown, had been influenced by them to some extent. The basic problem was that early Reformers like Luther and Calvin had expressed themselves intemperately about the Church of Rome and her doctrines, yet when their successors tried to put Protestant/Reformed beliefs into systematic theology, they had to use un-reformed medieval models, even sometimes sixteenth-century Roman Catholic models, as there were no others to use. In practice both sides, Arminius and his opponents, used such models to produce a form of Protestant scholasticism, as Muller has shown for Arminius in *God, Creation and Providence*, and for Reformed theology in *Christ and the Decree*. But they had to do this while strenuously denying that they were doing it! In this respect there was no difference between Arminius and his opponents, and twentieth-century Reformed theologians who have simply repeated their seventeenth-century predecessors' charges against Arminius, that his doctrine was essentially papist, have been selectively unjust.

The question is whether, and whether at this stage, he had actually recommended medieval and sixteenth-century Roman Catholic scholastic works to his students. The hostile Sibelius, who was his student at a slightly later date (1608-09), claimed that 'in the private theological class of doctor Arminius...we were utterly drawn away from Calvin, Beza, Zanchi, Martyr, Ursinus, Piscator, Perkins, and other learned and valuable theologians...and commanded to examine only Holy scripture and...Socinus, Acontius, Castellio, Thomas Aquinas, Molina, Suarez and other enemies of grace.'[62] As against this, Arminius himself denied any such thing:

> The report that I persuade the students to read the books of the Jesuits and Coornhert, I can only describe as a falsehood. None of them have interrogated me on this point, and I never of my own accord uttered a word on the subject. But after the Holy Scriptures, (which I encourage them to read more than anything else)...I exhort them to read the commentaries of Calvin.... I tell them that he is incomparable in the interpretation of Scripture, and his commentaries, more valuable than anything in the writings of the Fathers, so that in a certain spirit of prophecy he stands distinguished above all. His *Institutes*, so far as commonplaces [*loci communes*] are concerned, should be read after the Catechism as a more extended explanation. But here I add, with discrimination, as the writings of all men should be read.[63]

Whom should we believe? In support of Sibelius one may say that Gomarus (hardly a dispassionate witness!) had the same suspicions and voiced them in his appearance before the States of Holland and West

---

62 Quoted in C. Sepp, *Het Godgeleerd Onderwijs in Nederland gedurende de 16e en 17e Eeuw* ([2 vols in 1] Leiden, 1873-74), I, 118, as quoted in Muller, *God*, pp.27-8.
63 *Ep.Ecc.* 101, p.185; translated in *Works*, I, pp.295-6; Bangs, *Arminius*, p.287ff.

Friesland on 12 December 1608.⁶⁴ On the other hand, Sibelius was a theological opponent anyway, and would do himself no harm by a posthumous condemnation of someone the Synod of Dort had already condemned for heresy. What are interesting are Arminius' comments on Calvin in a private letter where there was no need to dissemble. He regards Calvin as the great commentator on Scripture. He also finds him useful as a systematic theologian, as the *Institutes* fill out the teaching of the *Catechism* in greater detail. But he is notably less enthusiastic about the *Institutes* than about the commentaries. He was not the last critic to make such a judgment. Undoubtedly Arminius, whether consciously or not, was exaggerating his admiration for Calvin at this point, for he had accepted Gomarus' claim that his (Gomarus') doctrine of predestination was that of Calvin:

> How well Calvin and Beza, those most excellent organs of God in His Church, treated the doctrine of predestination, we have partly seen in these annotations of ours; in which we have also examined their doctrine, which has here [i.e. by Gomarus] been propounded.⁶⁵

Arminius' examination and annotations are hardly those of an admirer!

Early in 1608, Arminius' opponent Lubbertus had written to Paraeus at the University of Heidelberg in the Palatinate making accusations against Arminius. The accusations were passed on to Hippolytus à Collibus, Palatine ambassador at The Hague, who, as a neutral but interested layman, invited Arminius to visit him and explain his position. From Arminius' later letter it appears that à Collibus was pleased with his answers and asked for a written statement, both for his own instruction and to explain and defend Arminius' views against the accusations. This was supplied by Arminius in a letter of 5 April 1608. The Ambassador had not supplied a list of the articles of doctrine which he wished to be expounded, and Arminius had to work from memory. It is noteworthy that predestination was not the first but the third of the five articles discussed, and that the first was the divinity of the Son of God (including the Trinity), which Arminius discussed at much greater length than any other; it was also the only one for which he quoted passages from other theologians—the Fathers Basil, Gregory Nazianzen, Ambrose, Augustine and Hilary. The important point is that Arminius approaches the question from God the Father's working through the other persons of the Trinity:

> My pupil...took the groundwork of his calumny from those things which I had publicly taught concerning the economy of our salvation as administered by the

---

64 See Muller, *God*, p.28; Bangs, *Arminius*, pp.319-20, for somewhat different interpretations of this.
65 *Examination of Gomarus, Consideration of the Corollary*; *Works*, III, p.656.

Father through the Son and the Holy Spirit.... I had said 'that we must have a diligent regard to the order which the Scriptures in every part most religiously observe, and...consider what things are considered as peculiar to [each person] in this matter.'[66]

On the question of God's providence, he refers to his two public disputations on the subject and expresses surprise that he is suspected of 'corrupt opinions', but guesses that this is because he had denied that Adam necessarily sinned. For the subject of predestination, he refers again to his public disputation 'in which no one found anything...false or unsound' — true enough *at the time*, but he is silent about Gomarus' reply. He grants that some thought that these *Theses* 'did not contain everything belonging to this decree', which was true, but he deliberately confined himself to Paul's doctrine in Romans 8 and 9 and Ephesians 1, the foundation of Christianity and of our salvation and assurance. He denies that these passages are about the predestination to salvation of particular persons; and says that there are many different views among Reformed divines about that. He describes creabilitarian, supralapsarian and infralapsarian views of both election and reprobation, but cannot with a safe conscience accept any of them, and is prepared to give a reason for this at the right time and place.[67]

Grace he interprets as the grace of Christ which belongs to regeneration, and he most approves of the teacher who ascribes as much as possible to it, so long as he does so without injuring God's justice and not taking away *the free will to do evil* (Arminius' italics).[68] That is, he rejects irresistible grace.

Finally, on justification he believes that faith and faith only is imputed for righteousness, that is, by faith alone we are justified before God, absolved from sin and accounted, pronounced and declared *righteous* by God from his throne of grace. While there is no faith alone without works, works play no part in justification. He refuses to go into questions of Christ's active and passive righteousness, or the righteousness of Christ's death and Christ's life. He will discuss such subjects, provided no attempt is made to enforce opinions.

The problem is that some charge him with saying that the act of faith, believing itself, is imputed for righteousness. He does so, and claims that Paul in Romans 4 did so before him. But those who charge him argue that if that is so, Christ and his righteousness are excluded from our justification, which is thus attributed to the worthiness of our faith. This he rejects, because the word 'impute' means that faith is not righteousness itself, but is graciously accounted by God for righteousness,

---

66 *Ep.Ecc.* 114, translated in *Works*, II, p.691.
67 *Ep.Ecc.* 114; *Works*, II, pp.698ff.
68 *Ep.Ecc.* 114; *Works*, II, pp.700-01.

and only with reference to Christ, in him, and on account of Christ whom God appointed as a propitiation through faith in his blood. Thus faith is imputed to us for righteousness on account of Christ and his righteousness. To say that God imputes Christ and his righteousness to us *for righteousness* is wrong, because it implies that Christ's obedience is not itself righteousness, which, in the most strict sense, it is.[69] This letter, then, summarises Arminius' late views on controversial subjects in a dispassionate way, free from the pressure of controversy, and so it acts as a useful foil to the *Declaration of Sentiments*.

The *31 Defamatory Theological Articles* are attributed by all critics to Lubbertus.[70] They were answered by Arminius, but as his friends persuaded him not to publish the reply (which appeared in the *Opera* after his death) the answers did not contribute to the ongoing controversy. Where they contribute significantly to an understanding of Arminius' own position, they have been noted in this study. The articles themselves show what Arminius was being accused of in the months before the *Declaration of Sentiments*:

> I-IV and XXVII-XXVIII are concerned with faith;
> V-VII with necessity and contingency;
> VIII with the grace sufficient for faith;
> IX with Christ's satisfaction for punishments;
> X-XI with Old Testament believers;
> XII with the scope of Christ's death;
> XIII-XIV with original sin;
> XV-XVII with the works of the heathen and unregenerate;
> XVIII with the conversion of those who do not hear the gospel;
> XIX with Adam's power to believe;
> XX with angels;
> XXI with the *autotheos* issue;
> XXII with God's freedom;
> XXIII with providence;
> XXIV-XXVI with justification;
> XXIX with perfection;
> XXX with semi-Pelagianism
> XXXI with the nature of original sin.

This is a ragbag of assorted accusations. Some of them seem to have been included simply on suspicion, to test Arminius' views, and he vehemently

---

69 *Ep.Ecc.* 114; *Works*, II, pp.701-02.

70 Nichols, *Works*, I, p.733, 'that practised and vile slanderer'; J.H. Maronier, *Jacobus Arminius* (Amsterdam: Y. Rogge, 1905), pp.248-9; Bangs, *Arminius*, p.300; Dekker, *Rijker dan Midas*, p.47 n.158. This shows that Plancius and Gomarus were not Arminius' only opponents who attacked him in print.

denies some and finds all carelessly expressed and in need of more accurate formulation. Some, however, like XII that 'Christ has died for all men and every individual', he would accept and assert in a certain sense. We should look briefly at XXX with its original accusation of 'semi-Pelagianism', because it is an accusation which has been frequently repeated over the years. The term was coined at this period (first appearing in English in 1600) to refer, not to what is now called by the name, what John Cassian and others taught in the fifth century as an alternative to the later doctrine of Augustine (and they regarded themselves as vigorous opponents of Pelagius and would have been highly offended by such an ascription!). The original reference was to the disputes in Spain in the later sixteenth century; Molina and others were called 'semi-Pelagian' by their more extreme Augustinian opponents. Arminius had said that it would be easy, under the pretext of Pelagianism, to condemn opponents, and to charge those who could defend themselves against the accusation of outright Pelagianism with being 'three quarters, four fifths Pelagian and so upwards', and added that something might be called 'semi-Pelagian' which did not depart from Christian truth. A true Catholic neither inflicts injury on grace like the Pelagians, nor on free will like the Manichaeans; Augustine as a true catholic wrote against both. He added that he could accuse his opponents of Stoicism as well as Manichaeanism if he wished, but he preferred everyone to abstain from such odious names.[71] It is possible that, knowing of the use of the term against Molina and others from whom he had learned something, he wished to come to their defence; but certainly he deplored this juvenile habit of theological name-calling.

For two years or more after he delivered his rectoral oration, the initiative seems to have passed to Arminius' opponents, but eventually, around April or May 1608, he and Uitenbogaert decided to take matters into their own hands. Arminius petitioned the States of Holland to institute a legal enquiry into his position. The States of Holland and West Friesland summoned a meeting of the Hoge Raad (High Court) for 30 and 31 May, and summoned Arminius, Gomarus and the delegates from Holland to the Preparatory Convention for the National Synod. This was what Arminius wanted, but Gomarus complained that as a civil court this had no jurisdiction over spiritual matters. Eventually the Court required both Arminius and Gomarus to submit their views in writing. The *Declaration of Sentiments* begins with Arminius' account of this, and follows with an account of various 'conferences' which had been proposed to him from 1605 onwards, and why he had felt obliged to refuse them.[72] Arminius later asked the States of Holland for permission

---

71 *Works*, II, pp.56-7.
72 *Works*, I, pp.581-613.

to submit his views to them in person also, which was granted. However, the Synod of South Holland, meeting in Dordrecht from 14-18 October, tried to forestall this by requiring all ministers to submit their opinions on the *Confession* and *Catechism* to their classis during the next month. This was not what Arminius wanted, and the States of Holland, who were sympathetic to him, reacted on 20 October by inviting him to appear before them on 30 October, giving Arminius ten days only for preparation.[73] This, however, seems to have concentrated his mind wonderfully, and the resulting *Declaration* is the clearest and most concise expression of his opinions.

All the subjects dealt with in it are in Arminius' mind aspects of the work and person of Christ. Apparent exceptions like human free-will and the revision of the *Confession* and *Catechism* are only apparent; human free-will is useless apart from regeneration and renewal by God in Christ through the Holy Spirit, and *Confession* and *Catechism* need to be made more Christocentric. Perseverance and perfection had been brought up in the *Defamatory Articles* that year. Arminius professed himself agnostic about final perseverance, which from his viewpoint was the question not whether a believer could fall from grace, but whether a believer could cease to be a believer.[74] He was also agnostic about whether it was possible for a believer to be free from sin in this life, but was sure that only by the grace of God could it be possible, and quoted Augustine against Pelagius to this effect.[75] Assurance of one's own salvation is possible through the testimony of the Holy Spirit in the believer, his own conscience and the fruits of faith, but can never be as certain as our knowledge that there is a God and that Christ is Saviour of the world.[76] On the divinity of the Son of God, the old arguments are rehearsed, but it is notable how Arminius—who did not mention his (now deceased) colleague Trelcatius the younger to Hippolytus à Collibus, and laid the blame on the unnamed student—now blames Trelcatius above all and indeed says that Gomarus, in his public disputation on the Trinity shortly afterwards, had expressed himself in a way incompatible with Trelcatius' views.[77] Providence is handled in much the same way as in the *Letter to Hippolytus à Collibus*, as is justification, though to the 'noble and potent Lords' present when the *Declaration* was delivered, Arminius passes over the recent controversy involving Piscator and others, and declares his complete support for Calvin's doctrine of justification contained in the

---

73 For a fuller account of the background of the *Declaration*, see Bangs, *Arminius*, pp.296-9, 307; Dekker, *Rijker dan Midas*, pp.49-50; and Hoenderdaal (ed.), *Verklaring van Jacobus Arminius*, pp.15-19.

74 *Works*, I, pp.664-7.

75 *Works*, I, pp.672-91.

76 *Works*, I, pp.667-71.

77 *Works*, I, pp.691-5.

third book of the *Institutes*.⁷⁸ Grace and free-will, which had been treated together in the *Letter to Hippolytus à Collibus*, are now separated. In his primitive condition man had free-will to understand, appreciate, consider, will and perform the true good, but only with the help of divine grace; in his lapsed and sinful state he can do none of these things, but must be regenerated and renewed in all his powers by God in Christ through the Holy Spirit. In the regenerate and renewed state he is delivered from sin and is again capable of thinking, willing and doing good, but again not without the continued aid of divine grace.⁷⁹ Grace is God's free and kindly affection to a sinner, by which he gives his Son as an object of faith, and justifies the sinner for Christ's sake and adopts him for salvation. Without the gifts of the Holy Spirit man cannot think, will or do anything good, and the Holy Spirit continues to work in a man thus regenerated. So Arminius 'ascribes to grace THE COMMENCEMENT, CONTINUANCE AND CONSUMMATION OF ALL GOOD' (his emphasis), so that even a regenerate man cannot conceive, will or do any good, or resist temptation, without 'this *prevenient and exciting, following and co-operating grace*' (his italics). What then is his difference with his opponents?

> The whole controversy [is contained in] this question, 'Is the grace of God an irresistible force?'.... I believe, according to the scriptures, that many persons resist the Holy Spirit and reject the grace offered.⁸⁰

Arminius makes it clear on many questions that he is prepared to tolerate different points of view, and hopes to receive the same toleration from his opponents. While he criticises the *autotheos* doctrine of Trelcatius and others quite harshly, his general tone in these sections (II-X) is mild. Yet the *Declaration* as a whole came as a bombshell which surprised his friends, his opponents and probably Arminius himself. Why did it cause such shock? Arminius himself explained in a letter six weeks later to Sebastian Egbertszoon, a magistrate of Amsterdam:

> In my Oration before the States I am said to have used not only the shield but the sword, and that immoderately. The occasion demanded that I use the sword, because I had to give my opinion about dogmas, which I think are guilty of error.... I earnestly condemned the dogma of predestination, in the form in which it is prevalent among us, because conscience dictates that it would be wrong to, even

---

78 *Works*, I, pp.657-8, 695-700.
79 *Works*, I, pp.659-60.
80 *Works*, I, pp.661-4.

orders me not to, keep silence when that dogma is discussed. But I observed moderation; I kept silent about many things that I could have said.[81]

He had to speak, because what he saw as truth about God, God's Son, God's Spirit and God's people took precedence for him over all considerations of ease or convenience. Not all readers will agree about his moderation (*moderationem*), any more than his hearers did in their comments about his using the sword (*gladio*). He had expressed himself as strongly in the *Examination of Gomarus's Theses*, but these were not published till much later and their contents were not generally known. Predestination was the first theological subject he spoke about, and almost half of the whole *Declaration* is taken up with it; the other articles that we have already considered are described as 'closely related to the doctrine of Predestination and in great measure dependent on it'.[82] Even more important than the sheer quantity, is the order he adopts. For most of the other articles, except for the divinity of the Son and justification, he gives his own opinion first, then sometimes considers an alternative opinion. In the case of predestination he considers no less than three other opinions (briefly mentioned in the *Letter to Hippolytus à Collibus*) before giving his own, and the first opinion in particular is given in great detail and fiercely criticised at even greater length. It is described as 'the very highest ground of predestination' and we may call it supralapsarianism in an explicitly creabilitarian form. Its first thesis is given thus:

> God by an eternal and immutable decree has predestinated, from among men [whom He did not consider as being then *created*, much less as *fallen*], certain individuals to everlasting life, and others to eternal destruction, without any regard whatever to righteousness or sin, to obedience or disobedience, but purely of His own good pleasure, to demonstrate the glory of His goodness and mercy, or (as others put it) to demonstrate His saving grace, wisdom, and free uncontrollable power.[83]

This is a reworking of Gomarus's *Theses* from *Thesis* VII onwards, which is here quoted: 'of His own right and good-pleasure...to the glory of His saving grace, wisdom, and most free power'. 'Not considered as created, much less as fallen' represents Gomarus' 'indefinitely foreknown'. The next three of Arminius' theses are concerned with the means common to the decree of election and that of rejection, of which the first is creation in original righteousness, since if men were not created they could not be subjects of either election or reprobation, and if they were not created in righteousness God would be the author of sin and would have no right to

---

81 *Ep.Ecc.* 123, 10 December 1608, p.218; partly quoted in the original in Hoenderdaal (ed.), *Verklaring van Jacobus Arminius*, p.19 n.28, translated by Nichols, *Works*, I, p.580 .
82 *Works*, I, p.657.
83 *Thesis* I; *Works*, I, p.614.

punish them, or to save them to the praise of his justice or mercy. The second is the permission of Adam's fall, or rather God's ordination that man should sin. The third is the loss of original righteousness and subjection to sin in the Fall. Again, all these elements can be found in Gomarus' *Theses*.[84]

Arminius then turns to the means for this decree of election; the pre-ordination of Jesus Christ as a Mediator and Saviour, who might by his merit purchase for all the elect and for them only, the lost righteousness and life, and communicate them by his own power; the effectual call through word and Spirit such that the elect person necessarily assents to it, and is justified and sanctified through the Spirit of Christ and his blood; and the preservation of the elect in faith, holiness and good works, so that they cannot sin 'with a full and entire will', or fall away completely from grace. Elect children who die young are saved only by the first of these means, without faith or perseverance, according to the covenant of grace.[85]

The means of the decree of rejection is desertion in sin, by denying them the necessary saving grace, because God is not willing that Christ should die for the reprobate or be their Saviour, and the price of his death was not offered for them (limited atonement). Nor is God willing to communicate the equally necessary Spirit of Christ to reprobates. In the case of reprobates who reach years of maturity, additional means are the illumination of their conscience to recognise the righteousness of the law, and their continuance in sin notwithstanding; and their rejection of the grace of the gospel by an ineffectual call, which they either cannot and do not wish to obey, or they believe it only with the faith of devils, or they taste the heavenly gift in certain measure, but necessarily return to their vomit and fall away from the faith.[86]

The result of all this is that the elect are necessarily saved and the reprobate necessarily damned, and all from the absolute determination of God. Those who hold these opinions regard them as the foundation of Christianity, salvation, and the certainty of salvation; the foundation of the consolation of all believers and of the tranquillity of their conscience; and the praise of God's grace. Any deviation from this robs God of the glory of his grace and attributes the merit of salvation to man's own power and strength, and that is Pelagianism. That is why those who hold such opinions are so concerned about their purity.[87]

This account is arguably more Christocentric than Gomarus' original *Theses*; it certainly introduces Christ at an earlier point, and as the first of the specific means for the salvation of the elect, not a 'subordinate cause'

---

84 *Theses* II–IV; *Works*, I, pp.614f.
85 *Theses* V-VI; *Works*, I, p.615.
86 *Theses* VII-VIII; *Works*, I, pp.616f.
87 *Thesis* IX; *Works*, I, p.617.

as Gomarus would have him. Yet Arminius proceeds to launch a fierce and sustained attack upon it in twenty heads, which must be carefully examined.

The starting-point is important. This doctrine is not the foundation of Christianity, which is the decree of God to appoint Christ as Saviour, Head and Foundation of those who will be made heirs of salvation, and through faith to insert them into him as lively stones built up into Christ, the only Cornerstone, as the members of the body are joined to their head. Nor is it the foundation of salvation, which is the decree of the good-pleasure of God in Christ Jesus on which alone our salvation depends. It is not 'the power of God to salvation to everyone that believes', for through it God's righteousness is not revealed from faith to faith. (Romans 1:16-17) That is, Arminius accuses supralapsarianism of being an alternative doctrine of salvation to the work of God through Christ, and he does this before saying anything about how the heirs of salvation come to faith. That comes when he turns to the certainty of salvation, which for him is not based on God's irresistible grace, but on the decree 'They who believe, shall be saved'.[88]

Not only is this doctrine not the whole of the gospel; it is no part of it. In the New Testament the gospel consists partly of a command to repent and believe, partly of a promise to grant forgiveness of sins, the Spirit of grace, and eternal life. This predestination belongs to neither, and here Arminius quotes Gomarus' admission in his *Thesis* XI that the gospel cannot be called the revelation and book of predestination absolutely, but only relatively, because it does not say how many or which particular persons (with a few exceptions) God predestinates, but only in general the kind of persons; an admission which, when repeated in *Thesis* XXXII, Arminius seized upon in his *Examination*.[89]

In his objections III-VI, Arminius objects that this doctrine of predestination was not approved in any council for the first 600 years after Christ, even those held against Pelagius and his errors, nor by any doctors or divines of the Church, not even Augustine. Nor was it included in the *Harmony of (Reformed) Confessions* published at Geneva (by Salnar in 1577), or with any one of them. He also challenges whether it is to be found in the *Belgic Confession*, which says in its Article 14 that man first sinned by listening to the devil's persuasion, not by necessity imposed by a preceding decree of predestination; or in the *Heidelberg Catechism*, which in its answers to Questions 20 and 54 says that only those are saved who are 'ingrafted into Christ by true faith' in 'a

---

[88] *Declaration* I.3.I.1-3; *Works*, I, p.618f.
[89] *Declaration* I.3:II; *Works*, I, pp.619f.

company chosen to eternal life and agreeing together in the true faith', but says nothing about whether election or faith comes first.[90]

He now returns to more directly theological matters. We see here that Muller is correct that Arminius' view of God's nature does strongly influence his work as a whole. But the supralapsarian doctrine is repugnant to God's nature, particularly to his wisdom, justice and goodness. It represents him as decreeing something (sin and damnation) which is not, and cannot be, good. It represents God as absolutely willing the salvation of certain men without the least regard to righteousness or obedience; therefore God loves such men more than his own justice; others he wills to subject to misery, which is also opposed to his justice. In fact, God's goodness wishes to communicate itself in accordance with his justice. Supralapsarianism, on the other hand, claims that of himself, without external pressure, God wills the greatest evil to his creatures, and that from all eternity he preordained that evil for them before he resolved to give them any portion of good. He willed to damn, and willed to create so that he might damn. God is simply not like that; this is contrary to the expansive goodness of God of which Jesus spoke in Matthew 5:45, by which he confers benefits not only on the unworthy, but on the evil, the unjust, and those who deserve punishment.[91]

It is also repugnant to the nature of man as God created him, in God's image, in the knowledge of God and righteousness, but notwithstanding this, this predestination makes God decree that man should become impure, unrighteous, and conformed to the image of Satan. It is inconsistent with the freedom of the will in which God created man, and the desire for and capacity for enjoying eternal salvation, with which God also created him. In fact, it is 'diametrically opposed to the act of creation'. Creation is a communication of good (here Arminius' Thomism again shows through clearly.) But the intention of such creation is not to communicate good in the case of the reprobates, but to condemn them to eternal perdition. This would be a preparation of the greatest evil according to the Creator's intention, the actual result, and to Christ's words in Matthew 26:24, 'It would have been better for that man never to have been born'. Reprobation is an act of hatred. Creation does not proceed from hatred, so is not a means to execute the decree of reprobation; in fact it is a perfect act of God, so is not subordinate to any other (whereas the Reformed make creation the stage on which God performs the action of salvation).[92]

This predestination is also opposed to the nature of eternal life, eternal death and sin. Eternal life is the inheritance of God's children (Titus 3:7),

---

90 *Declaration* I.3:III-VI; *Works*, I, pp.620-623.
91 *Declaration* I.3:VII; *Works*, I, pp.623ff.
92 *Declaration* I.3:VIII-IX; *Works*, I, pp.625ff.

but God gives to those who believe in Christ, adoption as children. It is the reward of obedience (Matthew 5:12), and of the labour of love (Hebrews 6:10), the crown of righteousness for those who fight the good fight and run well, (2 Timothy 4:7f; Revelation 2:10). Eternal death is the wages of sin (Romans 6:23), everlasting destruction for those who do not know God or obey the gospel (2 Thessalonians 1:8-9), everlasting fire prepared for the devil and his angels (Matthew 25:41), which shall devour God's enemies (Hebrews 10:27). The absolute decree ignores all this. Sin is disobedience and rebellion, the meritorious cause of damnation, inducing God, who abhors it, to will reprobation; as the cause of reprobation it cannot also be the means of executing it.[93]

In objection XIII Arminius challenges the 'specious pretence' that supralapsarianism is 'most admirably adapted and quite necessary for the establishment of divine grace'. On the contrary, as far as it can it destroys grace. Grace does not destroy free-will but corrects it, gives it a right direction and allows man freedom to be himself; this predestination takes all that away. According to Scripture grace is resistible (Acts 7:51) and may be received in vain (2 Corinthians 6:1); Jerusalem rejected it according to Jesus (Matthew 23:37), as did the Pharisees and lawyers in rejecting John's baptism (Luke 7:30). The warning of Hebrews 12:15 shows that the apostles believed that grace is resistible. God wants grace to help those to whom it is offered, and who receive it. So far from helping the reprobates, this doctrine of supralapsarianism makes their fall into the abyss heavier and their perdition greater.[94]

He now turns to God's glory, which does not consist in the declaration of liberty or authority, or demonstration of anger or power. This doctrine is so far from giving God glory, as to make him the author of sin. For according to supralapsarianism, God has absolutely decreed to demonstrate his glory by punitive justice and mercy, both of which presuppose sin. In order to attain this object, he ordained that man should sin, and from this the fall of man necessarily followed; God either denied to man or withdrew from him sufficient grace to enable him to avoid sin, and God performed certain 'operations' by forcing man to sin by a form of necessity called in scholastic theology 'consequential necessity antecedent to the thing itself'. This means that God really sins, because he moves man to sin by an unavoidable act, according to his own purpose and primary intention, without being induced to it by any preceding demerit or sin in man. God is the only sinner, for if man is impelled by an irresistible force, he cannot be said to sin himself, and sin is not sin, since whatever God does, it cannot be called sin.[95]

---

93 *Declaration* I.3:X-XII; *Works*, I, p.628.
94 *Declaration* I.3:XIII; *Works*, I, pp.628f.
95 *Declaration* I.3:XIV; *Works*, I, pp.629f.

So we come to the important point that 'this doctrine is highly DISHONOURABLE TO JESUS CHRIST our Saviour' (Arminius' emphasis). For

> 1. It entirely excludes Him from that decree of predestination which predestinates the end; and it affirms, that men were predestinated to be saved, before Christ was predestinated to save them; and thus it argues, that *He is not the foundation of election*.

> 2. It denies that Christ is the meritorious cause of salvation; it places Him as *only a subordinate cause* of a salvation already foreordained, and thus only a minister and instrument to apply that salvation to us.

Here Arminius quotes an opinion 'that God has absolutely willed the salvation of certain men, by His first and supreme decree, on which all His other decrees depend'. If so, that salvation could not have been lost, and Christ's work would have been unnecessary.[96]

The doctrine is also hurtful to the salvation of men. One who sins by unavoidable necessity cannot have consciousness of sin, or saving and godly sorrow for sins (2 Corinthians 7:10); he is entirely passive, like an automaton, and cannot have 'pious solicitude' about turning to God; he can have no concern or zeal for good works; he cannot pray for God's blessings, especially salvation, for which Jesus teaches us to pray in the Lord's Prayer; he has no fear and trembling by which we are commanded to work out our own salvation (Philippians 2:12); and if he knows what has happened to him, he despairs.[97]

In the next section, Arminius explains what he means by 'inverting the order of the Gospel of Jesus Christ'. God requires repentance and faith, and promises everlasting life in return, as in both beginning and end of Mark's Gospel (1:15 and 16:16). Supralapsarianism states that God's absolute will is to bestow salvation on certain individuals and to give them repentance and faith by irresistible force. God warns men in John 3:36 against impenitence and unbelief; supralapsarianism teaches that God has absolutely decreed condemnation for some and wills not to confer the necessary grace. Arminius parodies John 3:16: 'God so loved those whom He had elected to eternal life, that He gave His son to them alone, and by irresistible force produced within them faith in Him' — 'a real and most manifest inversion of the Gospel'.[98]

The concern of a former parish minister appears in the following objection, that 'this predestination is in open hostility to the ministry of the Gospel'. If God works by irresistible power, no man can be his

---

96 *Declaration* I.3:XV; *Works*, I, pp.630f.
97 *Declaration* I.3:XVI; *Works*, I, pp.631f.
98 *Declaration* I.3:XVII; *Works*, I, pp.632f.

fellow-worker (1 Corinthians 3:9); the ministry is made the savour of death unto death for most hearers (2 Corinthians 3:14ff); the baptism of reprobate children of believing parents seals and ratifies nothing; and public prayers cannot be offered with faith, whereas when Paul commands prayers and supplications to be made for all men, it is because God will have *all men* to be saved and to come to knowledge of the truth.[99]

The next objection is the longest so far, and is concerned with love. God's love is twofold: for righteousness and justice, necessitating hatred of sin; and for the rational creature, especially one who seeks (Hebrews 11:6). The latter is dependent on the former, but God wills to allow as abundant scope for love for his creatures as his love of righteousness will permit. But the doctrine that God wills absolutely to save certain individuals puts his love for them before his love of righteousness, whereas the doctrine that he wills absolutely to damn others detracts from his love for the creature without any necessity derived from his love of righteousness. One who thinks that 'My Father's love for me is so great that He is absolutely resolved to make me His heir, so I do not need to strive after obedience' is like the Pharisees and Sadducees who thought they were all right because Abraham was their ancestor—till they met John the Baptist. All this is concerned with religion in general. Christian faith takes into account the Fall. God's love of righteousness is declared in Christ, that sin should only be expiated by his blood and death, and that Christ should not be admitted as Advocate and Intercessor except when sprinkled with his own blood. God's love of creatures (now miserable sinners) is the love by which he gave his Son to them as Saviour. But supralapsarianism states that God has such love for certain sinners, that he willed absolutely to save them before he had satisfied his love of righteousness through Christ, making his love for justice, manifested in Christ, subordinate to his love for the elect. It also states that he has such hatred for others, that he willed absolutely to damn them, before complete satisfaction had been made in Christ Jesus. The 'two fiery darts of Satan' are security, in the bad sense that a man persuades himself that however much he neglects God he will be saved; and despair, that whatever reverence he shows towards God he will receive no reward. But if a man believes that God will inflict eternal death on those who do not seek him, he cannot indulge in security. If he believes that God will reward those who do seek him, he cannot despair. God's great love for man cannot prevent him from saving man, unless it is hindered by his still greater love for righteousness and justice.[100]

---

[99] *Declaration* I.3:XVIII; *Works*, I, pp.633f.
[100] *Declaration* I.3:XIX; *Works*, I, pp.634-638.

Finally, most Christians, even in Arminius' day, reject this doctrine: Lutherans, Anabaptists, Roman Catholics; Luther and Melanchthon themselves, who approved of it at the very beginning of the Reformation, but afterwards deserted it; Niels Hemmingsen in Denmark in his treatise on *Universal Grace* (1591); and the Dutch Churches:

> Of all the difficulties and controversies which have arisen in these churches since the Reformation, there is none that has not had its origin in this doctrine, or that has not at least been mixed with it.

Arminius gives examples, which are discussed by Bangs.[101] He also quotes from Melanchthon's letter to Caspar Peucer, written in Calvin's time, in which what Melanchthon calls 'stoical fate' was pressed at Geneva with 'such uncommon fervour' that someone had been imprisoned for rejecting it—which Melanchthon deplores. This final objection is, however, a weak feature. Hemmingsen by no means spoke for 'all the Danish churches'; some Roman Catholics like the opponents of Molina, held an Augustinian doctrine of predestination not too far removed from Reformed supralapsarianism; Melanchthon certainly abandoned his Augustinian beliefs on predestination fairly soon after becoming a Protestant, but Luther had produced *On the Bondage of the Will* from which Arminius extracted what he called the 'false assertion' that as by the light of nature we do not understand by what right God saves unworthy and sinful men, but do understand it by the light of grace; so by the light of grace we still do not understand by what right God can condemn an innocent person who has not merited damnation (absolute unconditional reprobation), but shall understand it by the light of glory.[102] Luther certainly put less emphasis on predestination than his Reformed successors, but as late as 1537 he could write to Capito that only the *Children's Catechism* and the *On the Bondage of the Will* were quite 'right' and worthy of preservation,[103] and he is not recorded as taking back this opinion.

Nevertheless, Arminius makes his objection to the supralapsarianism of Gomarus and others quite clear. It has little to do with the fact that, for Gomarus, faith follows election instead of the reverse order; it has everything to do with its unacceptable view of the nature of God, and of his dealings with man through Christ, and with the dishonour done to Christ by the subordinate role it gives him.

---

101 Bangs, *Arminius*, pp.311f.
102 *Articuli Nonnulli* VII:4; Works II p.713.
103 *W.A.Br.* 8.3162, p.99, as quoted in J.I. Packer and O.R. Johnston's translation of *De Servo Arbitro*, 1525, *Martin Luther's Reply to Erasmus of Rotterdam* in *Luther's Bondage of the Will* (London: James Clarke, 1957), Introduction, p.40.

Arminius then turns to two other doctrines of predestination. The first Bangs, following Nichols, calls a modified supralapsarianism, while Dekker finds that it resembles the position of Junius and the 'Thomists', as Arminius had analysed it in the *Collation*.[104] However, Arminius himself tells us whom chiefly he had in mind. His second paragraph runs,

> These persons use the word 'Predestination' in its special sense of *election*, and oppose it to *reprobation*. (1) In respect to its *end*, (salvation, and an illustration of the glorious grace of God), man is considered in common and absolutely, such as he is *in his own nature*. (2) But in respect to *the means*, man is considered as perishing from himself and in himself, and as guilty in Adam.[105]

This is a close quotation from a passage also quoted in the *Articuli Nonnulli* from the *Institutes* of Trelcatius, the late professor at Leiden. The sources used by Arminius sometimes lie closer to his immediate situation than later critics like Bangs and Dekker have recognised; Arminius thought of the doctrines he here criticised not, with Bangs, as varieties of supralapsarianism, nor, with Dekker, in the way he had once described them to Junius, but as Gomarus' doctrine and Trelcatius' doctrine. The difference between the full supralapsarian position and this first alternative is not primarily concerned with the elect; they are predestinated and saved in much the same way. The difference is in the reprobate: whereas in Gomarus' doctrine the reprobate are foreordained to perdition, and denied the necessary and sufficient grace by God's decree, in the first alternative they are passed by, left in their own nature which is incapable of anything supernatural; the saving and supernatural grace is simply not communicated to them. Thus God demonstrates his freedom; he is not obliged to do it and does not do it. Arminius finds Trelcatius' doctrine of reprobation difficult; Trelcatius speaks of two reprobations, one negative and passive, the other affirmative or active, and calls the first preterition and the second predamnation, the latter taking account of sin.[106]

In the second alternative doctrine of predestination, God willed within himself from all eternity (that is, it was not an afterthought after the Fall), to make a decree to elect certain men and reprobate the rest. So he viewed the human race not only as created but as fallen and corrupt, therefore deserving of damnation. As a God of grace and mercy, and also of justice, he wished to demonstrate both, and so determined to make some

---

104 Bangs, *Arminius*, p.312; cf. Nichols, *Works*, I, p.645 note; Dekker, *Rijker dan Midas*, pp.224ff.
105 *Declaration* I:2.2; *Works*, I, p.645; cf. *Articuli Nonnulli* XIII:1; *Works*, II, p.717, quoted from Trelcatius, *Institutes*, lib.2 *On Predestination*.
106 *Declaration* I:2.3-8, *A Second Kind of Predestination*; *Works*, I, pp.645-6; cf. *Articuli Nonnulli* section XIII; *Works*, II, pp.717-8.

sinners an example of his mercy, and others an example of his justice. There is no consideration of repentance and faith in the one case, or of impenitence and unbelief in the other. The difference is in the means; whereas the fall of man in supralapsarianism is a means foreordained for the execution of the decree of predestination, in this scheme it is the occasion for making it. Arminius gives no clue to the author of this scheme, but Dekker argues with justification that this is like the view which Arminius attributed in the *Collation* to Augustine and his followers, and at that time had regarded as the best position.[107] If so, it shows that a decade later, Arminius had changed his mind and now radically rejected all variants of Augustinianism.

Why have these alternatives tried to modify the supralapsarian position? Arminius considers that they are seeking to avoid any suggestion that God is the author of sin. But Adam's fall cannot, according to their views, be considered as other than a necessary means for the execution of the decree of predestination. In the first alternative man's transgression necessarily follows from God's decree not to bestow the necessary grace, and from the division of reprobation into preterition and predamnation; otherwise someone who had been passed by might not commit sin and so be left in a kind of limbo, neither saved nor damned—'a great absurdity'. At least supralapsarianism is consistent! The other alternative Arminius had been requested to refute nearly two decades earlier in the form of Corneliszoon and Donteklok's doctrine, and it is still put forward, for example by Jewett, as a morally more acceptable alternative to supralapsarianism. But infralapsarians speak of 'divine permission' (to sin), which leads to committing sin through necessity, and say that God's glory must be illustrated in the demonstration of mercy and punitive justice, neither of which have any place unless sin is in the world, so sin again is necessarily introduced, and the fall and creation are necessary for the execution of the decree of predestination. And all other arguments against the first doctrine are, after trifling modification, equally valid against the two latter.[108]

Arminius then proceeds to his own doctrine, which Bangs describes as a 'surprisingly brief affirmation'.[109] The likely reason is that it was prepared before the request on 20 October to deliver a statement, and that the original version is that in the *Articuli Nonnulli* Section 15, *On the Decrees of God which concern the Salvation of Sinful Men, according to his (God's) own sense*. Arminius translated this into Dutch to deliver the *Declaration*. He changed some expressions and made a few additions—for example, the first decree becomes 'absolute', and the

---

107 *Declaration* I:3:1-2, *A Third Kind of Predestination*, pp.646-7; cf. Dekker, *Rijker dan Midas*, pp.187, 223; and *Collation with Junius*; *Works*, III, pp.18, 234-5.
108 *Declaration* I.4; *Works*, I, pp.647-53.
109 Bangs, *Arminius*, p.312.

second 'precise and absolute', and Christ in the first decree is called 'King' in addition to his other titles, but there is no significant doctrinal difference. All four decrees (Articles I-IV of *Articuli Nonnulli* Section 15) and the substance of Articles VI and VII reappear in the *Declaration* as delivered, only Article V being omitted. The Dutch was translated back into Latin, not by Arminius, and this second Latin version is found in the *Opera*'s version of the *Declaration* and later translations made from it.[110] The decrees read:

> The FIRST absolute decree of God concerning the salvation of sinful man, is that by which He decreed to appoint His Son Jesus Christ for a Mediator, Redeemer, Saviour, Priest and King, who might destroy sin by His own death, might by His obedience obtain the salvation which had been lost, and might communicate it by His own virtue.

This is the most Christocentric statement of predestination that Arminius ever made, and it includes a beautifully concise summary of Christ's work. It would be difficult for any Christian to challenge this except possibly on the grounds that Christ himself also shared in the decreeing, which this neither excludes nor states; or on the other hand, on the grounds that it made Christ too central! But the second decree is more controversial. God decreed:

> to receive into favour *those who repent and believe*, and in Christ, for HIS sake and through HIM, to effect the salvation of such penitents and believers who persevere to the end; but to leave in sin and under wrath *all impenitent persons and unbelievers*, and to damn them as aliens from Christ.

Naturally Dekker finds *eigenschappen-predestinatie* here in the italicised phrases, but we need to see this in the light of the third divine decree, to administer in *a sufficient and efficacious manner* the *means* necessary to repentance and faith. The sinner does not repent and believe in his own strength; God makes him able to do it, but does not compel him to do so. Faith and repentance are not qualities but gifts; gifts which can, however, be rejected. The third decree runs in full:

---

110 Bangs, *Arminius*, p.307. The main evidence is that both the version in the *Articuli Nonnulli*, and the Dutch version as delivered, put the decrees in the indicative, but the version of the *Declaration* in the *Opera* puts them in the accusative and infinitive; thus the opening of the second decree runs, in *Articuli Nonnulli* (*Opera*, p.957): 'Secundum decretum est, quo...'; in the Dutch (Hoenderdaal [ed.], *Verklaring van Jacobus Arminius*, p.104): 'Het tweede precijs ende absoluyt decreet Gods is, dat...'; in the version of the *Declaration* in *Opera*, p.119: 'Secundum praecisum et absolutum Dei decretum esse, quo...'.

The THIRD Divine decree is that by which God decreed to administer *in a sufficient and efficacious manner* the MEANS...necessary for repentance and faith; and to have such administration instituted (1) according to the *Divine Wisdom*, by which God knows what is proper and becoming both to his mercy and his severity, and (2) according to *Divine Justice*, by which He is prepared to adopt whatever his wisdom may prescribe and to put it into execution.

So far predestination only affects groups of people, not particular persons. There is, therefore, need for a fourth decree, by which God decreed to save and damn particular persons:

This decree is founded in the foreknowledge of God, by which He knew from all eternity those individuals who would, through His preventing grace, believe, and, through His subsequent grace, persevere, according to the previously described administration of those means suitable and proper for conversion and faith; and by which foreknowledge, He likewise knew those who would not repent and persevere.[111]

This causes trouble even for a sympathetic critic like Bangs. 'Now why did Arminius have to say *that*? This is where all the trouble arises, and from every side.'[112] Bangs attempts to defend him in various ways, but the point should be added that faith and perseverance are only possible through the prevenient and subsequent grace of God, which however does not act irresistibly; and the reason it does not do so is that God is dealing with persons made in His own image. God is not like the celebrity asked in an interview, 'In the event of a natural disaster [e.g. fire or flood] what one *thing* would you rescue from your home?' In the actual occurrence of the disaster of the Fall into sin, God determines to rescue the persons he has made, but it is not just a case of transferring them like inanimate objects from a place of danger to a place of safety (which is how his opponents visualised salvation), but the restoration, in a better form, of the relationship with God lost at the Fall. And the relationship must be present in the actual process of salvation; the idea that someone could be saved by irresistible grace and then a relationship could be built afterwards on such a basis made no sense to Arminius.

It remains to consider the origins of this doctrine, and its links with contemporaries of Arminius. We may turn first to Aquinas, whose influence on Arminius is clear and who was aware of different approaches to the doctrine of predestination. In the *Summa*, section 1 on God and Question 23, *On Predestination*, he quotes from John of Damascus to the

---

111 *Declaration* I.5; *Works*, I, pp.653-4.
112 Bangs, *Arminius*, p.352. Bangs' difficulty is surprising; Arminius had said much the same many times before, if not in these precise terms. Neither he nor his opponents would have been satisfied with a statement which did *not* include the predestination of individuals.

effect that 'God foreknows everything, but does not predetermine everything', and among the things which he does not predetermine are human merits and demerits, 'and so the predestination of men disappears'.[113] Aquinas makes it clear that he disagrees. His next article poses the question, 'Does predestination suppose something in the predestinated?' Here he quotes from Origen on Romans 1:4 about the one who is predestinated, and understands him to mean that predestination, as distinct from simple destination, is of what is not, whereas Augustine says, 'What is predestination but the destination of someone?'[114] It may be doubted whether Aquinas understood Origen well, for in answer to the question in Article 5, 'Is the foreknowledge of (human) merits the cause of predestination?', he suggests that Origen believed that the effect of the predestination of an individual was preordained by God because of merits gained in another (presumably previous) life, an opinion which as he says, Paul specifically excludes in Romans 9:11ff.[115] However, he was aware that Origen held different opinions from Augustine on the subject.

Origen's actual doctrine is found in at least one passage of his predecessor Clement of Alexandria, and might therefore better be called the Alexandrian doctrine. It was developed against the background of Gnosticism, which, contrary to a widespread impression, had no doctrine of predestination strictly speaking, but instead had a fatalistic doctrine of different types of human beings, the spiritual who were bound for salvation, the earthy who had no hope of it, and (in some cases) an intermediate group who might go either way. As against this, more or less 'orthodox' Christians like Clement and Origen developed a doctrine to explain why some men were saved and others not, on the basis of the New Testament teaching of predestination. But like the Apostolic Fathers and the other Apologists, they were also under the influence of Greek ideas of free-will, which they considered the Bible also taught, so they reconciled this with predestination by interpreting God's foreknowledge in Romans 8:28 and other texts as a foreknowledge of how men would use their free-will. Thus Clement says:

> The ancient and Catholic Church...gathers together, by the will of one God through the one Lord...all those who are already enlisted in it, whom God foreordained, having known before the foundation of the world that they would be righteous.[116]

---

113 Aquinas, *Summa* Theologica, Book 1, Question 23, Article 1.
114 Aquinas, *Summa Theologica*, Book 1, Question 23, Article 2:2.
115 Aquinas, *Summa Theologica*, Question 23, Article 5, Conclusion.
116 *Miscellanies (Stromateis)*, Book 7, c.XVII, paragraph 107, in *Alexandrian Christianity* (Library of Christian Classics; trans. J.B. Mayor; rev. and ed. J.E.L. Oulton and Henry Chadwick; Philadelphia, PA: Westminster Press, 1954), p.163.

In one of many examples, mostly taken from his commentaries, Origen says,

> Such passages as [Romans 1:1 and Galatians 1:15] are seized on by those who do not understand that the man foreordained by the foreknowledge of God is really responsible for the happening of what is foreknown; and they imagine [on the basis of Romans 8:28ff] that God introduces men into the world who are already equipped by nature for salvation.... Let us observe the order of the words [in Romans 8].... It is not foreordination that is the start of calling and justification.... In fact foreknowledge precedes foreordination.... God observed beforehand future events, and noticed the inclination of some men towards piety, on their own responsibility.... He sees how they devote themselves to living a virtuous life, and He foreknew them.... If anyone asks whether it is possible for the events which God foreknew not to happen, we shall answer Yes, there is no necessity determining.... Romans 8:28 clearly makes us responsible causes of the predestination and foreknowledge of God.[117]

This Alexandrian doctrine of predestination preceded the Augustinian doctrine by a good two centuries and was held by most Christians during that time, including Ambrosiaster, Pelagius, and indeed by Augustine himself for about a decade after his conversion to Christianity, until he started to become dissatisfied with it when writing his answers to the questions of Simplicianus in 396, and eventually developed his own alternative doctrine of predestination.[118] That doctrine, however, was not fully developed till around 418 and was a novelty at the time.[119] Meanwhile, another doctrine of predestination had been hinted at by Athanasius in his *Discourses against the Arians* of about 355,[120] which was based much more on the predestination of Christ himself, and has been taken up by twentieth-century Reformed theologians like Maury and Barth as an alternative to the Calvinist doctrine. But the Alexandrian doctrine continued to be held by many earlier medieval theologians who

---

117 *Philocalia* XXV:I, *Commentary on the Epistle to the Romans* i:1-3, translated by Henry Bettenson, *The Early Christian Fathers* (London: Oxford University Press, 1969 [1956]), pp.195-6.

118 For a fuller account of this see my unpublished MPhil thesis, 'The Doctrine of Predestination from Paul to Augustine, A.D. 62-430' (University of Nottingham, 1982), *passim*, especially chs 7-10, 18-19.

119 It seems possible that if Clement and Origen had known of the later doctrine of Augustine and of the orthodox Reformed (Calvinist) doctrine of the sixteenth and seventeenth centuries, they would have suspected them of (Valentinian?) Gnosticism, because of the absolute and unconditional nature of the doctrines of predestination and reprobation.

120 Athanasius, *Four Discourses against the Arians*, Discourse II, c.22 paragraphs 75f on Proverbs 8:22-30; translated J.H. Newman and revised A. Robertson, *The Nicene and Post-Nicene Fathers*, second series, volume 4 (Grand Rapids, MI: Eerdmans, 1978), p.389.

were unhappy with Augustinianism, like John of Damascus, and remained an alternative till about the thirteenth century, when, in the West, Aquinas' general support for Augustine (with modifications), and the realist-nominalist controversy, sent the Alexandrian doctrine of predestination under a cloud for a time. Arminius' own fourth decree can be seen as a revival of this doctrine, but in a Protestant form which emphasises God's foreknowledge of a man's faith in Christ, rather than of that man's merits, or righteousness. In his first three decrees he is closer to the Christocentric doctrine of Athanasius than to either Augustine or the Alexandrians.

We should also look briefly at the sixteenth-century context of Arminius' doctrine. As early as 20 May 1593 someone in the consistory of Amsterdam objected to Arminius that 'Martinists' (Lutherans) 'as well as Anabaptists and followers of Coornhert, gloried in his discourses on the ninth chapter of Romans',[121] and Arminius continued to be accused of Lutheranism from time to time. When Gomarus appeared before the States of Holland on 12 December 1608 to deliver his counterblast to Arminius' *Declaration*, he claimed that Arminius had borrowed his doctrine of predestination from the 'Ubiquitists'.[122] Not much notice has been taken of these accusations, and Bangs, who records them and others, can claim that Arminius had 'no rootage in Lutheranism'. Certainly on most subjects which divide the two camps, Arminius falls firmly into the Reformed category, and can lambast 'Ubiquitists' as strongly as his Reformed colleagues; and, unlike them, he strongly disapproved of Luther's *On the Bondage of the Will*. But, for better or worse, orthodox Lutheranism had moved away from Luther's views on predestination to some extent, as can be seen from their final confession, the *Formula of Concord*:

> We must always take as one unit the entire doctrine of God's purpose, counsel, will and ordinance concerning our redemption, call, justification and salvation, as Paul treats and explains this article [of election] (Romans 8:28ff, Ephesians 1:4ff)...that in His purpose and counsel God has ordained the following:—
>
> 1. That through Christ the human race has truly been redeemed and reconciled with God, and that by His innocent obedience, suffering and death, Christ has earned for us 'the righteousness which avails before God' and eternal life.
>
> 2. That this merit and these benefits of Christ are to be offered, given and distributed to us through His word and sacraments.

---

121 See Bangs, *Arminius*, p.148.
122 Bangs, *Arminius*, p.319.

3. That He would be effective and active in us by His Holy Spirit through the Word when it is preached, heard and meditated on, would convert hearts to true repentance, and would enlighten them in the true faith.

4. That He would justify and graciously accept into the adoption of children and into the inheritance of eternal life all who in sincere repentance and true faith accept Christ.

5. That He also would sanctify in love all who are thus justified (Ephesians 1:4).

6. That He would protect them in their great weakness against the devil, the world, and the flesh....

7. That He would also strengthen and increase in them the good work begun, and preserve them to the end, if they cling to God's Word, pray diligently, persevere in the grace of God, and use faithfully the gifts they have received.

8. That finally He would eternally save and glorify in eternal life those whom He has elected, called and justified.

In this...God has not only prepared salvation in general, but has also graciously considered and elected to salvation each and every individual among the elect who are to be saved through Christ....[123]

There is no direct verbal dependence of Arminius on this; if Arminius had it in mind when composing the *Declaration*, he must have been deliberately trying to avoid its terminology. But there is the same emphasis of predestination or election as 'one unit' with the other work of God in Christ for us, and on the activity of the Holy Spirit and the word preached; the same emphasis on grace as necessary for conversion and faith, and the hint in 4. that not all who receive this grace will respond positively; the same stress on the sufficiency of grace to preserve the justified, but the condition in 7. that the elect have responsibilities and cannot presume on their security in Calvinist fashion; and the same insistence that election is to be understood both generally, and in respect of particular individuals. There may also be a few differences from Arminius; certainly he used 'predestination' sometimes to include reprobation, as the Lutherans did not; but there was some truth in the suspicion that in this doctrine at least, Arminius was a crypto-Lutheran.

Arminius lived for nearly a year after the delivery of the *Declaration*, but they were twelve months of continuing controversy and increasing ill-health, which gave little opportunity for further development of his

---

[123] *Formula of Concord*, Solid Declaration, Article XI on *Election*, sections 14-23, translated Theodore G. Tappert *et al.*, *The Book of Concord: The Confessions of the Evangelical Lutheran Church* (Philadelphia, PA: Muhlenberg Press, 1959), p.619.

theology. The one work he produced which perhaps adds something to our understanding is his final *Public Disputation* XVI, *On the Vocation of Men to Salvation* (25 July 1609), whose contents have already been considered. Whether he wished it or not, the doctrine of predestination had become for good or ill that for which he would be remembered; perhaps the way in which it dominates his *magnum opus*, the *Declaration of Sentiments*, indicates that he had become reconciled to that. The ultimate reasons for this were his beliefs in the goodness of God to humankind, and the centrality of Christ's work in human salvation.

Do not all Christians believe this? In practice, says Arminius, *No*! He had come to see the Calvinistic (Reformed) doctrine of predestination, for all its long antecedents stretching back to Augustine, as the enemy of what he believed, and therefore to be opposed and refuted. This doctrine had dominated Christian theology, though not without opposition, for over a thousand years, and had apparently survived the crisis of the Reformation, and even emerged from it strengthened. The revelation that it could be opposed so fiercely, and by someone who appeared orthodox on the work of Christ and in many other respects, was the shocking element in the *Declaration of Sentiments*. Arminius came to this point slowly, gradually, reluctantly. But he succeeded in his last great struggle, in that never again could one claim that supralapsarian Calvinism is universally recognised as the Church's creed. His lasting achievement was to provide, from then on, an alternative to the Augustinian doctrine of predestination for Protestants, as Molina and others had done for Roman Catholics. It is something for which the Reformed have never forgiven him.

CHAPTER 6

Epilogue:
How Great the Harvest

> How great the harvest is
> Of him who came to save us!
> The hearts of men are his,
> Our law the love he gave us.
> The world lay cruel, blind,
> Nought holding, nought divining;
> He came to human kind,
> And now the light is shining.[1]

Since Arminius' death, his name, particularly in the forms Arminian/ Arminianism, has been used frequently in contradistinction to Calvin/Calvinism.

Arminius would have been surprised at this. He never wrote against Calvin, and seems to have made it a rule not to attack any deceased theologian. He would only respond directly to contemporaries like Perkins and Gomarus. Even in personal letters his recorded statements about Calvin, though not uncritical, are generally positive.[2] The development in the use of these terms has less to do with Arminius than with the rise and rise of Calvin's reputation in the Reformed Churches. In Arminius' time Calvin was of course regarded as a great Reformed leader, but not exactly as one who towered head and shoulders above all his contemporaries. Shortly before Beza's death in 1605, Gomarus could bracket his name with Calvin's as theologians 'who have deserved very well of the Church and of the truth of predestination against the Pelagians', and as 'illustrious restorers of the Churches'.[3] Reputations have a habit of plummeting after death, but Beza had led both the Church and Academy of Geneva for forty years, far longer than Calvin, and had represented the Reformed Churches in discussions with opponents at, for example, the Colloquy of Montbéliard in 1586. He had had a smoother

---

[1] Dutch seventeenth-century carol, *Hoe groot de Vruechten zijn*, verse 1, translated in *Oxford Book of Carols* (Oxford: Oxford University Press, 1928), no.152, p.307

[2] See *Ep.Ecc.* 101 of 3 May 1607 to Egbertszoon, already quoted, p.141.

[3] *Theses on Predestination* of 31.10.04, *Corollary*; *Works*, III, p.654.

passage than Calvin, and it could be argued that he had been more consistently successful than his master. But later generations of the Reformed tradition have esteemed Calvin more than Beza or anyone else. Some see Calvin as almost if not quite perfect in his beliefs, and would hold others responsible for all that can be fairly criticised in traditional Reformed theology. That view is represented in this study by Kendall. Others have more respect and admiration for Calvin's contemporaries and immediate successors. For example, Muller, in *Christ and the Decree*, considers his contemporaries Bullinger, Wolfgang Musculus, and Vermigli, the slightly later Beza and the Heidelberg theologians, and finally Polanus and Perkins. Yet he virtually ignores Zwingli, Calvin's Reformed predecessor, and begins study of 'Reformed Theology in its First Codification' with Calvin, before passing to the 'systems' (sic) of Calvin's contemporaries.[4]

As we have seen, Arminius esteemed Calvin very highly as a biblical commentator, somewhat less, but still highly, as a systematic theologian, and he was glad in such contexts as the *Declaration of Sentiments* to express agreement with Calvin on subjects like justification. On some subjects where he was conscious of disagreement with Calvin, like the *autotheos* issue, he refrained from public criticism of Calvin and chose rather to criticise his own contemporaries. But there was one subject on which his disagreement with Calvin was profound and far-reaching, predestination, and on this he did not restrain himself. It will no doubt have become clear in the course of this study that, whatever disagreements I myself have with Arminius on other subjects, on the subject of predestination I consider his objections to the opposing doctrines almost entirely correct and his criticisms of them well-deserved. Some contemporaries regarded him as impudent to attack a doctrine which in various forms had over a thousand-year history in the Church since Augustine. But opposition to it had continued for almost as long, from the so-called 'semi-Pelagians' of the fifth century, to the opponents of Gottschalk in the ninth, to Bernard of Clairvaux in the twelfth and his belief that God's grace 'saves' free-will to choose again. The Eastern Churches had followed John of Damascus, the first well-known Christian convert from Islam, in rejecting an Augustinian doctrine which to them was too strongly reminiscent of Muslim fatalism. However, from about the thirteenth century in the West, differing schools of thought, for example Thomist and Nominalist, tended to unite in agreeing with Augustine against his opponents. This roughly coincided, perhaps not accidentally, with the West's discovery, through the Crusades, of Muslim

---

4 Muller, *Christ and the Decree*; the word 'system' as used by others, e.g., Toplady, suggests a dangerous impersonality in the orthodox Reformed approach. However, the phrase 'systematic theology' has become traditional.

philosophy and of the classical Aristotelian philosophy which it had preserved. The Augustinian consensus continued into the early sixteenth century, past the Reformation; it had its critics, but late in that century criticism of Augustinian views of predestination was still considered bold in the Reformed Churches.

In private notes (the *Articuli Nonnulli*) if not in public statements, Arminius named Calvin directly. He had, as we have seen, agreed with Gomarus that the latter had propounded the doctrine of Calvin and Beza in his *Theses*, and commented,

> Doctors...may deserve well of the Church, and yet be entangled in some error: and the illustrious restorers of the churches perhaps did not spy out everything with which the Church was deformed, and perchance themselves built a superstructure of some errors upon a true foundation; which might easily happen...[5]

That is, a theologian may be right about some things, even the great majority of things, and yet be seriously wrong about others.

Along with Gomarus' statement that 'the way of reprobation is creation in an original state of righteousness',[6] and a similar statement from Beza, Arminius attacks as 'horrid' (*horrendum*) Calvin's statement that 'men are predestinated to eternal death by the naked will of God, irrespective of any demerit of their own'.[7] The use of *horrendum* here echoes Calvin's use of *horribile* in the so-called 'horrible decree' passage of *Institutes* II.xxiii.7, then as now apparently Calvin's most offensive passage to his critics, where he says,

> it is impossible to deny that God foreknew what the end of man was to be *before he created him*, because He had so ordained by His decree[8]

—the words in (my own) italics indicating that Arminius was right to hold that Calvin shared Gomarus' creabilitarian view.

The word 'horrible' now has overtones of 'obscene, loathsome, disgusting', which Calvin certainly did not intend, but translations like

---

5 *Examination of Gomarus*; *Works*, III, p.656
6 *Examination of Gomarus*, Thesis XXIII; *Works*, III, p.588.
7 *Articuli Nonnulli* V, *On Predestination to Salvation, and on Damnation, Considered in the Highest Degree*, paragraphs 7-9. Arminius' references to the *Institutes* in the version of the *Articuli* in the *Opera*, reproduced in Nichols's translation, *Works*, II, pp.710-1, 716, are scrappy and different from the references in modern editions, so it is not always easy to judge where Arminius is quoting from the *Institutes*. *Articuli Nonnulli* V:9ff are from *Institutes* II.xxiii.7.
8 *Institutes of the Christian Religion* (Library of the Christian Classics; trans. F.L. Battles; ed. J.T. McNeill; 2 vols, Philadelphia, PA: Westminster Press. 1961), quoted G.R. Potter and M. Greengrass, *John Calvin* (Documents of Modern History; London: Edward Arnold, 1983), p.30.

'awesome'[9] are both too mild and too positive. As a Latinist, Calvin meant, literally, a decree to make one shudder. But he also provokes his critics by his way of putting it; so far from this being 'impossible to deny', it had already been denied, frequently, as Calvin himself very well knew. It is this attempt to browbeat possible critics into submission that invites objection. Arminius' 'horrendum' has something of the later overtones.

The other two subjects connected with predestination, on which Arminius directly challenges Calvin, are the fall of Adam, on which Calvin had said: 'God not only foresaw the fall of the first man, but by His own will ordained it'; 'God foreknew what end (*exitum*) man would have, because He thus ordained it by His decree'; 'It was decreed by God that Adam should perish by his own defection'; and 'By the will of God all the sons of Adam have fallen into this miserable condition in which they are bound and fastened': and the necessity of sinning for the reprobate:

> The reprobate cannot escape the necessity of sinning, especially since this kind of necessity, and similar things, [are] caused by the appointment of God (*ex Dei ordinatione iniiciatur*).[10]

Is, then, Arminius' objection to Calvin's doctrine what it has to say about fallen and reprobate man? Not entirely; he also objects to the way it depicts God, his nature and his work, and to what it says about Christ. The Calvinist stress on the 'sovereignty' of God fails to take into account the different ways in which sovereignty (human or divine) may be exercised. There is the sovereignty of the *tyrannus*, the *despotes*, the modern dictator, who rules by imposing his will on his subjects, and this is the sovereignty Calvinism too often ascribes to God. There is also the sovereignty of the *rex*, the *basileus*, the constitutional monarch or president, who has the same power but normally chooses not to exercise it, but to hold it in reserve because he prefers to rule in relationship with his subjects. This, we have seen, is a distinction made by Arminius, and it is the latter sovereignty he ascribes to God; the despotic power is reserved for the recalcitrant. And in Section V of the *Articuli* Arminius also asserts that 'no small injury is inflicted on Christ as Mediator, when He is called "the subordinate cause of destined salvation".'[11] Arminius does not specifically attribute this description to Calvin, but it is clear from *Concerning the Eternal Predestination of God* that Calvin, like Gomarus, could express himself in such terms. Calvin says that Christ

---

9 J.K.S. Reid (ed.), *Concerning the Eternal Predestination of God* (London: James Clarke, 1961), Introduction p.20.
10 *Articuli Nonnulli* XI:5-8, X:6; *Works*, II, p.716.
11 *Works*, II, *Articuli Nonnulli* V:16, p.711.

is the manner in which God discharges His work of grace. But why He takes [the elect] by the hand has another superior cause, that eternal purpose...by which He destined them to life.'[12]

As Reid says, this makes the primary ground of predestination the secret counsel in the depths of the divine wisdom (*arcanum consilium...divinae sapientiae adyta*), into which Christ has not been admitted. Arminius himself quotes a similar statement from Calvin about the reprobate, 'preparation unto destruction is not to be referred to any other thing, than to the secret counsel of God'.[13] In short, Arminius objects to Calvin's doctrine of predestination that it is creabilitarian, deciding on the destinies of individuals even before their creation; that it claims that Adam and his posterity fell by the will of God; that God has appointed that the reprobate cannot escape the necessity of sinning; and most of all, that Christ is not the ultimate cause of the salvation of the elect, but that the *arcanum consilium Dei* is. As a friend has remarked, to contrast Christ with this *arcanum consilium* is disastrous theology, pointing in the same general direction as Arius in denying the co-eternity of the three Persons of the Trinity.

Yet extreme Augustinian views of predestination continue and prosper to some extent, particularly in the Calvinist/orthodox Reformed form and among theologians, because they seem to them the only way of explaining and safeguarding certain important truths; the freedom of God, the priority of grace, the inability of man to save himself, and the observation from both Scripture and experience that when the gospel is proclaimed some make a positive response and others do not. Whether these truths are actually safeguarded by such views is debatable. The view of grace as irresistible power can be as damaging to the freedom of God as it is to the freedom of man, making grace a kind of independent force which compels God himself to make it irresistible, instead of what it really is, the benevolent activity of a God who has both right and power to make his grace irresistible or not, as and when he chooses; and, whether he sometimes chooses to make it so, or he never does, Scripture indicates that he does *not* invariably choose to determine human response (e.g., Luke 7:30). The suggestion of 'rationalist' tendencies in Arminius' theology, with which Muller concludes his study,[14] is one which Arminius might well have thrown back at his critics. He found the doctrine of irresistible grace deeply 'rationalistic' and impersonal, compared with his own view of grace as expressing the personal care of God for each person he has made. Whether later so-called 'Arminianism' became rationalistic, is

---

12 J. Calvin, *Concerning the Eternal Predestination of God* (ed. J.K.S. Reid; London: James Clarke, 1961), paragraph VIII:4, p.114; cf. Introduction pp.39-44.
13 *Articuli Nonnulli* V:11; *Works*, II, pp.710-11: 'ad arcanum consilium Dei'.
14 Muller, *God*, pp.282-5.

another matter, but Arminius himself is no rationalist. He *has* certain links with the later kind of humanism, for both stress the importance of personal relationships; the vital distinction is that for Arminius the fundamental personal relationship for a human being is one with God the Father through the Lord Jesus Christ; which in turn is based on the original mysterious relationship between God the Father and his Word and Spirit.

Those who hold Calvinist views are nowadays generally prepared to concede that there are 'difficulties' or 'problems' in their implications at least,[15] but would argue that such must be accepted for the sake of the positive statements of the doctrine. They also say that a critic must look at the positive side (the salvation of the elect) *before* turning to the dark shadow (the absolute unconditional damnation of the reprobate). Thus Sell follows Cunningham[16] in complaining that critics like Wesley had unduly emphasised reprobation and failed entirely to take the force of the Calvinist 'insistence' (my inverted commas) on stating election positively and then regarding reprobation as a legitimate deduction from it. To call objections to this doctrine 'problems' and 'difficulties' is too positive and too mild an understatement, and neither Calvin nor Cunningham nor Sell has a right to 'insist' or dictate how a critic must approach their doctrine; the critic is free to begin criticism at whatever point he or she chooses. As the television programme 'Going for a Song' illustrated, an antique chair may look beautiful from the normal standpoint, until the critic turns it upside down and reveals the poor workmanship underneath; so the orthodox Reformed doctrine of election may look fine until it is inverted and attention is directed to what it says or necessarily implies about reprobation; then it is revealed in all its shoddiness.

When Augustine first put forward views on predestination somewhat resembling Calvin's, he was attacked by Julian of Eclanum for the picture he was giving of God. 'Tell me, who is this person who inflicts punishment on innocent creatures?... You answer, God. God, you say! God! He Who "commended his love to us", Who "has loved us", Who "has not spared His own Son for us".... He it is, you say, Who judges in this way; He is the persecutor of new-born children; He it is who sends tiny babies to eternal flames.'[17] We do not need to accept all the views Julian held, which made posterity, for all its misgivings, largely side with

---

15 E.g., in Packer and Johnston's Introduction to their translation and edition to Luther's *Bondage of the Will*, p.54.

16 Alan P.F. Sell, *The Great Debate: Calvinism, Arminianism and Salvation* (Worthing: H.E. Walter, 1982), pp.81-2.

17 Peter Brown, *Augustine of Hippo* (London: Faber and Faber, 1975), p.391; Brown's own translation of *Contra secundam Juliani responsionem opus imperfectum*, I.48f, pp.429-30.

Augustine, to recognise the force of his objection that Augustine's doctrine implies an unacceptable view of God. Over a millennium later, from a rather different standpoint from Julian's, Arminius, whose views were also less than perfect at some points, revived the objection that his opponents' view of God creating men for destruction, and forcing both the elect and the reprobates to sin by his decree, will not do because God is just not like that. Only the clearest statement in God's own revelation that he *is* like that, could overturn the objection, and Arminius' opponents fall far short of demonstrating that. But if they are right, then we may believe in God, Father, Son and Holy Spirit; we may believe that, to modify Arminius' own parody, God so loved the elect that he gave his only-begotten Son, that whosoever is gifted with faith in him by irresistible grace should not perish but have everlasting life. We may even believe that we ourselves are among such elect—and yet remain quite agnostic as to whether it would be better to be saved than to be damned by a God who unconditionally reprobated some of his creatures quite literally for the hell of it.

Arminius' opinion of Calvin was, therefore, a combination of extremes of both admiration and repugnance. He was not alone in this; Calvin was essentially an extremist,[18] and his power to repel has remained as strong as his power to attract, so he excited and continues to excite strong and contradictory reactions, sometimes in the same people. Calvin has seemed to many like the little girl with the little curl right in the middle of her forehead (the Calvinist poet's daughter Jemima Longfellow?), and Arminius was not the last to think that when Calvin was right he was often very very right, but that when he was wrong he could be blasphemously so.

The ultimate justification given for the Calvinist doctrine of predestination is that, while it may confine hope of final salvation to the elect, it at least secures it for them with a cast-iron guarantee, whereas Arminius' doctrine secures it for no-one.[19] This, as we have seen, misinterprets the nature of Christian salvation as security, not relationship; security without any necessary relationship, or with one imposed which is in fact no relationship at all. The relationship with God through Christ *is* salvation, and nothing else is. Whatever New Testament words like predestination, election, grace etc. may mean, they cannot be taken in a

---

18 So-called 'moderate Calvinism' would have been to Arminius a contradiction in terms!

19 See, e.g., J.I. Packer's introductory essay to John Owen's *The Death of Death in the Death of Christ* (London: Banner of Truth Trust, 1959), pp.3-6, 10, 13ff, which argues against Arminius in this way; Neal Punt, *Unconditional Good News* (Grand Rapids, MI: Eerdmans 1980), pp.66-73, regards Packer's comparison of the two 'sides' as 'helpful', but says that Packer 'does not address himself to the universal emphasis found in Scripture' and as a result he, like other Calvinists, uses certain unhappy expressions'.

sense which denies this fundamental relationship, even implicitly. Evangelism based on Calvinist presuppositions, though often fervently sincere and effective in its own terms, is often directed to a perceived or supposed concern with one's own personal salvation, to the exclusion of others; so long as *I* am saved others don't matter; a concern all the more blasphemous for being theological. The Christian is called to desire the salvation of all, as Arminius and those who follow him believe that God himself does. If his opponents were right, God is not only the author of sin, but he is as much Hatred towards the reprobate as he is Love towards the elect; quantitatively more Hatred, if, as many Augustinians have thought, the reprobate are more in number. Their teaching may have the additional objection that it makes our salvation depend on the damnation of others, rather than on the saving work of Christ; 'you see clearly that if God did not choose some and reject others, there would be salvation for none', as a pamphlet put it; but in fact Christ has died for all, salvation, covenant and power to use them are all in place, and all we have to do is to accept or not.

This has all been negative. What is Arminius' positive belief about God's dealings with man?

As Muller recognises, Arminius' view of God's nature strongly influences his thought as a whole; I would add, it strongly influences his view of Christ's work as an expression of God's love and his other qualities. He believed in God's goodness and the expression of his goodness through creation, especially in making creatures—human beings and angels—to which he could relate. God's nature is to be in relationship; therefore he made the universe so that he could relate to it; and he made man in his own image for relationship with him. The potential to share in relationship with God is part of what 'being made in God's image' means. The relationship was to be codified in the form of covenant, a word which, as we have seen, Arminius interprets differently from Calvin and from orthodox Reformed theology. Calvin and others had a horror and fear of anything which might imply that man made any contribution to his salvation, and interpret covenant as a promise of God to man which God confirmed with an oath. Arminius' definition was nearer the secular sense of an agreement between two individuals or groups by which both made promises and accepted obligations. To him Muller's concept of 'monopleuric covenant' would have been nonsense. But while the covenant in Arminius' understanding must be two-sided in the sense that the human partner(s) make a response, there is no suggestion that any man could ever lay down his own conditions to God. Of course, Arminius could not be expected to possess our modern knowledge of ancient Near Eastern suzerain-vassal treaties, one-sided covenants in which the suzerain laid down all the conditions; but in this sense, his view of God's covenants is equally one-sided; God lays down all the conditions. Where he would regard the opposing view as going wrong, is in denying the human response which God specifically requires in the conditions which he lays down.

The relationship of the first covenant broke down through man's sin, as God in his foreknowledge knew (but did not determine) that it would, so God in his mercy chose to restore it in a new and better form. Man in his sin and ignorance would not have had a clue how to do it; God's wisdom must find the way. The second person of the Godhead, God's Word and Son, should become incarnate as the Lord Jesus Christ, and act as Mediator between God and man in the covenant of grace, the new covenant. Thus, Christ's work becomes the centre of Christian faith, the *fundamentum electionis* (ground of election):

> The first relationship (*relatio*)...was that between God and man...in a state of innocency.... But that relationship was changed, through the sin of man.... Therefore after sin, either man could have had no hope of access to God and to a union with Him...or a new relationship of man to his Creator was to be founded by God, through His gracious restoration of man, and a new religion was to be founded on that relationship. This is what a merciful (*misericors*) God has done, to the praise of His glorious grace.[20]

Much of this may seem fairly standard, unexceptionable Christian theology. The problem arises when we see that for Arminius the salvation of men consists, not in a mere transfer to a place of safety—as works of art are removed from museums etc. for safe storage underground during wartime—but in the restoration of such a relationship with God. Because it is essentially such a relationship, it must be restored in an appropriate way, not by any irresistible 'grace', but including a response on the part of the one saved. That such a response contains no human merit or 'works', that God does everything to provide the Person and means of salvation, that it is God who makes someone who has been helpless in sin, and whose will has therefore been bound, able to choose again; Arminius is not only willing to concede these points, he wishes to assert them. Indeed, he insists on doing so, as forcefully as any of his opponents. But he will not say what appears to many of them the logical conclusion of all this, that God also makes the final choice for us. That denies what has gone before, and goes against the whole nature of salvation, and any doctrine of 'irresistible grace' that asserts it must be rejected.

---

20 *Public disputation* XXXII:III; *Works*, II, p.376: 'Relatio prima....inter Deum et hominem fuit....At mutata illa relatio est, nempe per peccatum hominis....Unde post peccatum aut nullus homini sperandus ad Deum et eiusque unionem aditus fuit....aut Deo per hominis gratiosam restitutionem nova sui ad illum fundanda fuit relatio, novaque super illam relationem instituenda fuit Religio. Id quod et fecit misericors Deus, ad laudem gloriosae suae gratiae.'

Such was the Augustinian doctrine of predestination, as re-emphasised in the sixteenth century by Calvin and his successors, which was a matter of controversy in the Dutch Churches around 1589-91, just as Arminius began his ministry. For a few years he fought shy of involvement, and contented himself with objecting that it failed to stress the importance of human faith, but by 1596 he had become convinced that he had to tackle the subject himself, at the deepest level. He wanted a doctrine of predestination that did justice to what the Bible said on the subject, and at the same time did not override the relationship between man and God. Most of all he wanted a doctrine of which Christ himself should be the ground and ultimate cause, and not merely the agent of a purpose formed in his absence. How far he succeeded, in the doctrine of predestination put forward in the *Declaration of Sentiments*, we must all judge; but the work is one which, in my opinion, all theologians should study. In any case, Arminius has had a (largely unacknowledged) influence on later covenant theologians; the debt of John and Charles Wesley to him *is* acknowledged, though he has been imperfectly understood by the Wesleys and their followers; he may still have a contribution to make to fuller Christian understanding.

Certainly there are faults in Arminius' theology, especially in his doctrine of the Persons of Christ and of his Holy Spirit, and, therefore, also in his doctrine of the Trinity. It is strange that one who insisted so strongly that Christ was the primary and ultimate cause of human salvation, and not subject to any secret counsel or hidden purpose of a predestinating God, should also be so anxious to stress Christ's subordination, and that of his Holy Spirit, to God the Father in all respects. As we have seen, the latter is required by his imperfect understanding of the needs of the situation. Crudely stated, Arminius believed that Christ had to be subordinate to his Father for salvation to work at all. A modern understanding should reject both Arminius' error of the complete subordination of Christ and his Spirit to his Father, and his opponents' error of the subordination of Christ, as cause of election and salvation, to the *arcanum consilium,* in favour of recognising him as primary in both aspects. Yet, like his Father, Christ does not impose himself upon man, but is prepared to be frustrated in his desire to save a Jerusalem who 'would not' (Matthew 23:37//Luke 13:34).

Because his work logically precedes it, Christ is the *fundamentum electionis,* the ground of election. A gracious God wills to choose him and through him to choose us, so restoring the relationship with God for which we were made. This restoration is completed by our acceptance, and God's will is fulfilled. So Arminius' insight is concluded, not to man's glory but to God's.

Praise be to You, O Christ. Amen.

Bibliography

Writings of Arminius
Works

Verclaringhe Iacobi Arminii (Leiden, 1610) [Dutch text of the *Declaration of Sentiments*]

Opera Theologica (Frankfurt, 2nd edn, 1631)

Examen Thesium D. Francisci Gomari De Praedestinatione (n.p., 1645) [Nichols' translation (see below) Vol. 3, p.521, suggests Amsterdam: Louis Elzevir, Jr]

The Works of James Arminius (vols 1 and 2; trans. and ed. James Nichols; London: Longman, Hurst, Rees, Orme, Brown and Green, 1825 and 1828; vol. 3; trans. and ed. William Nichols; London: Thomas Baker, 1875)

Nichols, James (ed.), *The Works of Arminius* (ed. W.R. Bagnall; 3 vols; Grand Rapids, MI: Baker Book House, 1991 [1853])

Verklaring van Jacobus Arminius afgelegd in de Vergadering van de Staten van Holland op 30 october 1608, opnieuw uitgegeven door G.J. Hoenderdaal (Lochem: De Tijdstroom, 1960)

Bangs, C.O., *The Auction Catalogue of the Library of J. Arminius* (facsimile edition with introduction, Utrecht: HTS Publishers, 1985) (Catalogi Redivivi 4)

The Works of James Arminius (3 vols; Grand Rapids, MI: Baker Book House, 1991) [Reprint of the London edition above, translated by James and William Nichols, with new (1986) introduction by Carl Bangs]

Letters

Bibliotheca Historico-Philologico-Theologica (Bibliotheca Bremensis; Classis Tertiae, Fasciculus Secundus; Amsterdam, 1720) [contains early letter of Arminius to Grynaeus, pp.384-388]

De Vries de Heekelingen, Herman, *Genève: Pépinière du Calvinisme Hollandais. Volume 1: Les Etudiants des Pays-Bas à Genève au Temps de Théodore de Bèze* (Fribourg: Fragnière Frères, 1918) [contains earliest known letter of Arminius, pp.240-42]

Limborch, Ph. van and Christian Hartsoecker (eds), *Praestantium ac eruditorum virorum epistolae ecclesiasticae et theologicae* (Amsterdam, 1660, 3rd edn, 1704) [contains most known letters from and to Arminius]

Rogge, H.C., *Brieven en onuitgegeven stukken van Johannes Uitenbogaert* (Eerste deel 1584-1618; Utrecht, 1868) [also contains important letters of Arminius to Uitenbogaert]

General Bibliography

Aquinas, Thomas, *Somme Théologique* (Texte latin et traduction française avec notes et appendices par le Père A.D. Sertillanges, OP; Paris, Tournai, Rome: Société Saint Jean L'Evangeliste, Desclee et Cie., 3rd edn, 1925-)

Athanasius, *Select Works and Letters*, in *The Nicene and Post-Nicene Fathers*, second series, volume 4 (trans. J.H. Newman; rev. A. Robertson; Grand Rapids, MI: Eerdmans, 1978)

Augustine, *Writings against the Pelagians*, in *The Nicene and Post-Nicene Fathers: 1st Series, Volume 5* (trans. Peter Holmes and Robert Ernest Wallis; Grand Rapids, MI: Eerdmans, 1973)

Aulen, G., *Christus Victor: An Historical Study of Three Main Types of the Idea of the Atonement* (trans. A.G. Hebert; London, SPCK, 1953 [1931])

Bangs, Carl, 'Arminius: An Anniversary Report', *Christianity Today* 10 October 1960

—, 'Arminius and the Reformation', *Church History* 30.2 (June, 1961)

—, *Arminius: A Study in the Dutch Reformation* (Nashville, TN: Abingdon Press, 1971; 2nd edition rev. and ed. Joseph D. Allison; Grand Rapids, MI: Zondervan, 1985)

Barrett, C.K., *The Gospel according to St. John: An Introduction with Commentary and notes on the Greek Text* (London: SPCK, 2nd edition 1978)

Barth, Karl, *Church Dogmatics. Volume 2: The Doctrine of God*, Part 2 (trans. G.W. Bromiley, J.C. Campbell and Iain Wilson; Edinburgh: T&T Clark, 1957)

Basinger, David and Randall Basinger (eds), *Predestination and Free Will: Four Views of Divine Sovereignty and Human Freedom* (Downers Grove, IL: Inter-Varsity Press, 1986)

Bertius, Petrus, *Petri Bertii Liick Oratie over de Dood van den Heere Iacobus Arminius* (Leiden, 1609) [Latin version in *Opera Theologica* (Leiden, 1st edn, 1629), fol. 001-0004; English in Nichols translation, *Works*, I, pp.13-47]

Brandt, Caspar, *The Life of James Arminius, D.D.* (trans. John Guthrie; London 1854, and Nashville 1857)

Brandt, Gerard, *Historie der Reformatie en andre Kerkelijke Geschiedenissen in en ontrent de Nederlanden* (4 vols; Amsterdam, 1671-1704)

Breward, Ian, *The Work of William Perkins* (Courtenay Library of Reformation Classics; Abingdon: Sutton Courtenay Press, 1970)

Brown, Peter, *Augustine of Hippo* (London: Faber and Faber, 1975)

Brunner, Emil, *Dogmatics. Volume 1: The Christian Doctrine of God* (trans. Olive Wyon; London: Lutterworth Press, 1964)

Bullard, John M., 'Arminius', in John H. Hayes (ed.), *Dictionary of Biblical Interpretation* (2 vols; Nashville, TN: Abingdon Press, 1999).

Calvin, J. *Concerning the Eternal Predestination of God* (ed. J.K.S. Reid; London: James Clarke, 1961)

—, *Institutes of the Christian Religion* (Library of Christian Classics; trans. F.L. Battles, ed. J.T. McNeill; 2 vols; Philadelphia, PA: Westminster Press, 1960/London: SCM Press. 1961)

Cameron, Charles M., 'Arminius: Hero or Heretic?', *Evangelical Quarterly* 64.3, (1992), pp.213-28
Clarke, F. Stuart, 'The Doctrine of Predestination from Paul to Augustine, A.D. 62-430' (MPhil, University of Nottingham, 1982)
Clement of Alexandria, *Stromateis* VII, in *Alexandrian Christianity* (Library of Christian Classics; trans. J.B. Mayor; rev. and ed. J.E.L. Oulton and Henry Chadwick; Philadelphia, PA: Westminster Press, 1954)
Dakin, A., *Calvinism* (London: Duckworth, 1940)
Dekker, Evert, Rijker *dan Midas: Vrijheid, Genade en Predestinatie in de Theologie van Jacobus Arminius (1559-1609)* (Zoetermeer: Uitgeverij Boekencentrum BV, 1993)
Dorner, I.A., *A History of Protestant Thought particularly in Germany* (2 vols; trans. George Robson and Sophia Taylor; New York: AMS Press, 1970 [1871]),
Geyl, Pieter, *The Revolt of the Netherlands* (London: Ernest Benn, 2nd ed., 1962)
Graafland, C., *Van Calvijn tot Barth: Oorsprong en ontwikkeling van de leer der verkiezing in het Gereformeerde Protestantisme* ('s-Gravenhage: Uitgeverij Boekencentrum BV, 1987)
Goodwin, John, *Banner of Justification* (n.pl., 1659)
Harrison, Archibald H.W., *The Beginnings of Arminianism to the Synod of Dort* (London: University of London Press, 1926)
—, *Arminianism* (London: Duckworth, 1937)
Hicks, John Mark, 'The Righteousness of Saving Faith: Arminian versus Remonstrant Grace', *Evangelical Journal* 9 (1991), pp.27-39
Itterzon, G.P. van, *Franciscus Gomarus* ('s-Gravenhage: Martinus Nijhoff, 1930)
Jewett, Paul K., *Election and Predestination* (Grand Rapids, MI: Eerdmans/Exeter: Paternoster Press, 1985)
Jones, Ivor H., and Kenneth B. Wilson (eds.), *Freedom and Grace* (London: Epworth Press, 1988)
Kendall, R.T., *Calvin and English Calvinism to 1649* (Oxford: Oxford University Press, 1979; 2nd edn in Studies in Christian History and Thought; Carlisle: Paternoster Press, 1997)
Loonstra, B., *Verkiezing-Verzoening-Verbond: Beschrieving en Beoordeling van de leer van het PACTUM SALUTIS in de gereformeerde theologie* ('s-Gravenhage: Boekencentrum BV, 1990)
Loosjes, J., *Lutherschen en Remonstranten in den tijd van de Dordtsche Synode*. ('s-Gravenhage: Martinus Nijhoff, 1926)
Luther, Martin, *Luther and Erasmus, Free Will and Salvation* (Library of Christian Classics 17; London: SCM Press, 1969)
Maronier, J.H., *Jacobus Arminius, een Biographie* (Amsterdam: Y. Rogge, 1905)
McCracken, G.E. and A. Cabaniss (eds), *Early Mediaeval Theology* (Library of Chroistian Classics IX; London: SCM Press, 1957)
McGonigle, Herbert Boyd, *Sufficient Saving Grace: John Wesley's Evangelical Arminianism* (Studies in Evangelical History and Thought; Carlisle: Paternoster Press, 2001)

The Manifold Grace of God, papers read at the Puritan and Reformed Studies Conference, (n.pl.: n.p., 1968)

Montgomery, John Warwick (ed.), *Chytraeus on Sacrifice: A Reformation Treatise in Biblical Theology* (St Louis, MO: Concordia, 1962)

Muller, Richard A., *Christ and the Decree: Christology and Predestination in Reformed Theology from Calvin to Perkins* (Studies in Historical Theology 2; Durham, NC: Labyrinth Press, 1986; 2nd edition Grand Rapids, MI: Baker Book House, 1988)

—, 'The Christological Problem in the Thought of Jacobus Arminius', *Nederlands Archief voor Kerkgeschiedenis* 68 (1988), pp.145-63

—, 'The Federal Motif in Seventeenth Century Arminian Theology', *Nederlands Archief voor Kerkgeschiedenis* 62 (1982), pp.102-22

—, *God, Creation and Providence in the Thought of Jacob Arminius: Sources and Directions of Scholastic Protestantism in the Era of Early Orthodoxy* (Grand Rapids, MI: Baker Book House, 1991)

Nichols, James, *Calvinism and Arminianism Compared* (London, 1824)

Olson, Roger E., *The Story of Christian Theology: 20 Centuries of Tradition and Reform* (Downers Grove, IL: Apollos, 1999)

Origen, *Comm. in Ep. ad Romanos* in *Philocalia*, in Henry Bettenson, *The Early Christian Fathers* (London: Oxford University Press, 1969 [1956])

Owen, John, *The Death of Death in the Death of Christ* (London: Banner of Truth Trust, 1959)

Packer, J.I. and O.R. Johnston, [Martin Luther] *The Bondage of the Will* (London: James Clarke, 1957)

Pinnock, Clark H. (ed.), *Grace Unlimited* (Minneapolis, MN: Bethany Fellowship, 1975)

—, (ed.), *The Grace of God and the Will of Man* (Minneapolis, MN: Bethany House, 1995)

Potter, G.R. and M. Greengrass (eds), *John Calvin* (Documents of Modern History; London: Edward Arnold, 1983)

Punt, Neal, *Unconditional Good News* (Grand Rapids, MI: Eerdmans 1980)

Rogge, H.C., *Brieven en onuitgegeven stukken van Johannes Uitenbogaert* (Utrecht, 1868),

—, *Johannes Uitenbogaert en Zijn Tijd* (3 vols; Amsterdam, 1874-6)

Rouse, R., and S.C. Neill (eds), *A History of the Ecumenical Movement, 1517-1948* (London: SCM Press, 1954)

Sanday, William and Arthur C. Headlam, *A Critical and Exegetical Commentary on the Epistle to the Romans* (International Critical Commentary; Edinburgh: T&T Clark, 1895, 5th edn, 1930)

Schmidt, Heinrich, *Doctrinal Theology of the Evangelical Lutheran Church* (trans. Charles E. Hay and Henry E. Jacobs; Philadelphia, PA: Augsburg Publishing House, 1961 [3rd edn, 1899])

Sell, Alan P.F., *The Great Debate: Calvinism, Arminianism and Salvation* (Worthing: H.E. Walter, 1982)

Sepp, C., *Het Godgeleerd Onderwijs in Nederland gedurende de 16e en 17e Eeuw* ([2 vols. in 1] Leiden, 1873-74)
Shank, Robert, *Elect in the Son* (Minneapolis, MN: Bethany House, 2nd ed. 1989)
Starreveld, J.C.R. (ed.), 'Een Verslag van de Conferentie Tussen Gomarus en Arminius Op 6 en 7 Mei 1603', *NAKG* 62.1 (1982), pp.65-75.
Tappert, Theodore G. et al., *The Book of Concord: The Confessions of the Evangelical Lutheran Church* (Philadelphia, PA: Muhlenberg Press, 1959)
Thomas, G. Michael, *The Extent of the Atonement: A Dilemma for Reformed Theology from Calvin to the Consensus* (Paternoster Theological Monographs; Carlisle: Paternoster Press, 1997)
Watkin-Jones, Howard, *The Holy Spirit in the Mediaeval Church...from the post-Patristic Age to the Counter-Reformation* (London: Epworth Press, 1922)
—, *The Holy Spirit from Arminius to Wesley* (London: Epworth Press, 1929)
Williamson, G.I., *The Heidelberg Catechism: A Study Guide* (Phillipsburg, NJ: Puritan and Reformed Publishing, 1993
Wood, Arthur Skevington, 'The Declaration of Sentiments: The Theological Testament of Arminius', *Evangelical Quarterly* 65.2 (1993), pp. 111-29
Yonge, Charlotte M., *Landmarks of History, Modern History: Volume 3. From the Reformation to the Fall of Napoleon* (London, 1857)

General Index

Acontius 141
adiaphora 114
adoption 58, 100, 112, 126, 132, 135, 163
Aetius 43
Alexandrian doctrine 160, 161, 162
Ambrose of Milan 114, 142
Ambrosiaster 161
Amsterdam xx, 12, 13, 19, 23, 40, 45, 50, 51, 59, 61, 147, 162
Amsterdam Consistory 3
Anabaptists 5, 155, 162
Anchi 141
Andreae 131
Anglicanism/Anglicans 2
Anglo-Catholics 3
Anselm 56
Apostles' Creed, the 82, 85
Aquinas, T. 24, 141, 160
Arius 43, 135
Arminianism xvii, 2, 3, 6, 7, 8, 30, 128, 165, 169
assurance 13, 101-102, 143
Athanasius 162
atonement xviii, 1, 56, 63, 73, 88-89, 149
Augustine 19, 24, 25, 33, 42, 55, 107, 108, 131, 137, 142, 145, 150, 157, 160, 162, 164, 166, 171
Augustinianism 30, 71, 157, 162, 167, 169, 172, 174
Aulen, G. 56, 89

Bangs, C. xvii, 2, 4, 5, 6, 11, 14, 15, 16, 19, 20, 23, 30, 41, 42, 45, 49, 50, 51, 73, 74, 75, 76, 95, 108, 119, 125, 126, 127, 128, 129, 132, 138, 140, 155, 156, 157, 159, 166
baptism 18, 67, 119, 120, 154
baptism of John 115, 120
Barneveldt 3

Barth, K. 6, 7, 87, 110, 161
Basil the Great 43, 142
Belgic Confession, the 14, 21, 22, 73, 134, 140, 150
Bellarmine 8, 75, 76
Bernard of Clairvaux 166
Bertius 13, 14, 15, 23
Beza, T. 13, 17, 24, 25, 26, 51, 95, 126, 130, 131, 133, 137, 140, 141, 142, 165, 166, 167
Borrius 91
Brandt, C. 2, 13, 40, 41, 50, 108, 128
Brandt, G. 1, 2
Bullinger, H. 51, 71, 72, 166

Calvin, J. 1, 3, 4, 7, 8, 13, 17, 24, 25, 42, 43, 49, 71, 72, 90, 95, 103, 104, 119, 126, 133, 137, 140, 141, 142, 146, 155, 165, 166, 167, 168, 169, 170, 171, 172, 174
Calvinism/Calvinists 1, 2, 3, 4, 6, 8, 14, 16, 30, 46, 84, 89, 93, 129, 161, 163, 164, 165, 168, 170, 172
Capito 155
Carlstadt, A. 114
Cassian, John 145
Castellio 133, 141
Christology xvii, xviii, xix, xx, 1, 8, 10, 11, 15, 17, 19, 20, 22, 25, 26, 27, 28, 29, 30, 31, 32, 33, 34, 35, 36, 37, 38, 39, 40-60, 61-124, 146, 174
Chrytraeus, D. 51
Church of England, the 2
Classis of Dordrecht, the 138
Clement of Alexandria 160, 161
Collibus, Hippolytus à 64, 104, 142, 146, 147, 148
Colloquy of Montbeliard, the 165
communion 98-100

concupiscence 19
Consistory of Amsterdam, the 50
consubstantiation 86
conversion 16, 35, 76, 94, 104, 163
Conyers, T. 1
Coolhaes 4
Coornhert, D.V. 13, 14, 16, 50, 133, 140, 141, 162
Corneliszoon, A. 6, 10, 13, 14, 50, 157
Council of Trent, the 5
covenant(s) xviii, xix, 7, 22, 23, 69-79, 108, 111, 112, 113, 119, 120, 123, 172, 173, 174
creabilitarianism 15, 130, 143, 148, 167, 169
creation xvii, xviii, xix , 26, 31, 39, 41, 47, 49, 69, 70, 136, 157, 172
Cuchlinus, J. 23
Cyril of Jerusalem 43

de Molina, L. 8, 122
de Witt, J.R. 6
Dekker, E. xvii, xviii, 5, 8, 10, 11, 19, 20, 22, 23, 24, 30, 45, 50, 51, 75, 76, 77, 89, 90, 91, 122, 123, 126, 128, 129, 132, 133, 138, 141, 156, 157, 158
divine knowledge xviii
divine will xviii
Donne, J. 65
Donteklok, R. 6, 10, 13, 14, 23, 50, 157
Dorner, I.A. 63, 73, 74, 88
Drusius, J. 11, 12, 23, 30
Dutch Reformed Church 1, 24, 45

ecclesiology xix, 59, 108-121
ecumenical movement 140
Edwards, J. 2
Egbertszoon, S. 147
election 7, 21, 24, 25, 26, 28, 32, 33, 34, 35, 37, 38, 39, 49, 57, 87, 92, 96, 99, 110, 126, 127, 130, 131, 132, 134, 135, 136, 143, 148, 149, 151, 153, 163, 170, 171, 174
Episcopius 1, 88, 91

Eucharist, the 121
eucharistic sacrifice 53
Eunomius 43
Evangelical Revival, the 2
evangelical theology 61, 62, 63
evangelicals 109
exaltation xviii
expiation 34, 35, 36, 53, 56, 88, 105, 113

faith xviii, xix, 6, 7, 12, 13, 15, 16, 33, 35, 40, 46, 47, 48, 49, 76, 92, 95-96, 100, 101, 103, 104, 112, 117, 123, 126, 143, 144, 147, 149, 150, 158, 159, 163
Fall, the xviii, xix, 26, 31, 61, 75
foreknowledge 24, 31, 35, 75, 126, 159, 160, 161, 162, 173
foreordination 153, 156, 161
free will xvii, 14, 16, 77, 107, 162
freedom 111-15, 151, 169

Gnosticism 160, 161
God, doctrine of xvii, xx, 10, 41, 42, 59, 69 123
Gomarus, F. xvii, xx, 16, 22, 23, 47, 50, 51, 76, 90, 99, 104, 122, 125, 127, 128, 129, 131, 132, 133, 134, 135, 136, 137, 138, 142, 143, 145, 146, 148, 149, 150, 155, 156, 162, 165, 167
Goodwin, J. 1
Gottschalk 166
Graafland, C. 7
grace xvii, xviii, 6, 8, 19, 20, 22, 27, 28, 35, 36, 37, 45, 46, 48, 75-78, 83, 84, 88, 91, 92, 99, 101, 106, 107, 112, 113, 120, 123, 127, 134, 141, 143, 147, 149, 150, 152, 153, 155, 156, 159, 163, 169, 173
Gregory Nazianzan 142
Gregory of Nyssa 31
Gregory of Rimini 122
Grotius, H. 3, 88
Grynaeus 14, 19, 20, 38, 75, 96

Hakes, J. 1

General Index   183

Hallam 3
Harrison, A.W. 4
Headlam, A.C. 3
Heidelberg Catechism, the 14, 103, 104, 107, 134, 140, 150
Heidelberg theologians 95
Hemmingsen, N. 155
Heshusius, T. 17
Hicks, J.M. 7, 8, 88, 89, 105
Hilary 142
Hoenderdaal, G.J. xx, 5
holiness 99, 105-108, 132, 149
humanism 5
humiliation xviii

Illyricus 33, 34
imputed righteousness 99, 103, 104, 143, 144
incarnation 62, 87, 115
infant baptism 107
infants 108
infralapsarianism/infralapsarians 15, 30, 50, 143, 157
initiation 120
International Congregational Council 5

Jacobsdr, G. 23
Javellus 131
Jesuits 140, 141
Jewett, P.K. 6, 157
John of Damascus 159, 162, 166
Julian 171
Junius, F. 16, 19, 20, 21, 23, 24, 25, 26, 27, 28, 29, 30, 33, 38, 39, 45, 48, 50, 87, 88, 100, 126, 128, 129, 133, 135, 156
justification by faith xx, 4, 17, 27, 34, 38, 40, 46, 47, 48, 77, 90, 99, 100, 102-105, 106, 143, 144, 146, 147, 148, 149, 157, 161, 162, 163, 166

Keble, J. 2
Kendall, R.T. 6, 10, 95, 96

Lake, D.M. 7
Law 8, 108, 114, 149

Leemann, B. 13
legal theology 62
Leiden xx, 3, 11, 23, 39, 40, 41, 48, 50, 60, 61, 69, 110, 125, 138, 156
Limborch, Ph. van 103
Loonstra, B. 51, 71
Lord's Supper, the 120
Lubbertus 12, 22, 142, 144
Luther, M. 89, 141, 155, 162
Lutheranism/Lutherans 5, 7, 17, 51, 79, 84, 85, 86, 87, 114, 131, 133, 136, 155, 162, 163
Lydius, M. 13

Major 131
Manichaeanism/Manichaeans 135, 137, 145
Maronier 4
Martinius of Bremen 128
Martyr, P. 141
Maurice of Nassau 3
Maury 161
McDonald, H.D. 88
McGonigle, H.B. 8
Medenblik, T. 46
Melancthon, P. 43, 155
mercy 127, 149, 156, 157
Methodists 2, 4, 6
moderate Calvinism 171
Molina 75, 76, 141, 145, 155, 164
More, Thomas 117
mortification 106, 113
Muller, R.A. xvii, xx, 5, 7, 8, 10, 11, 41, 42, 54, 61, 62, 63, 68, 69, 64, 70, 71, 72, 76, 78, 79, 86, 87, 88, 95, 110, 121, 122, 123, 125, 141, 151, 166, 169, 172
Müntzer, T. 114
Musculus, W. 51, 166

new covenant xix, 53, 89, 103
Nicene (Constantinopolitan) Creed 43
Nichols, J. xx, 2, 40, 41, 44, 46, 50, 51, 61, 63, 68, 126, 128, 135, 156
Nichols, W. xx, 4
nominalism 121, 122, 162, 166

Oldenbarneveldt 3

Olson, R.E. 7
Origen 160, 161
original righteousness 99, 136, 148, 149
original sin 14, 15, 16, 74, 144
Oxford Movement, the 2

papacy, the 116
Paraeus 142
Paul of Samosata/Samosatenians 135, 136
Pelagianism 5, 135, 137, 145, 149
Pelagius 107, 108, 145, 146, 150, 161
penal substitution 89
perfection 146
Perkins, W. xviii, xx, 6, 8, 16, 30, 31, 32, 33, 34, 35, 36, 37, 38, 39, 40, 75, 76, 85, 88, 95, 98, 100, 105, 122, 133, 135, 141, 165, 166
perseverance 102, 146, 159, 163
Peucer, C. 155
Pezelius 43
Pinnock, C.H. 7
Piscator 86, 141
Plancius 16, 20, 21, 135, 144
Polanus 43, 85, 166
Praamsma, L. 103, 104
predestination xvii, xviii, xix, xx, 6, 8, 10, 11, 13, 14, 15, 16, 17, 20, 21, 22, 23, 24, 26, 28, 29, 30, 32, 38, 39, 40, 57, 59, 69, 73, 90, 91, 99, 104, 110, 122, 126, 127, 129, 130, 131, 132, 133, 134, 135, 137, 138, 140, 142, 143, 148, 150, 151, 153, 155, 156, 157, 158, 159, 160, 161, 162, 163, 164, 165, 166, 167, 169, 171, 174
prelapsarianism 119
preodination 131, 149
priesthood of all believers 52
propitiation 81, 104, 144
Prosper of Aquitane 33
Protestant scholasticism 141
providence xvii, xviii, 69-79, 76
Puccius, F. 20
Purtanism/Puritans 1, 2, 6

Ramism 59, 121
Ramus, P. 59
realism 162
reconciliation 7, 32, 34, 36, 37, 38, 58, 135, 162
redemption xix, 27, 31, 32, 33, 34, 35, 36, 37, 38, 45, 80, 91, 98-100, 110, 113, 114, 162
Reformed Churches 1, 4, 125, 131, 133, 140, 165, 167
Reformed theology 102, 103, 121-22, 133, 155, 162, 164, 166, 169, 170, 172
Reformed theology 16, 31, 37, 38, 40, 48, 50, 51, 72, 76, 77, 78, 79, 85, 86, 90, 95
Reformed tradition, the 1, 2, 5, 6, 7, 10, 17
regeneration 17, 18, 19, 27, 33, 100-101, 146, 147
Reid, J.K.S. 169
remission of sins 32, 34, 36, 37, 47, 83, 94, 99
Remonstrant Brotherhood 1, 2, 4, 5
Remonstrants 11, 88, 103
repentance xix, 91-108, 158, 163
reprobation/reprobate, the 37, 127, 131, 132, 134, 136, 143, 148, 151, 152, 154, 156, 157, 163, 167, 168, 169, 170, 172
righteousness 3, 7, 18, 27, 28, 35, 36, 46, 55, 56, 74, 77, 80, 81, 94, 103, 104, 105, 106, 112, 130, 131, 143, 144, 148, 152, 154, 162
Rogge, H.C. 4
Roman Catholicism/Roman Catholics xix, 5, 7, 8, 20, 75, 76, 95, 102, 116, 117, 121, 131, 141, 155
Rungius 131

Sabellianism 42, 43, 65
sacerdotalism 57
sacraments xix, 33, 95, 116, 119-21, 162
Salnar 150
salvation 28, 29, 32, 33, 35, 54, 57, 79, 80, 83, 84, 87, 90, 91, 92, 93,

94, 95, 96, 97, 103, 106, 110, 112, 123, 125, 127, 132, 135, 137, 143, 149, 150, 151, 153, 158, 159, 161, 162, 163, 164, 168, 170, 171, 172, 174
sanctification xix, 17, 27, 37, 77, 81, 90, 99, 103, 105, 149
Sanday, W. 3
satisfaction 37, 89, 94, 113, 144, 154
scholasticism 8, 51, 70, 82, 122
Second Helvetic Confession, the (1675) 1, 140
Sell, A.P.F. 170
semi-Pelagianism 144, 145, 166
Sibelius 141, 142
Simplicianus 161
Smetius, A. 76, 93
Snecanus 21
Socinus 135, 141
soteriology 3, 7, 16, 20, 21, 22, 62, 86
Suarez 8, 75, 76, 141,
subordinationism xviii, 62, 87, 88, 174
supralapsarianism 10, 13, 15, 129, 130, 133, 135, 137, 143, 148, 150, 151, 152, 153, 154, 155, 156, 157
Synod of Dort, the (1618–19) 1, 4, 128, 137, 142
Synod of South Holland, the 138, 146

Taffinus, J. 45
Thomism/Thomists 30, 69, 121, 134, 156, 166
transubstantiation 86
Trelcatius 42, 140, 146, 147, 156
Trinity, the xviii, 3, 5, 40, 42, 43, 44, 45, 54, 60, 63-67, 68, 77, 78, 88, 134, 146, 169, 174

Ubiquitists 162
Uitenbogaert xvii, 4, 11, 12, 13, 21, 23, 29, 30, 40, 42, 44, 45, 46, 47, 48, 49, 50, 62, 95, 121, 127, 129, 138, 140, 145
Unitarianism/Unitarians 43
Ursinus 47, 51, 141

Vermigli 166
Viguerius 131
voluntarism 95
Vorstius 63

Watkin-Jones, H. 5, 65, 66
Wesley, C. 2, 138, 174
Wesley, J. 2, 5, 8, 138, 174
Wood, A.S. 7

Zanchius 47, 51
Zwingli 166
Zwinglianism 89

Studies in Christian History and Thought
(All titles uniform with this volume)
Dates in bold are of projected publication

David Bebbington
Holiness in Nineteenth-Century England
David Bebbington stresses the relationship of movements of spirituality to changes in their cultural setting, especially the legacies of the Enlightenment and Romanticism. He shows that these broad shifts in ideological mood had a profound effect on the ways in which piety was conceptualized and practised. Holiness was intimately bound up with the spirit of the age.
2000 / 0-85364-981-2 / viii + 98pp

J. William Black
Reformation Pastors
Richard Baxter and the Ideal of the Reformed Pastor
This work examines Richard Baxter's *Gildas Salvianus, The Reformed Pastor* (1656) and explores each aspect of his pastoral strategy in light of his own concern for 'reformation' and in the broader context of Edwardian, Elizabethan and early Stuart pastoral ideals and practice.
2003 / 1-84227-190-3 / xxii + 308pp

James Bruce
Prophecy, Miracles, Angels, *and* Heavenly Light?
The Eschatology, Pneumatology and Missiology of Adomnán's Life of Columba
This book surveys approaches to the marvellous in hagiography, providing the first critique of Plummer's hypothesis of Irish saga origin. It then analyses the uniquely systematized phenomena in the *Life of Columba* from Adomnán's seventh-century theological perspective, identifying the coming of the eschatological Kingdom as the key to understanding.
2004 / 1-84227-227-6 / xviii + 286pp

Colin J. Bulley
The Priesthood of Some Believers
Developments from the General to the Special Priesthood in the Christian Literature of the First Three Centuries
The first in-depth treatment of early Christian texts on the priesthood of all believers shows that the developing priesthood of the ordained related closely to the division between laity and clergy and had deleterious effects on the practice of the general priesthood.
2000 / 1-84227-034-6 / xii + 336pp

Anthony R. Cross (ed.)
Ecumenism and History
Studies in Honour of John H.Y. Briggs
This collection of essays examines the inter-relationships between the two fields in which Professor Briggs has contributed so much: history—particularly Baptist and Nonconformist—and the ecumenical movement. With contributions from colleagues and former research students from Britain, Europe and North America, *Ecumenism and History* provides wide-ranging studies in important aspects of Christian history, theology and ecumenical studies.

2002 / 1-84227-135-0 / xx + 362pp

Maggi Dawn
Confessions of an Inquiring Spirit
Form as Constitutive of Meaning in S.T. Coleridge's Theological Writing
This study of Coleridge's *Confessions* focuses on its confessional, epistolary and fragmentary form, suggesting that attention to these features significantly affects its interpretation. Bringing a close study of these three literary forms, the author suggests ways in which they nuance the text with particular understandings of the Trinity, and of a kenotic christology. Some parallels are drawn between Romantic and postmodern dilemmas concerning the authority of the biblical text.

2006 / 1-84227-255-1 / approx. 224 pp

Ruth Gouldbourne
The Flesh and the Feminine
Gender and Theology in the Writings of Caspar Schwenckfeld
Caspar Schwenckfeld and his movement exemplify one of the radical communities of the sixteenth century. Challenging theological and liturgical norms, they also found themselves challenging social and particularly gender assumptions. In this book, the issues of the relationship between radical theology and the understanding of gender are considered.

2005 / 1-84227-048-6 / approx. 304pp

Crawford Gribben
Puritan Millennialism
Literature and Theology, 1550–1682
Puritan Millennialism surveys the growth, impact and eventual decline of puritan millennialism throughout England, Scotland and Ireland, arguing that it was much more diverse than has frequently been suggested. This Paternoster edition is revised and extended from the original 2000 text.

2007 / 1-84227-372-8 / approx. 320pp

Galen K. Johnson
Prisoner of Conscience
John Bunyan on Self, Community and Christian Faith
This is an interdisciplinary study of John Bunyan's understanding of conscience across his autobiographical, theological and fictional writings, investigating whether conscience always deserves fidelity, and how Bunyan's view of conscience affects his relationship both to modern Western individualism and historic Christianity.

2003 / 1-84227-223-3 / xvi + 236pp

R.T. Kendall
Calvin and English Calvinism to 1649
The author's thesis is that those who formed the Westminster Confession of Faith, which is regarded as Calvinism, in fact departed from John Calvin on two points: (1) the extent of the atonement and (2) the ground of assurance of salvation.

1997 / 0-85364-827-1 / xii + 264pp

Timothy Larsen
Friends of Religious Equality
Nonconformist Politics in Mid-Victorian England
During the middle decades of the nineteenth century the English Nonconformist community developed a coherent political philosophy of its own, of which a central tenet was the principle of religious equality (in contrast to the stereotype of Evangelical Dissenters). The Dissenting community fought for the civil rights of Roman Catholics, non-Christians and even atheists on an issue of principle which had its flowering in the enthusiastic and undivided support which Nonconformity gave to the campaign for Jewish emancipation. This reissued study examines the political efforts and ideas of English Nonconformists during the period, covering the whole range of national issues raised, from state education to the Crimean War. It offers a case study of a theologically conservative group defending religious pluralism in the civic sphere, showing that the concept of religious equality was a grand vision at the centre of the political philosophy of the Dissenters.

2007 / 1-84227-402-3 / x + 300pp

Byung-Ho Moon
Christ the Mediator of the Law
Calvin's Christological Understanding of the Law as the Rule of Living and Life-Giving

This book explores the coherence between Christology and soteriology in Calvin's theology of the law, examining its intellectual origins and his position on the concept and extent of Christ's mediation of the law. A comparative study between Calvin and contemporary Reformers—Luther, Bucer, Melancthon and Bullinger—and his opponent Michael Servetus is made for the purpose of pointing out the unique feature of Calvin's Christological understanding of the law.

2005 / 1-84227-318-3 / approx. 370pp

John Eifion Morgan-Wynne
Holy Spirit and Religious Experience in Christian Writings, c.AD 90–200

This study examines how far Christians in the third to fifth generations (c.AD 90–200) attributed their sense of encounter with the divine presence, their sense of illumination in the truth or guidance in decision-making, and their sense of ethical empowerment to the activity of the Holy Spirit in their lives.

2005 / 1-84227-319-1 / approx. 350pp

James I. Packer
The Redemption and Restoration of Man in the Thought of Richard Baxter

James I. Packer provides a full and sympathetic exposition of Richard Baxter's doctrine of humanity, created and fallen; its redemption by Christ Jesus; and its restoration in the image of God through the obedience of faith by the power of the Holy Spirit.

2002 / 1-84227-147-4 / 432pp

Andrew Partington,
Church and State
The Contribution of the Church of England Bishops to the House of Lords during the Thatcher Years

In *Church and State*, Andrew Partington argues that the contribution of the Church of England bishops to the House of Lords during the Thatcher years was overwhelmingly critical of the government; failed to have a significant influence in the public realm; was inefficient, being undertaken by a minority of those eligible to sit on the Bench of Bishops; and was insufficiently moral and spiritual in its content to be distinctive. On the basis of this, and the likely reduction of the number of places available for Church of England bishops in a fully reformed Second Chamber, the author argues for an evolution in the Church of England's approach to the service of its bishops in the House of Lords. He proposes the Church of England works to overcome the genuine obstacles which hinder busy diocesan bishops from contributing to the debates of the House of Lords and to its life more informally.

2005 / 1-84227-334-5 / approx. 324pp

Michael Pasquarello III
God's Ploughman
Hugh Latimer: A 'Preaching Life' (1490–1555)

This construction of a 'preaching life' situates Hugh Latimer within the larger religious, political and intellectual world of late medieval England. Neither biography, intellectual history, nor analysis of discrete sermon texts, this book is a work of homiletic history which draws from the details of Latimer's milieu to construct an interpretive framework for the preaching performances that formed the core of his identity as a religious reformer. Its goal is to illumine the practical wisdom embodied in the content, form and style of Latimer's preaching, and to recapture a sense of its overarching purpose, movement, and transforming force during the reform of sixteenth-century England.

2006 / 1-84227-336-1 / approx. 250pp

Alan P.F. Sell
Enlightenment, Ecumenism, Evangel
Theological Themes and Thinkers 1550–2000

This book consists of papers in which such interlocking topics as the Enlightenment, the problem of authority, the development of doctrine, spirituality, ecumenism, theological method and the heart of the gospel are discussed. Issues of significance to the church at large are explored with special reference to writers from the Reformed and Dissenting traditions.

2005 / 1-84227-330-2 / xviii + 422pp

Alan P.F. Sell
Hinterland Theology
Some Reformed and Dissenting Adjustments

Many books have been written on theology's 'giants' and significant trends, but what of those lesser-known writers who adjusted to them? In this book some hinterland theologians of the British Reformed and Dissenting traditions, who followed in the wake of toleration, the Evangelical Revival, the rise of modern biblical criticism and Karl Barth, are allowed to have their say. They include Thomas Ridgley, Ralph Wardlaw, T.V. Tymms and N.H.G. Robinson.

2006 / 1-84227-331-0 / approx. 350pp

Alan P.F. Sell and Anthony R. Cross (eds)
Protestant Nonconformity in the Twentieth Century

In this collection of essays scholars representative of a number of Nonconformist traditions reflect thematically on Nonconformists' life and witness during the twentieth century. Among the subjects reviewed are biblical studies, theology, worship, evangelism and spirituality, and ecumenism. Over and above its immediate interest, this collection provides a marker to future scholars and others wishing to know how some of their forebears assessed Nonconformity's contribution to a variety of fields during the century leading up to Christianity's third millennium.

2003 / 1-84227-221-7 / x + 398pp

Mark Smith
Religion in Industrial Society
Oldham and Saddleworth 1740–1865

This book analyses the way British churches sought to meet the challenge of industrialization and urbanization during the period 1740–1865. Working from a case-study of Oldham and Saddleworth, Mark Smith challenges the received view that the Anglican Church in the eighteenth century was characterized by complacency and inertia, and reveals Anglicanism's vigorous and creative response to the new conditions. He reassesses the significance of the centrally directed church reforms of the mid-nineteenth century, and emphasizes the importance of local energy and enthusiasm. Charting the growth of denominational pluralism in Oldham and Saddleworth, Dr Smith compares the strengths and weaknesses of the various Anglican and Nonconformist approaches to promoting church growth. He also demonstrates the extent to which all the churches participated in a common culture shaped by the influence of evangelicalism, and shows that active co-operation between the churches rather than denominational conflict dominated. This revised and updated edition of Dr Smith's challenging and original study makes an important contribution both to the social history of religion and to urban studies.

2006 / 1-84227-335-3 / approx. 300pp

Martin Sutherland
Peace, Toleration and Decay
The Ecclesiology of Later Stuart Dissent

This fresh analysis brings to light the complexity and fragility of the later Stuart Nonconformist consensus. Recent findings on wider seventeenth-century thought are incorporated into a new picture of the dynamics of Dissent and the roots of evangelicalism.

2003 / 1-84227-152-0 / xxii + 216pp

G. Michael Thomas
The Extent of the Atonement
A Dilemma for Reformed Theology from Calvin to the Consensus

A study of the way Reformed theology addressed the question, 'Did Christ die for all, or for the elect only?', commencing with John Calvin, and including debates with Lutheranism, the Synod of Dort and the teaching of Moïse Amyraut.

1997 / 0-85364-828-X / x + 278pp

David M. Thompson
Baptism, Church and Society in Britain from the Evangelical Revival to *Baptism, Eucharist and Ministry*

The theology and practice of baptism have not received the attention they deserve. How important is faith? What does baptismal regeneration mean? Is baptism a bond of unity between Christians? This book discusses the theology of baptism and popular belief and practice in England and Wales from the Evangelical Revival to the publication of the World Council of Churches' consensus statement on *Baptism, Eucharist and Ministry* (1982).

2005 / 1-84227-393-0 / approx. 224pp

Mark D. Thompson
A Sure Ground on Which to Stand
The Relation of Authority and Interpretive Method of Luther's Approach to Scripture

The best interpreter of Luther is Luther himself. Unfortunately many modern studies have superimposed contemporary agendas upon this sixteenth-century Reformer's writings. This fresh study examines Luther's own words to find an explanation for his robust confidence in the Scriptures, a confidence that generated the famous 'stand' at Worms in 1521.

2004 / 1-84227-145-8 / xvi + 322pp

Carl R. Trueman and R.S. Clark (eds)
Protestant Scholasticism
Essays in Reassessment

Traditionally Protestant theology, between Luther's early reforming career and the dawn of the Enlightenment, has been seen in terms of decline and fall into the wastelands of rationalism and scholastic speculation. In this volume a number of scholars question such an interpretation. The editors argue that the development of post-Reformation Protestantism can only be understood when a proper historical model of doctrinal change is adopted. This historical concern underlies the subsequent studies of theologians such as Calvin, Beza, Olevian, Baxter, and the two Turrentini. The result is a significantly different reading of the development of Protestant Orthodoxy, one which both challenges the older scholarly interpretations and clichés about the relationship of Protestantism to, among other things, scholasticism and rationalism, and which demonstrates the fruitfulness of the new, historical approach.

1999 / 0-85364-853-0 / xx + 344pp

Shawn D. Wright
Our Sovereign Refuge
The Pastoral Theology of Theodore Beza

Our Sovereign Refuge is a study of the pastoral theology of the Protestant reformer who inherited the mantle of leadership in the Reformed church from John Calvin. Countering a common view of Beza as supremely a 'scholastic' theologian who deviated from Calvin's biblical focus, Wright uncovers a new portrait. He was not a cold and rigid academic theologian obsessed with probing the eternal decrees of God. Rather, by placing him in his pastoral context and by noting his concerns in his pastoral and biblical treatises, Wright shows that Beza was fundamentally a committed Christian who was troubled by the vicissitudes of life in the second half of the sixteenth century. He believed that the biblical truth of the supreme sovereignty of God alone could support Christians on their earthly pilgrimage to heaven. This pastoral and personal portrait forms the heart of Wright's argument.

2004 / 1-84227-252-7 / xviii + 308pp

Paternoster
9 Holdom Avenue,
Bletchley,
Milton Keynes MK1 1QR,
United Kingdom
Web: www.authenticmedia.co.uk/paternoster

www.ingramcontent.com/pod-product-compliance
Lightning Source LLC
Chambersburg PA
CBHW060607230426
43670CB00011B/2014